W9-ANH-413

WITH-

WITHDRAWN

Eighteenth-Century Fiction on Screen

Eighteenth-Century Fiction on Screen offers an extensive introduction to cinematic representations of the eighteenth century, mostly derived from classic fiction of that period, and sheds new light on the process of making prose fiction into film. The contributors provide a variety of theoretical and critical approaches to the process of bringing literary works to the screen. They consider a broad range of film and television adaptations, including several versions of *Robinson Crusoe*; three films of *Moll Flanders*; American, British, and French television adaptations of *Gulliver's Travels*, *Clarissa*, *Tom Jones*, and *Jacques le fataliste*; Wim Wenders' film version of Goethe's *Wilhelm Meister's Apprentice Years*; the controversial film of Diderot's *La Religieuse*; and French and Anglo-American motion pictures based on *Les Liaisons dangereuses* among others. This book will appeal to students and scholars of literature and film alike.

ROBERT MAYER is Associate Professor of English at Oklahoma State University. He is the author of *History and the Early English Novel: Matters of Fact from Bacon to Defoe* (Cambridge, 1997).

Peter O'Toole as Robinson Crusoe in Jack Gold's *Man Friday*

Eighteenth-Century Fiction on Screen

Edited by

Robert Mayer

Oklahoma State University

CAMBRIDGE
UNIVERSITY PRESS

PUBLISHED BY THE PRESS SYNDICATE OF THE UNIVERSITY OF CAMBRIDGE
The Pitt Building, Trumpington Street, Cambridge, United Kingdom

CAMBRIDGE UNIVERSITY PRESS
The Edinburgh Building, Cambridge CB2 2RU, UK
40 West 20th Street, New York, NY 10011-4211, USA
477 Williamstown Road, Port Melbourne, VIC 3207, Australia
Ruiz de Alarcón 13, 28014 Madrid, Spain
Dock House, The Waterfront, Cape Town 8001, South Africa

http://www.cambridge.org

First published 2002

Printed in the United Kingdom at the University Press, Cambridge

Typeface Plantin 10/12 pt   *System* LaTeX 2$_\varepsilon$ [TB]

A catalogue record for this book is available from the British Library

Library of Congress Cataloguing in Publication data

Eighteenth-century fiction on screen / edited by Robert Mayer.
     p.   cm.
Includes bibliographical references, filmography, and index.
ISBN 0 521 79316 5
1. Motion picture adaptations.   2. Motion pictures and literature.
3. European fiction – 18th century – History and criticism.   I. Title: 18th
century fiction on screen.   II. Mayer, Robert
PN1997.85 .E39 2002   791.43′6 – dc21   2002019252

ISBN 0 521 79316 5 hardback

For Eleanor and Susanna

Contents

Illustrations

Contributors

MARTIN C. BATTESTIN is William R. Kenan, Jr., Professor Emeritus at the University of Virginia. An authority on the life and works of Henry Fielding, he is the author of *Henry Fielding: A Life*, and he has edited Fielding's three major novels: *Joseph Andrews*, *Tom Jones*, and *Amelia*.

ALAN D. CHALMERS received his doctorate from the University of Southern California and is currently Associate Professor of English at the University of South Carolina at Spartanburg. He is the author of *Jonathan Swift and the Burden of the Future* (Delaware, 1995).

PETER COSGROVE received his doctorate from Columbia University and has taught English literature of the eighteenth century for many years at Dartmouth College. His book, *Impartial Stranger*, is about the sense of the historical past in Edward Gibbon's *Decline and Fall*. He has also published articles on music, photography, and Edmund Burke's theory of the sublime.

RICHARD FROHOCK teaches Restoration and eighteenth-century British literature, and early American literature, at Oklahoma State University. He has written articles on Aphra Behn, Woodes Rogers, and Sir William Davenant. Currently he is working on a book on British literary representations of the Americas in the late seventeenth and early eighteenth centuries.

KEVIN JACKSON has wide experience of television and radio as producer, writer, and presenter. He was associate arts editor of the London *Independent* and is currently film critic for the *Independent on Sunday*. The books he has published include *The Humphrey Jennings Film Reader* (1993), *The Language of Cinema* (1998), and *Invisible Forms: A Guide to Literary Curiosities* (1999). He recently wrote and narrated a film on the life and work of Anthony Burgess, and is writing an authorized biography of Humphrey Jennings.

MARGARET MCCARTHY is Associate Professor of German language, literature, and film at Davidson College. She has published articles on Ingeborg Bachmann, Jutta Brückner, Luc Besson, G. W. Pabst, and Doris Dörrie. At present she is co-editing an anthology on German popular film.

ROBERT MAYER is Associate Professor of English at Oklahoma State University where he teaches literature and film. He has published articles on early modern historiography, the novel, Daniel Defoe, Tobias Smollett, and Walter Scott. His book, *History and the Early English Novel: Matters of Fact from Bacon to Defoe*, was published by Cambridge in 1997. He is currently writing a study of Scott and the transformation of the reader and the author.

CATHERINE N. PARKE, Professor of English and Women Studies at the University of Missouri-Columbia, writes on later eighteenth-century British literature, modern British and American women writers, and biography and autobiography. Her publications include *Samuel Johnson and Biographical Thinking*, a critical edition of Zoë Akins' essays on American poetry, *In the Shadow of Parnassus*, and *Biography: Writing Lives*. She is at work on a study of early twentieth-century American motion pictures.

ALAN J. SINGERMAN is Professor of French at Davidson College. He has published numerous studies on eighteenth-century French fiction, including a monograph on the novels of the Abbé Prévost, a critical edition of Prévost's *Histoire d'une Grecque moderne*, and a series of articles on film adaptations of eighteenth-century French novels. He has recently served as guest editor for a "Film Forum" on Jacques Rivette's adaptation of Diderot's *La Religieuse*, published in *Eighteenth-Century Life*, and is at work on a textbook for the teaching of French film classics.

JANET SORENSEN, Associate Professor of English at Indiana University, Bloomington, has published essays on eighteenth-century culture, Daniel Defoe, Samuel Johnson, and the Scots poet Robert Fergusson, and a book-length study entitled *The Grammar of Empire in Eighteenth-Century British Writing* (Cambridge University Press, 2000). She has also published essays on film and video.

CYNTHIA WALL is Associate Professor of English at the University of Virginia. She is the author of *The Literary and Cultural Space of*

Restoration London (Cambridge, 1998), the editor of the Bedford Cultural Edition of Pope's *The Rape of the Lock* (1998), and co-editor (with J. Paul Hunter) of the forthcoming *Bedford Anthology of Eighteenth-Century Literatures in English*. She is currently working on the history of spatial description in novels and poetry.

Acknowledgments

I wish to thank the Oklahoma Humanities Council and the College of Arts and Sciences and the Department of English at Oklahoma State University for support of my work on this volume. I am also grateful to the staff of the University Library at OSU, especially David Oberhelman and the staff of Interlibrary Services. I am particularly indebted to the staff of the Motion Picture, Broadcasting, and Recorded Sound Division of the Library of Congress, and especially Rosemary Hanes, reference librarian in the Moving Image Section, who was extraordinarily helpful and friendly. Thanks are also due to Charles Silver at the Museum of Modern Art. I wish to thank the staff of the English Department at OSU, particularly Shirley Bechtel and Dale McLaughlin, for help in the preparation of the manuscript. Linda Bree at Cambridge University Press has been wonderfully helpful, and patient with this first-time editor. The contributors to this volume have been stimulating company and admirably cooperative. I cannot thank Kevin Jackson enough for helping me and the other contributors with the thorny problem of finding appropriate stills. My greatest debt is to my family. Elizabeth Williams helps me in countless ways and shares this life with me. My daughters, Eleanor and Susanna, are lovely, bright, curious, capable, strong, and loving; I dedicate this book to them.

The illustrations are provided by or reproduced with the assistance of the British Film Institute, Kevin Loader (*Clarissa*), Hallmark Entertainment (*Gulliver's Travels*), and Carlton International (*Man Friday*).

Introduction
Is there a text in the screening room?

Robert Mayer

On film, the eighteenth century, especially in Anglo-American culture, has often been an occasion for representing the stately, the lavish, the sensuous, and even the lubricious. Hollywood's most memorable, certainly its most fevered, rendering of this eighteenth century is probably still Josef von Sternberg's *The Scarlet Empress* (1934), although many subsequent motion pictures have competed with that one in lavishness, including several based on eighteenth-century novels such as *Tom Jones* (1963) and *Dangerous Liaisons* (1988). The latter two films, which either won or were nominated for an Academy Award for best art direction, as well as films not based on literary sources like *The Draughtsman's Contract* (1982) and *Restoration* (1995), revel in the opportunity to represent the long eighteenth century in terms of opulent settings, dazzling costumes and makeup, and spectacularly amoral characters. Such films often function as peculiarly eighteenth-century versions of the "heritage film," either because they "sell" prestigious literary properties or because in them "the past is delivered as a museum of sounds and images, an iconographic display."[1] Many adaptations of eighteenth-century fiction, to be sure, do not qualify as heritage films of this sort. Films discussed in this volume based on Diderot novels, on Goethe's *Wilhelm Meister's Apprentice Years*, and on Defoe's *Robinson Crusoe*, among others, happily capitalize on the status of their literary sources but forgo the opportunity provided by the classic to "transform the past into a series of commodities for the leisure and entertainment market."[2] Certain of these films, furthermore (including some of the heritage films, such as *Dangerous Liaisons*) explore the works they "adapt" in a critical spirit, and even sometimes turn against them, adapting them in such a way as to make the films vehicles for a critique either of the ideological positions or values associated with the text or of twentieth-century aesthetics or politics.

Film adaptations of eighteenth-century fiction, therefore, are far from being easy either to describe in a general sense or to classify; the question of "fidelity" to a text is only one of a large number of critical or ideological questions raised by these motion pictures. The films are shaped by, among

other factors, the culture in which the adaptation is produced, the aims
and values of filmmakers, the demands of a studio or network, and the
standing of a particular literary work or artist. They are also, often, as
much *about* the beauty, wit, ambition, or artistic will to power of a movie
star (like Marlene Dietrich) or a director (like Stanley Kubrick) as they are
about the eighteenth-century texts or characters, fictional or otherwise,
referenced in the films. These films thus serve to remind us just how
vexed an issue "adaptation" is for students of cinema. Christopher Orr
describes films based upon literary sources as "a privileged site for a
comparative investigation of the discursive practices of film and literature"
but also laments the fact that commentary on such motion pictures often
takes the form of what he labels "fidelity studies": a line of inquiry that
suggests that the worth of an adaptation of a major, canonical novel is
largely traceable to the skill and imaginative power of the author of the
original text.[3] While "fidelity studies" are often disparaged by students
of film-and-literature, the question of how a film makes use of a work of
fiction, and indeed the question of whether a film is or is not in one way
or another "faithful" to a book has not gone away and probably never
will, especially since, according to one estimate, upwards of 30 percent
of all films are based on novels.[4] The present collection of essays enters
the discussion of films based upon fiction, mainly by treating films based
upon classic English, French, and German eighteenth-century fictional
texts, although the first essay and the last also discuss at least one film
that constructs a cinematic eighteenth century without an eighteenth-
century text in mind. Approaching this topic from a variety of critical
perspectives, the authors of these essays explore the relationship between
fiction and cinema, the process of moving from fiction to film, and the
cultural uses to which the eighteenth century, literary or otherwise, has
been put in American and western European cinema. The purpose of this
introduction is to examine some basic elements of adaptation theory and
to discuss certain problems associated with the "discourse on adaptation"
along with some solutions to those dilemmas proposed by various scholars
and theorists. This essay builds upon one such approach to the issue
of adaptation – the view of a film as a reading of a novel (discussed
below) – and offers its own version of this approach by employing recent
contributions to reading theory by Hans Robert Jauss, Harold Bloom,
and Stanley Fish, all of which have the virtue, from the standpoint of the
student of film, of refusing theoretically to privilege a text over any reading
of that text. I shall argue that reading theory may make it possible to put
aside all consideration of the "transfer" of elements of a literary text to a
motion picture, as well as all questions of fidelity, in favor of the view that
films that derive from novels and other forms of fiction are distinct works

of art with no debt to texts even though they have a clear and important link to those texts. I shall conclude by surveying the approaches to the fiction-to-film problematic that are used by the authors of these essays and the arguments of the essays that make up this volume.

Critics and theorists who have written about adaptation in the last half century have tended, at least formally, to reject the premises of fidelity criticism and assert that any discussion of adaptation must start from the proposition that literature and cinema are radically different, even incommensurable, art forms. The foundation text for this line of argument (at least in English-language scholarship) is George Bluestone's *Novels into Film*, which cites, as many have done, the strikingly similar assertions of Joseph Conrad and D. W. Griffith, each of whom asserted that the aim of his art was "before all, to make you *see*." Bluestone observes that despite the apparent kinship of these remarks, both the concept of "seeing" ("the percept of the visual image" [in film] as opposed to "the concept of the mental image" [in fiction]) and the "you" or audience each artist had in mind were distinctly different.[5] Bluestone argues that "the end products of novel and film represent different aesthetic genera, as different from each other as ballet is from architecture." He therefore rejects the view that there is such a thing as "a separable content that may be detached [from novels] and reproduced [in films]" as well as the related assumption that "the novel is a norm" from which "the film deviates at its peril."[6] In a similar vein, Dudley Andrew identifies the most common view of the move from literary text to film as the belief "that the task of adaptation is the reproduction of something essential about an original text," but then insists upon the dissimilarity of the two art forms: "film . . . work[s] from perception toward signification . . . Literary fiction works oppositely. It begins with signs, graphemes and words, building to propositions which attempt to develop perception."[7]

Yet although such declarations as these without doubt constitute the dominant, "official" view of adaptation in film theory and criticism in the last few decades, if one examines the arguments of at least some scholars who adopt this line, one frequently discovers that despite an obvious desire to give cinema its due, writers continue to efface the difference between fiction and films, privilege literature over film in important ways, and assume that a film adaptation has a certain responsibility to remain faithful to either the letter or the spirit of the text upon which it is based. Brian McFarlane, for example, notes with dismay the habit of "using words like 'tampering,' 'interference,' and even 'violation'" in discussions of cinematic renderings of fictional texts, giving "the whole process an air of deeply sinister molestation." He argues that "such dissatisfactions resonate with a complex set of misapprehensions about . . . the irreducible differences between the two" forms.[8] Yet McFarlane's work, relying as it does upon categories drawn from narratology, still, seemingly almost against the author's will, has recourse to a kind of fidelity criticism. He distinguishes between what can be "transferred" in moving from novel to film (narrative) and what cannot be (enunciation) and argues in respect to a film based upon a literary text "that a true reading of the film will depend on a response to how the cinematic codes and aspects of mise-en-scène work to create this particular version of the text."[9] This comment is revealing in two ways: first, it assumes that "a true reading" of a film or a text is possible, and, second, it implies that a film can and perhaps should be a "version" of a literary text. McFarlane himself notes in respect to Bluestone's work that although the latter insists on "the fundamental difference between the way images are produced in the two media," he nevertheless concludes that the different kinds of images, in the end, "'can scarcely be distinguished'" from each other.[10]

The problem here is *not* fuzzy thinking on the part of Bluestone or McFarlane, both of whom are rigorous and thoughtful analysts of the move from novel to film. Rather the problem is with the terms that commentators on adaptation have at their disposal and the models that have been adopted to theorize this issue, which generally derive from literary theory and not surprisingly tend to privilege the literary text over the cinematic work. Some scholars, for example, have argued that one can understand adaptation as an essentially interpretive act. Neil Sinyard approvingly cites a comment by the screenwriter Daniel Taradash in which the latter explains that adaptation involves the screenwriter's "discovery" of "the basic theme" of a text and the dramatization of that theme; Sinyard himself concludes that "the best film adaptations provide a critical gloss on the novel."[11] This way of looking at adaptation is in its way both illuminating and liberating; it, after all, views adaptation as a creative (albeit critical) act and not just as a transposition or transfer of at least some elements of a novel to the screen. But it also reduces the adaptation itself to the status of a commentary on another work of art. Geoffrey Wagner identifies "commentary" through "restatement" or "alteration" as one of three possible modes of adaptation, but then revealingly observes that such renderings often seem like "tampering with an original" or "infringement on the work of another."[12] Another line of argument that implicitly marks the literary text as a privileged site is the suggestion that adaptation is a process not unlike the translation of a text from one language into another.[13] Once again, this view of adaptation recognizes the inevitable alteration of the original through translation and grants to the adapters the same creative role that readers grant to a translator. Still, when readers have recourse to widely praised versions of poems such as Richmond Lattimore's *The Iliad* or A. Poulin, Jr.'s translation of Rilke's *Duino Elegies*, they mostly go to those texts for Homer and Rilke, not for the poetry of the twentieth-century translators. Thus, both the commentary and translation models contain a bias in favor of the text as against the cinematic work even though at least some of the writers who employ these models mean to distance themselves from the tendency of fidelity criticism to privilege fiction over film.

Narratology is another paradigm derived ultimately from the study of texts that has been suggested as a way out of the impasse of fidelity criticism. McFarlane's work, as well as that of Seymour Chatman, demonstrates that narratological theory can yield rich results by highlighting the particular narrative techniques available to each art form.[14] Not infrequently, however, there emerges from such analyses a sense – often not enunciated – that that which *is* transferable *ought to be* transferred, or, at the very least, that it is not unreasonable for viewers of a film who know a work of fiction to expect that the narrative elements of a work of fiction that can be presented in a film will be. Thus, McFarlane argues that an important potential dividend of distinguishing between "narrative" and "enunciation" is that such discussions "could deflect reviewers and critics from pointlessly chastising a film for not reproducing their sense of the original text" by making it clear "that some elements are more likely than others to survive transfer." A conclusion that one might draw from this line of argument (although it is *not* a conclusion that McFarlane does draw) is that critics and reviewers might well be justified in chastising filmmakers for failing to transfer those narrative elements that can "survive transfer."[15] A novel, in short, might indeed function as at least one norm against which a film is judged, and a filmmaker might legitimately be charged with violating the letter or spirit of a text.

Such favoring of fiction over film seems almost inescapable in discussions of adaptation; the very word, after all, suggests alteration or adjustment in order to make something fit its new context or environment without, however, changing that something into something else – one "adapts," that is, one does not "transform" or "metamorphose." No wonder, then, that Orr declares: "one is tempted to call for a moratorium on adaptation studies."[16] And indeed not a few filmmakers and theorists have rejected the very idea of adaptation. Ingmar Bergman, for example, has asserted that "film has nothing to do with literature" and declared "we should avoid making films out of books."[17] Béla Balázs denies that there can be any transfer or transposition from one art form to the other. He insists that when a novel is "turned into" a film, although "the subject, or story, of both works is identical, their *content* is nevertheless different." Balázs believes that when what is putatively the same material is approached by artists using different forms and media that material is conceived by each artist "from the specific angle of his own art form," and is, therefore, comprehensively reconceived.[18]

Other models indebted to literary theory help to move discussions of the "metamorphosis of fiction into cinema" beyond the concept of adaptation.[19] For many critics, the way out of the problematic embodied in the "discourse on adaptation" is a recourse to the concept of intertextuality. Thus, Orr argues:

> By placing the notion of adaptation within the theory of intertextuality, we can describe the literary source [of a film] as one of a series of pre-texts which share some of the same narrative conventions as the film adaptation. This description obviously does not exhaust the film's intertextual space, which also includes codes specific to the institution of cinema as well as codes that reflect the cultural conditions under which the film was produced.[20]

In important ways the intertextuality model solves the main problems associated with adaptation theory by treating the literary text as one of many items in the "multidimensional space in which a variety of writings, none of them original, blend and clash" that is the intertextual matrix from which a film emerges.[21] No longer is the novel privileged, and the problem of fidelity criticism therefore recedes because there can be no sense of responsibility to a text within such a model. Yet the use of this concept presents other problems to the critic who wishes to focus on the relationship between film and fiction. Once one highlights Roland Barthes's "multidimensional space," the relationship between a particular text and a particular film may get lost; at the very least, the task of describing any film's emergence from its intertextual matrix seems at best daunting, and in some cases colossal. While intertextuality allows one at least theoretically to place a film that draws upon a work of fiction within its proper context, seeing the cinematic work as shaped not only by a particular text but also by a multitude of elements within a cultural setting – including other films, a star's persona, political discourse, and potentially almost innumerable narratives and other items from popular and elite culture – use of the intertextuality model might in some cases tend to obscure the relationship between the two works. McFarlane recognizes the potential of the concept of intertextuality for opening up a discussion of a filmic adaptation of a literary work into a consideration of how a film is a product of its cultural moment. He argues, however, that such matters as "other texts (literary, cinematic, non-fictional) and ... other pressures (e.g. genre conventions, auteurist predilections, studio style, 'industry' matters such as use of certain stars, let alone extra-cinematic influences such as the prevailing ideological climate)" are not susceptible to the kind of rigorous analysis that he attempts in his use of narratological theory. In other words, one can identify with some ease "those novelistic elements which can be *transferred* and those which require *adaptation proper*" but the description of a film's intertextual space is at best an intimidating enterprise.[22]

Recent reading theory may offer a solution to the problems posed by the intertextuality model's account of the fiction-to-film problematic. Jauss, Bloom, and Fish refuse to privilege one reading (or work or form) over another but they nevertheless remain focused to a significant degree upon particular works and the distinct ways they have been received. These conceptualizations of reading return us to the idea of adaptation as hermeneutical act, but in this case with a radically different sense of that process, one that may help students of film-and-fiction escape from the bias toward the literary text inherent in most accounts of adaptation and still allow them to theorize the historically crucial relationship between literature and cinema and between particular films and texts. Reading theory in recent years has been dominated by the view that reading is not a matter of the decoding of signs that yields something essential about a text (such as its "basic theme") but is instead a creative act that in "concretizing" a work remakes it and indeed remakes the artistic field in which it appears.[23] Jauss, for example, describes reading or reception as an evolving dialogue of question and answer: texts of whatever character pose questions to readers – formal, aesthetic, thematic, sociological, historical questions – and acts of reception constitute answers to those questions. Acts of reception, furthermore, pose, in their turn, new questions.[24] "Reception" includes both individual concretizations of texts and critical or theoretical commentaries, and also includes new works of art that "respond" to earlier works, without, in many cases, "transferring" anything substantial from the works that they answer. Thus, in his discussion of the treatments of the Faust legend by Goethe and Valéry, Jauss denies that the relationship between the two texts is "a matter of two variations of one and the same substance"; he declares, indeed, that "Goethe's voice and Valéry's clearly don't speak *to one another at all.*" As a result, Jauss argues that describing the relationship between two or more texts, as well as the link between the texts themselves and any reading of those texts, requires

a rehistoricization [of all three], such that one discovers the hermeneutic relation of question and answer, problem and solution, which mediates not only Goethe and Valéry, but also the different meanings of their similar works ... with the contemporary horizon of interest of the questioner who is comparatively questioning them.[25]

According to Jauss, then, all texts-as-answers necessarily alter not only the field(s) in which the texts exist (cinematic genres, particular novelistic traditions, American popular culture, island myths) but also the texts-as-questions themselves. Everything, in fact, is at least potentially changed by every act of reception: "the appearance of a new work . . . can result in a 'change of horizons' through negation of familiar experiences or through raising newly articulated experiences to the level of consciousness."[26] But one can escape from the impossible task of describing a vast textual space that is constantly changing by focusing, as Jauss frequently does, on the relationship (within a stipulated larger field) among a few particular works or readings of works, such as the two Faust texts, or, to cite examples from the present collection, Goethe's *Wilhelm Meister's Apprentice Years* and Wim Wenders' *Wrong Move*, or the novel *Les Liaisons dangereuses* and the several cinematic transformations of Laclos's narrative. One escapes, furthermore, from the problem of privileging text over film (or one text over another) because the new work, in whatever medium, with its particular answers to the questions posed by the earlier work(s), alters the prior work(s) and as a result the several works are, in effect, contemporary with each other and each exists in a field that has likewise been transformed by the act of reception. Following Jauss, one is bound to see a film based upon an eighteenth-century novel, with its own long history of transformation through reception, as a work that both responds to the earlier work, casting that work, at least potentially, in a new light, and yet functions at the same time as its own set of questions posed to an historically distinct audience through the vehicle of a unique work of art.

Bloom's discussions of reading also suggest an alternative approach to the problem of how critics might construe the fiction-to-film problematic. Like Jauss, Bloom focuses on individual acts of creation (poems by Collins, Blake, Wordsworth, Shelley) as species of reading or, as Bloom sees it, *mis*reading of earlier poets (Spenser, Milton, Wordsworth). Bloom investigates these "intra-poetic relationships" and sees them as unfolding by means of individual creative acts in the course of which poets misread powerful "precursor poets" in the process of creating their own art. Thus, Bloom views poetic influence – the debt one artist has to an earlier artist, the ways in which a later poet's work depends upon, starts from, imitates, revises, completes, or rejects an earlier poet's work – in terms of fruitful misconstruing; he sees one artist using another through "creative correction" and "misinterpretation." There can be no real question of "adaptation" or "transfer" or of the responsibility of one artist or work to another according to this view of reading, unless one is discussing one work that is no more than a slavish imitation of another.[27] Thus Bloom's

model insists upon the right of (and the need for) every reader, especially strong readers (that is, major artists), to misconstrue whatever text
is being read. Bloom seeks to account for influences or relations between
artists and works, and yet he sees those connections as opportunities for
one artist to move beyond, rather than demonstrate her or his indebted-
ness to, another artist. What Bloom and Jauss have in common, then,
is a habit of mind that rejects ordinary ideas of influence and obligation or shared contents, forms, and styles, and instead sees the history of
art in terms of responses to earlier works and artists that are themselves
autonomous creations with no responsibility to the earlier works even
though they may evince a powerful interest in, likeness to, interrogatory
attitude toward, or anxious view of, those earlier works.

Yet a third model of reading, elaborated by Fish, complements, at least
for our purposes, the two models already reviewed here. In his famous
essay, "Is There a Text in This Class?" Fish responds to literary theorists who argue in favor of "literal or normative meanings" of texts by
asserting that an "utterance's meaning is not a function of the values its
words have in a linguistic system that is independent of context; rather,
it is because the words are heard as already embedded in a context that
they have a meaning." For Fish context is, if not everything, then at the
very least inescapably important; in different contexts different meanings will be "obvious and accessible" and each of these can be normative
in its particular environment.[28] Different cultural moments, institutional
and national settings, and historical epochs yield distinct concretizations
of texts, sometimes strikingly different from each other and sometimes
seemingly at odds with the texts themselves.

These accounts of how texts are read suggest an approach to the novel-
to-film problematic. The theories of reading elaborated by Jauss, Bloom,
and Fish allow the student of film to reject all consideration of "transfer" or "transposition," "interference" or "violation" – in theory at least,
all discussion of "adaptation" – in favor of the view that a film derived
from a literary text is a particular "reading" of that text that issues from
its unique context and distinct artistic consciousness, emerges within a
particular cultural moment, responds to a text that possesses its own history, and, crucially, employs radically different artistic means. In Fish's
essay, the colloquy between the young woman who asks the question, "Is
there a text in this class?" and her professor reveals that the question has
multiple meanings and a variety of answers. So too with the question,
"Is there a text in the screening room?" Filmmakers read novels both
before and as they make films – the very act of making a film based upon
a work of fiction is an act of reading. Some films, like David Lean's *Great
Expectations* (1946), will at least apparently strive to be scrupulously

faithful to a text, while others, like Billy Wilder's *Sunset Boulevard* (1950), which Sinyard argues "comes very close to the spirit as distinct from the content" of Dickens's *Great Expectations,* may appropriate the text and yet leave it far behind.[29] As McFarlane asserts: "There are many kinds of relations which may exist between film and literature, and fidelity is only one – and rarely the most exciting."[30] The act (and art) of reading a text by making a film, therefore, brings with it no responsibility to that text. Rather such concretizations remake both texts and the contexts – filmic, political, and cultural – in which both films and texts appear and are apprehended. Fish's student explains her sense of the question she asks: "'I mean in this class do we believe in poems and things, or is it just us?'" The student of film might well ask, in a similar vein: "Do we believe in novels and other works of fiction, or is it just the movies?"[31] The correct answer would seem to be that often there *is* a text in the screening room, but that in "reading" a novel or any other work of fiction a film believes not in the text but in itself.

Nevertheless, however sound theoretical declarations of the incommensurable nature of film and fiction may be, for many filmgoers the relationship between a literary text and a motion picture is both important and compelling, and this includes more than just naive members of the audience objecting to the omitting, altering, or reconceiving of treasured characters, incidents, or scenes. Many directors, including such unimpeachable *auteurs* as Alfred Hitchcock and Orson Welles, have made one film after another based on fictional texts.[32] Welles's comments on the making of *The Magnificent Ambersons* bespeak his determination to do justice to a beloved text: "If the movie of *Ambersons* has any quality, a great part of it is due to [the author of the book, Booth] Tarkington. What doesn't come from the book is a careful imitation of his style."[33] What is more, no less a theoretician than André Bazin and no less a *cinéaste* than François Truffaut have argued forcefully for the filmmaker's responsibility to give a faithful rendering of a text. Bazin has declared that infidelity is a betrayal of both literature and cinema, and Truffaut once defended Robert Bresson's intention to follow the text "page by page, even phrase by phrase," in adapting Georges Bernanos's *Diary of a Country Priest.*[34]

Critics, furthermore, remind us that "from its beginnings the feature film was associated with literary and dramatic classics," and since motion pictures based on fiction were often undertaken with an eye toward securing or holding on to an audience, the films were commonly made and presented in such a way as to encourage potential viewers to expect fidelity to a text. If, that is, novels were "pre-sold stories" that "promised to deliver a ready-made audience of people who had read the book" (the classic, but hardly the only, example is, of course, *Gone with the Wind*), one premise of this strategy was an implicit promise to deliver a faithful filmic "version" of the book.[35] Such films have done well at the box office, John Izod observes, by offering the audience "identifiable and sure attractions."[36] Thus, the movie business – at least in America never separable from the art of making moving pictures – valorized fidelity to an original text through its use of well-known works of fiction. What is more, as we have already seen, certain film scholars have argued or at least implied that filmmakers and students of film might well distinguish between what in a work of fiction can and cannot be transposed in the move from text to film, and have also shown that the former elements can be brought to the screen in a fairly straightforward fashion. Thus while in a theoretical sense one can assert a radical disjuncture between film and text, in practice one must acknowledge that when viewing or analyzing a film that refers to a work of fiction, consideration of questions of how the text has been rendered on film, what has been retained and what has been discarded, and the relationship between fictional and cinematic technique are inevitably raised.

The question becomes, then, what kind of criticism treating the move from novel to film is likely to be illuminating once one embraces the view that the film has no responsibility to, even though it often has a compelling relationship with, a text. In a sense, this book constitutes an answer to that question, and it is a response that is necessarily multiform. Some critics, of course, will always find the issue of what has or has not been transferred from a particular novel to a particular film a compelling one, especially since, as McFarlane notes, there are always filmmakers who "legitimately feel challenged to represent in audio-visual images as close a correspondence" as possible to what the novel "has created in purely verbal terms."[37] One of the contributors to this collection – Martin Battestin – enunciates a now virtually classic account of how filmmakers can in fact turn a novel into pictures. Other contributors explore the ways in which some responses to fiction constitute if not fidelity to a text then at least a deep engagement with it. Cynthia Wall is interested in the way that the BBC *Clarissa* (1991) enacts a visual interpretation of Richardson's text through its distinctly filmic treatment of time and space but she at the same time shows how the television drama uses cinema to highlight possibilities in the narrative not fully realized in the novel itself. Maggie McCarthy examines the relationship between the *Bildungsroman* of Goethe and Wim Wenders' road movie, *Wrong Move* (1974), and provides a new map for reading both works. Alan Singerman's essay is particularly interested in Claude Santelli's film, *Jacques le fataliste* (1984), as a metacinematic response to Diderot's metafictional novel. Peter Cosgrove's essay, finally, focuses primarily on what film does rather than on the relationship

between novel and film. He treats cinema's capacity for apparent historical authenticity and indeed shows that that capacity in film – rooted in
its fixation on the image – actually undermines a film's narrative drive.

The remaining essays in this collection tend to illustrate a point made
by Andrew (and others) about what happens to the "discourse of adaptation" when questions of fidelity cease to be central. Andrew dismisses
adaptation as "frequently the most narrow and provincial area of film
theory," and concludes that "it is time for adaptation studies to take a sociological turn" and investigate "what conditions . . . warrant and demand
the use of literary prototypes."[38] He is principally concerned with "film
culture" and the choices made by filmmakers (Bresson, Truffaut) and the
positions elaborated by critics and theorists (Bazin, Alexandre Astruc).
Christopher Orr, however, argues that a "possible alternative to fidelity
criticism" is to approach the move from novel to film "from an ideological
perspective," according to which "the issue is not whether the adapted
film is faithful to its source, but rather how the choice of a specific source
and how the approach to that source serve the film's ideology . . . [and]
provide clues to the ideology embedded in the text."[39] The idea that
once film theorists and critics rid themselves of a concern with fidelity
the door opens to political and cultural criticism is anticipated in Walter
Benjamin's "The Work of Art in the Age of Mechanical Reproduction."
Benjamin argues that "technical reproducibility" undermines the "concept of authenticity" which is predicated on a sense of the presence and
the uniqueness of "the original"; mechanical reproduction shatters the
idea that a work possesses an "aura," the "unique value of the 'authentic'
work of art" that imparts to that work "a ritual function." As a result,
the very character and function of art change: "instead of being based on
ritual, it begins to be based upon another practice – politics."[40] In light of
Benjamin's argument, it is not surprising that many theorists and critics
have suggested that once one abandons the idea that the prior work of
art has a privileged status and character, fidelity criticism is likely to be
replaced by "sociological" or "ideological" commentary – by Benjamin's
"politics." And many of the essays in this volume bear that contention out.

Catherine Parke examines how Moll Flanders has been constructed in
several films as a "female/feminine/feminist" character, and my essay on
three cinematic Robinsonades treats those films as post-colonial readings
of Defoe's novel. Alan Chalmers describes how even the most ostensibly faithful rendering of *Gulliver's Travels* – the 1996 two-part television
mini-series – censors Swift even as it seemingly affirms the principle of
free expression as well as the value of fidelity to a text. Kevin Jackson focuses on the controversy surrounding Jacques Rivette's film of Diderot's
La Religieuse (1966) both as an ideological struggle in France that echoes

Enlightenment battles and also as an occasion for a contest between those who decry the political power of the cinema and those who relish it. Richard Frohock shows that Laclos's novel has repeatedly provided twentieth-century filmmakers with an opportunity to explore the philosophy of libertinism in order to engage in cultural criticism. Janet Sorensen, finally, argues that the film *Rob Roy* (1998) is in some ways a typical and typically conservative heritage film even though it at first glance appears to offer a distinctly different and seemingly radical vision of eighteenth-century Britain. Thus, many of the essays in this collection suggest that one obvious alternative to "fidelity studies" is the analysis of the ideological significance of specific moves from fiction to film, whether one focuses on the text, the film, or both.

But of course these various approaches to eighteenth-century fiction on screen are far from being mutually exclusive. Questions about "fidelity" would not be totally out of place in any of these essays. And all the contributors to this volume focus on the different means used by film artists to render the subjects and stories derived from classic works of fiction. What is more, none of these essays is unmindful of ideological issues, either as reflected in the practice of studios and networks or individual artists or as examples of the cultural uses to which the eighteenth century in general or eighteenth-century fiction in particular have been put by filmmakers and audiences.

A focus on the move from fiction to film, in short, yields a number of theoretical positions and methodological approaches, and this collection attempts to embody if not all of those approaches then at the very least a representative selection of ways of approaching the novel-to-film problematic as well as a mix of essays on both the continental and the British novel. On balance, these essays reveal that at this stage in film history and theory the issue of fidelity is of less direct concern to most scholars investigating the move from novel to film than it has been in times past. Nevertheless, these essays are obviously focused on the vexed and yet undeniably important link between literary texts and motion pictures, and they make it clear that treating that relationship continues to be a fruitful line of inquiry for students of both cinema and prose fiction. This volume is presented as a fresh contribution to the ongoing discussion of the relationship between film and fiction as well as an examination of the particular enterprise of putting eighteenth-century fiction on screen.

NOTES

1 Andrew Higson, "Re-Presenting the National Past: Nostalgia and Pastiche in the Heritage Film," in *Fires Were Started: British Cinema and Thatcherism*, ed. Lester Friedman (Minneapolis: University of Minnesota Press, 1993), p. 115.

2 Higson, "Re-presenting the Past," p. 112.
3 Christopher Orr, "The Discourse on Adaptation," *Wide Angle* 6 (1984), 73, 74.
4 Morris Beja, *Film and Literature: An Introduction* (New York and London: Longman, 1979), p. 78; Beja's figure refers to the American film industry, but it seems likely that similar statistics would emerge from an examination of the film industries of western Europe.
5 George Bluestone, *Novels into Film* (1957; reprinted Berkeley and Los Angeles: University of California Press, 1971), pp. 1–2. The quoted phrase is from Conrad's preface to *The Nigger of the Narcissus*; Griffith's variant is "above all to make you see."
6 Bluestone, *Novels into Film*, p. 5.
7 J. Dudley Andrew, "The Well-Worn Muse: Adaptation in Film History and Theory," in *Narrative Strategies: Original Essays in Film and Prose Fiction*, ed. Syndy M. Conger and Janice R. Welsch (Macomb: Western Illinois University, 1980), p. 12.
8 Brian McFarlane, *Novel to Film: An Introduction to the Theory of Adaptation* (Oxford: Clarendon Press, 1996), p. 12.
9 McFarlane, *Novel to Film*, pp. vii, 13, 22.
10 McFarlane, *Novel to Film*, p. 4; McFarlane quotes Bluestone, *Novels into Film*, p. 47.
11 Neil Sinyard, *Filming Literature: The Art of Screen Adaptation* (New York: St. Martin's, 1986), p. 117.
12 Geoffrey Wagner, *The Novel and the Cinema* (Rutherford, NJ: Farleigh Dickinson University Press, 1975), p. 223.
13 Beja, *Film and Literature*, p. 84; Michael Klein , "Introduction: Film and Literature," in *The English Novel and the Movies*, ed. Klein and Gillian Parker (New York: Frederick Ungar, 1981), p. 3.
14 Seymour Chatman, "What Novels Can Co That Films Can't (And Vice Versa)," in *Film Theory and Criticism: Introductory Readings*, 5th edn., ed. Leo Braudy and Marshall Cohen (New York and Oxford: Oxford University Press, 1999), pp. 435–51. See, for example, Chatman's discussion of Jean Renoir's adaptation of a Maupassant story in *A Day in the Country* (1946).
15 McFarlane, *Novel to Film*, p. 196.
16 Orr, "Discourse on Adaptation," 72.
17 Ingmar Bergman, "Introduction," in *Four Screenplays*, trans. Lars Malmstrom and David Kushner (New York: Simon & Schuster, 1960), pp. 17, 19.
18 Béla Balázs, *Theory of the Film* (New York: Arno Press; New York Times, 1972), p. 260.
19 The phrase serves as the subtitle to Bluestone's book, *Novels into Film*.
20 Orr, "Discourse on Adaptation," 72.
21 Roland Barthes, *Image–Music–Text*, ed. and trans. Stephen Heath (New York: Hill and Wang, 1977), p. 146.
22 McFarlane, *Novel to Film*, p. 201.
23 My use of the concept of "concretizing" a work of art comes from Felix Vodička, "The Concretization of the Literary Work: Problems of the Reception of Neruda's Work," in *The Prague School: Selected Writings, 1929–1946*,

ed. Peter Steiner, trans. John Burbank et al. (Austin: University of Texas Press, 1982), p. 105. For Vodička, the crucial part of the "biography" of a work is an account of "how the work has changed in the minds of those following generations who have dealt with it... lived on it, fed on it."

24 Hans Robert Jauss, *Toward an Aesthetic of Reception*, trans. Timothy Bahti (Minneapolis: University of Minnesota Press, 1982), p. 19.

25 Jauss, *Reception*, pp. 112–13 (emphasis in original).

26 Jauss, *Reception*, p. 25.

27 Harold Bloom, *The Anxiety of Influence: A Theory of Poetry* (London: Oxford University Press, 1973), pp. 8, 30, and *passim*.

28 Stanley Fish, *Is There a Text in This Class? The Authority of Interpretive Communities* (Cambridge, MA, and London: Harvard University Press, 1980), pp. 305, 309, 308.

29 Sinyard likens Lean to F. R. Leavis (who, Sinyard argues, shared with Lean a distaste for "the flamboyant aspects of Dickens's art" and a preference for a Dickens-as-realist constructed by both critic and filmmaker). In respect to Wilder's film, on the other hand, he argues that its "outrageous melodrama and decadence has a true Dickensian spirit" and concludes that *Sunset Boulevard* is an "imaginative transformation" of the novel. Sinyard, *Filming Literature*, pp. 124, 119. See also John Orr, who discusses films that come "closer to fiction by not adapting it" than other, seemingly more faithful, films; John Orr, "Introduction: Proust, the movie," in *Cinema and Fiction: New Modes of Adapting, 1950–1990*, ed. Orr and Colin Nicholson (Edinburgh: University of Edinburgh Press, 1992), p. 6.

30 McFarlane, *Novel to Film*, p. 11.

31 Fish, *Is There a Text?* p. 305.

32 John Huston rarely made a film that was not an adaptation of some sort of text. Hitchcock's run of films from the 1950s and 1960s included many, such as *Rear Window*, *Vertigo*, *Psycho*, and *The Birds*, that started from some work of fiction, although it must be said that Hitchcock generally used texts that few members of his mass audience knew. Welles, by contrast, tended to adapt classics like *The Trial*, *Othello*, and *Macbeth*.

33 Orson Welles and Peter Bogdanovich, *This is Orson Welles*, ed. Jonathan Rosenbaum (New York: HarperCollins, 1993), p. 96.

34 André Bazin, *What is Cinema?*, vol. 1, trans. Hugh Gray (Berkeley and Los Angeles: University of California Press, 1967), pp. 68, 54; Beja, *Film and Literature*, p. 83.

35 John Izod, "Words Selling Pictures," in *Cinema and Fiction*, ed. Orr and Nicholson, pp. 97, 99, 96.

36 Izod, "Words Selling Pictures," p. 97.

37 McFarlane, *Novel to Film*, p. 194.

38 Andrew, "Well-Worn Muse," pp. 14–15.

39 Christopher Orr, "Discourse on Adaptation," 73.

40 Walter Benjamin, *Illuminations: Essays and Reflections*, ed. Hannah Arendt, trans. Harry Zohn (New York: Schocken, 1969), pp. 222–4.

1   The cinema of attractions and the novel in *Barry Lyndon* and *Tom Jones*

Peter Cosgrove

Novel and film have had a long symbiotic relationship, which no doubt is affected by the commercialism of the studios. Novels become properties, pre-existent stories like rough first drafts which studios rewrite to reach the widest popular audience. Book lovers and academic critics consequently decry the misconstrual of the novel by filmmakers. Yet in doing so they tend to react as if films ideally should do no more than illustrate the book. The visual impact of the screen, however, has attractions far superior to the handmaidenly role of mere illustration. Lacunae and redistributed emphases are not merely a matter of cinematic mistranslation or misinterpretation. Films encourage a kind of fetishism of the image, a fixation on the film spectacle that renders nothing to the literary original. This may be the enchantment with a location, or the desire for the repetition of a camera angle on an actor's features, or a momentary regret for a formal composition whisked away by the exigencies of the plot. Literature, Roland Barthes claims, also offers opportunities to disregard the "integrity of the text... [W]e boldly skip... descriptions, explanations, analyses, conversations; doing so, we resemble a spectator in a nightclub who climbs onto the stage and speeds up the dancer's striptease, tearing off her clothing, but in the same order."[1] The image in film and narrative in the novel invite us to a variety of pleasures, pleasures almost illicit insofar as they wander outside the kinds of careful reading that insist on the integrity of the text. In what follows I will question what Barbara Stafford calls the "anti-ocular suspicion" of visual representation perpetuated by overestimation of linguistic artifacts. By analyzing film adaptation of novels on their own visual terms, I hope to contribute to Stafford's program of "reawakening a deadened appreciation for *meraviglia*."[2]

Taking Barthes's provocative analogy at face value we see that the pleasures of skipping in a book and fetishizing the movie image employ exactly opposed tactics. The reader wants to speed the narrative up while the viewer struggles to slow it down. Indeed, the slowing down process is built into the medium of film. Despite the emphasis on narrative techniques in film history and theory, films are always more disposed to the spectacle than to the story; where the book fails to provide an opportunity for spectacle, the film will supply one. In considering two films adapted from novels, Tony Richardson's *Tom Jones* and Stanley Kubrick's *Barry Lyndon*, I shall argue that narrative integrity is not essential for an informed response to the film image. Films set in the past lure historically minded viewers to fetishize costume and settings, the success of the illusion, and the appearance of authenticity. They peer around and behind the foregrounded drama for glimpses of the set or tune in to the rhythm of spectacle rather than to the progression of the plot. While exploring the vagaries of historical authenticity in the cinema, I hope to show the prevalence of an odd paradox: the visual modes best suited to historical reenactment are those that are incidental to the narrative and consequently in some respects are least faithful to the text.

Film theorists believe that the film image and the narrative are at cross-purposes or even locked in conflict. For Tom Gunning, "The primary task of the filmic narrator must be to overcome the initial resistance of the photographic material to telling by creating a hierarchy of narratively important elements within a mass of contingent details."[3] The resistance arises from an "inherent photographic tendency towards mimesis." Gunning's "photographic mimesis" differs from the traditional use of the word. Mimesis in Gunning's usage refers to a viewer's fascination with the "mass of contingent details" on the screen. Unlike verbal representation or painting, the camera lens is inherently hostile to organizing the representation. The camera records everything before it regardless of what we might call theme, the ordering principle for foregrounding the object of most interest to the photographer. Gunning believes that unthematized objects on the screen elicit pleasure in representation for its own sake. John Ford's Monument Valley is an object of interest regardless of why John Wayne and Richard Widmark are pacing across it. The appeal of visuals without theme gives rise to what Gunning calls the "cinema of attractions," a form going back to the prehistory of films when early experimenters played with special effects or put a naive *cinéma-vérité* on the screen as a sample of the marvelous. The cinema of attractions, Gunning stresses, evokes "other possibilities of the cinema than its storytelling potential. Such apparently different approaches as the trick film and actuality filmmaking unite in using cinema to present a series of views to audiences, views fascinating because of their illusory power... and exoticism."[4] Galloping horses, moving trains, military reviews were all sufficient for early movie audiences. And while film narrative has come a long way from the days when movies were a carnival sideshow, the cinema of attractions still has a grip on us. From the grand hotel in *Last Year at Marienbad* to the special effects of *Independence Day*, directors continue to

1. The British troops advance in Stanley Kubrick's *Barry Lyndon*

attract the audience with spectacle, and audiences continue to respond. For fetishists of the spectacle, the narrative can be an unnecessary distraction. As Harold Rosenberg comments: "I could have watched *Barry Lyndon* for another two hours without the slightest interest in what was happening to its hero."[5]

Spectacle, as this remark suggests, is the primary difference between the film and the book. The film, notably, will expand upon quite minor incidents in the novel. The filmmaker goes to great lengths to perfect scenes relatively insignificant for the purposes of the exposition. In *Tom Jones*, the most famous scene, though not, to my mind, the most compelling, is the largely irrelevant supper where Albert Finney and Joyce Redman eat their way into bed with each other, a scene not in the book. Similarly, a skirmish between British and French troops in *Barry Lyndon* is visually compelling far beyond its significance to the narrative. A line of British redcoats marches towards a stationary line of white-clad French soldiers. There are five separate volleys from the French and at each volley more British troops fall, yet the line maintains its shape and marches forward with bayonets fixed. The superb visual effect is an achievement of the sheer laboriousness of cinematic illusion – "three cameras moving with the troops on an 800-foot track," laid by Kubrick's studio hands for just this two and a half minutes of screen time.[6] The set-up enables the viewer to observe the moving lines of troops from the side. The contrast between the rigid mobile line and the falling men – registered sometimes in close-up by the zoom – is remarkable and not to be conveyed through mere verbal description. So compelling is the mise-en-scène that the personal drama of the death of Major Grogan seems like an interruption of the camerawork. In one sense this is film's achievement, the world without the narrator that presents itself to the viewer as an immediacy that depends not at all on narrative continuity or thematic appropriateness.

These examples suggest that movies exist to feed our fetishes in ways the novel does not. At the movies we are all in attendance at that interactive striptease evoked by Barthes. Even the publicity material invites decoupage and misreading. We go for the star, for the director, for the desire to see Venice again or San Francisco, to see a beloved novel animated, or we respond to the enticement of one of those strange new genres invented by Hollywood to fill market niches. The films this essay engages, versions of novels set in or written about the eighteenth century, invite their own misreading. They become period films, costume dramas, which, according to Leonard Maltin, are "more fanciful than factual, but entertainingly and lavishly produced."[7] Even so, one feature of costume drama that appeals to historically minded viewers is some shadow of cultural memory that inheres in the representation of that particular slice of the past. The cinema, it is hoped, has the potential to evoke the past in all its immediacy. No matter how shallow the interpretation, how distorted the characterization, historically minded viewers are delighted to see the past in motion, antique costumes worn by living people, and sets that convey a little of what it was like to live in a world without automobiles or electricity. Urging us to acknowledge the importance of set design in the historical film, C. S. Tashiro argues, "To pretend that somehow the viewer (or the critic) does not take surfaces as an integral part of the historical message is self-deceiving, and ultimately damaging, since at least one consequence of the designed historical image is to make the past appealingly pretty."[8] Historical appeal in film seems to lie in the moving image whose subversive shallowness convinces the eye of the pleasure of "being there."

One aspect of the debate between print and pictures is the argument that the printed word has the power to convey mental states while the film is confined to representing external signs, an argument that often leads to the observation that the novel is vastly superior to film because of the higher value we put on interiority and subjectivity. This view raises philosophical and ideological problems that will be apparent to most readers. Yet even if we respect this distinction, written historiography will fall on the pictorial side of the debate. History is not often the record of subjectivities, and a strand of thought on the representation of the past from Lord Kames to Simon Schama supports the importance of visualization to historical representation. Kames remarks that "a good historical painting makes a deeper impression than words can, though not equal to that of theatrical action." Schama in a recent issue of the American cultural monthly, *Harper's*, praises the depiction in Tacitus of the fallen legions of Augustus in the Teutoberg Forest for being almost "a page from the directorial notebook of an Eisenstein or a Kurosawa."[9] The "lively and distinct images" of the cinema are even more capable than the theater of throwing the viewer, in Kames's words, "into a kind of reverie... precisely as if he were an eye-witness."[10]

The visual experience, I propose, accounts for a lot of films about the eighteenth century, whether these are drawn from novels or from history. The particular fetish of students of history is to ask not whether Tony Richardson was faithful to the original, but: is this the way an inn looked for Fielding? Does this masquerade truly represent a social event that has become so important to our studies since Terry Castle first drew our attention to this aspect of eighteenth-century culture? We do not in a sense follow the story at all but look past it to the costumes and the sets. We are anxious to see in background motion the quotidian details of the period that we have pored so much over in print: we "intensify our attention to the apprehension of the detail" in order to catch a glimpse of the evocative fragments of the past.[11] By this means the film promises some sensation of both the having-been-there of the actors and events and the being-there-ourselves in imagination. We hope that the vivacity of the moving image will convey something of the period. We go to *Tom Jones* or *Barry Lyndon* to achieve some version of the historian's dream of annihilating the interval between ourselves and an age that is both so familiar and so alien.

Historical movies in general can be said to be resolutely non-historical even with the great effort to which producers and directors go to achieve authentic sets, props, and costumes, often with the help of accredited historians. The production values, the exigencies of the camera, the formulaic narratives all tend to thwart any real loyalty to recuperating the past: Roman forums are always too large; romances between historical personages and undocumented characters, such as between Commodus's sister, Lucilla, and Russell Crowe in *Gladiator*, merely accommodate the star qualities of the latest Australian hard man; neither Lord Cornwallis nor Nathanael Greene was present at the battle of the Cowpens as *The Patriot* would have it. Yet these problems do not prevent movie makers from making claims for authenticity that are very similar to those made by legitimate academic historians. D. W. Griffith on the release of *Birth of a Nation* had the hubris to remark that henceforward "Instead of consulting all the authorities... and ending bewildered... you will actually see what happened. There will be no opinions expressed. You will merely be

present at the making of history."[12] Stanley Kubrick said much the same
thing in remarking that "*Barry Lyndon* offered the opportunity to do the
things that movies can do better than any other art form, and that is, to
present historical subject matter. Description is not one of the things that
novels do best, but it is something that movies do effortlessly, at least
with respect to the effort required of the audience."[13] For both of these
influential directors the historian's dream of "things as they really were"
lies in the power not of print but of the spectacle in motion.

What inspires these assertions is not necessarily any claim to an ex-
planatory narrative, but the peculiar power of the visual to support our
notions of the real in rendering the mise-en-scène through the mimetic
capacities of the camera lens. Griffith's remarks were made not on the
basis of the plot of *Birth of a Nation* but with regard to his claim to have
accurately reconstructed Ford's Theatre on the night of Lincoln's assas-
sination. "Things as they were" applies here not to the plot but to the
set. Words may convey a narrative but only the movies can set a scene.
In a return to the cinema of attractions, Kubrick and even Griffith, the
great inventor (by his own account) of narrative cinema, see description,
mise-en-scène, the visual as what is most historical about the historical
film. We will of course be extremely cautious about accepting these filmmakers' attempts to elevate their art to the status of history. We know
how often we are disappointed by the historical inaccuracy of the result.
But these images provide the opportunity for what Tashiro calls the "connoisseur's moment," a complex response that involves both pleasure and
critical evaluation.[14] That connoisseur's moment will be the spirit of the
following pages. I shall set aside questions of narrative and theme in order
to assess the strengths and weaknesses of the filmmakers' claims for the
historical fidelity of sets and costume, not to carp but to appreciate. And
I shall conclude with an analysis of an extended sequence from both
movies to illustrate two points: first that even with the lacunae in
authenticity it is within the power of spectacle to override our informed
skepticism, and second, that the success of the illusion of reenactment
may owe little or nothing to the original narrative. Indeed, the most memorable scenes in a movie may neither be essential to the development of
the film narrative nor play a significant part in the novel.

Tony Richardson's *Tom Jones* and Stanley Kubrick's *Barry Lyndon* offer
an opportunity to explore both sides of these issues: the role of spectacle
in novel adaptations and the display of historical authenticity in costume
drama. Though they are very different in their approach to filmmaking, both directors are remarkable for the number of films they adapted
from novels. Yet fidelity to the original does not seem to have been up-
permost in their minds. *Barry Lyndon* completely reverses the theme of

Thackeray's book. Instead of being a satire on upward mobility, Kubrick's adaptation becomes an elegy for the destruction of the low-born hero by an unyielding class system. Alan Sillitoe, the author of the short story on which Richardson based his previous film, *The Loneliness of the Long-Distance Runner*, commented sourly on Richardson's method of adaptation that "the novel was merely a blueprint."[15] Richardson himself says of *Tom Jones* that by the time he had completed his initial "breakdown of the main events, characters, and even scenes I thought usable...a lot of the details of the narrative were missing."[16] We suspect that the director thought first in terms of "scenes" rather than narrative. Though he claims to have been attracted by "Fielding's great sprawling love-of-life comic odyssey with its wild range of characters and its unstoppable narrative," this consideration seems secondary to a primarily filmic desire: "It would give me a chance to use colour, and colour film was becoming faster and more sensitive."[17]

Despite the directors' insouciance about the fidelity of the adaptations, great claims were made for the films' historical authenticity, and the productions went to some lengths to achieve an eighteenth-century look. In his autobiography Richardson remarks that "we had determined to make the English countryside look as if it was unchanged from the eighteenth century and the people as real as today."[18] In respect to Kubrick's film, Ken Adam, the set designer for both *Dr. Strangelove* and *Barry Lyndon*, says that "Stanley wanted [*Barry Lyndon*] in a way to be a documentary on the eighteenth century."[19] Yet similar though these avowals of formal intent appear to be, the results diverge substantially according to the styles of the two filmmakers. Kubrick is a much more formal director than Richardson, obsessed with the technical details almost to the exclusion of any other consideration. Vincent LoBrutto explains that "*Barry Lyndon* would reach the screen in all its glory with a disciplined, though some thought overwrought, aesthetic and a concept of presenting history through the rigors of the zoom lens, candlelight and the narrator's distinctive voice."[20] Richardson by contrast was an improvisatory filmmaker, following "the dict[um] that perfection is not an aim." John Tibbetts quotes Richardson on the advantages of location as contributing exactly to this effect: "by improvising one's way out of the impossibilities of real conditions you get something on the screen that is more true, somehow, than something contrived on a set."[21]

If Richardson sought a fortuitous equivalence between documenting rural England and the immediacy of the past, Kubrick opted for the alienation of history. The more authentic historical movies tend to alienation since the modes of display are outdated and foreign to contemporary viewers no matter how familiar they are with the period. (Recall the monstrous but accurate Queen Anne wigs in Peter Greenaway's *Draughtsman's Contract* or the slightly repellent beauty spots on Lady Bellaston in *Tom Jones* and Balibari in *Barry Lyndon*.) For most directors this alienation is an opportunity to achieve visual effects that would be unmotivated in movies with contemporary subjects. Kubrick adheres to the alienation effect of authentic props somewhat more than Richardson. The stylized poses and compositions, the exaggerated slowness of the pace emphasize the dreamlike condition of the past. Alan Spiegel argues that this effect is one of the achievements of the film: "Kubrick's aesthetics...seek to preserve not the immediacy, but the pastness of the past, its remoteness and irretrievability."[22]

The pleasure of the two films lies not in their presentation of some "truth" of history but in the specific forms their partial versions take. When two styles are equally successful, as in the two films under consideration, we are faced with difficulties that belong as much to theories of representation as to ideals of historical authenticity. The fact that the distinct approaches of Richardson and Kubrick both lay claim to documentary status only alerts us to the truth that mimesis is never quite mimesis; it is also the art of photography. The difference between improvisation and technical discipline is most obvious in the director's choice of cinematographer: John Alcott for Kubrick and Walter Lassally for Richardson. There is no question about their credentials: both are superb professionals. Each film is its own evidence of their gifts. But they have very different styles. Alcott as a director of cinematography was well practiced in studio techniques. He had been the assistant director on *2001: A Space Odyssey* for Geoffrey Unsworth, the leading studio cinematographer of British (and, from the early 1960s, US) cinema, whose credits include *Becket, The Return of the Pink Panther,* and *Superman.* Alcott was agreeable to shooting that aspect of Kubrick's film that was most in the tradition of the studio, the recreation of the period through the reliance on period paintings. Another studio cinematographer, Ossie Morris, was Richardson's first choice for *Tom Jones,* but when he found that Morris "was trying to steer [him] back towards a more conventional studio-based production," he turned to Lassally who had worked on *The Loneliness of the Long Distance Runner.*[23] In fact, Richardson expresses his dissatisfaction with Morris as the antithesis of Kubrick's method: "after a few discussions when there were too many art books consulted and too much aesthetics talked we realized that our philosophies were even farther apart than before."[24]

Walter Lassally participated in Lindsay Anderson's Free Cinema movement, the cinematic equivalent of Britain's postwar Angry Young Man period, that advocated a neorealist style and working-class subject matter.

Lassally's neorealist training favored a documentary style of camerawork that fitted in with Richardson's conviction that location was the key to making it new. Not everyone admired Lassally's work on this movie, though George Perry seems to be in error when he blames him for the "intrusion of jump cuts, freeze frames, speeded up movement . . . in short the whole bag of fashionable self-indulgent tricks."[25] According to Lassally's autobiography, however, Richardson himself added most of these tricks in the editing process: "Tony went through agonies in the editing, worrying whether it would stand its length of over two hours, trying to speed it up, adding optical tricks, and so on."[26] Despite the tricks and somewhat against the grain of Fielding's romance plot, Lassally and Richardson succeed in providing *Tom Jones* with a neorealist foundation that gives the movie a remarkably contemporary feel. The hero transmogrifies into an eighteenth-century Jimmy Porter (the working-class antihero of John Osborne's *Look Back in Anger*) whose morganatic marriage has a happier outcome. Richardson found in documentary what Alan Spiegel attributes to Renoir and Griffith, a "dramatic form that translates the historical past into the immediate present."[27]

If Lassally can be said to use his camera to make Albert Finney's Tom Jones a more fortunate contemporary of the dispossessed heroes of the Angry Young Man era, Alcott worked with Kubrick on mastering the alienation effect of the zoom. This camera technique, says LoBrutto, "replaced the renowned Kubrick dolly and tracking shots."[28] Alcott and Kubrick used a 20:1 zoom that Alcott explains "became an image in itself and not, as is usually the case, a means of moving from one point in space to another."[29] *Barry Lyndon* frequently features a reverse zoom that begins with an extreme close-up. For example, after the close-up of a pistol in Barry's duel with Captain Quin the camera slowly draws back to frame the participants and then pulls further and further away until the tension of the human situation is resolved in a balanced composition of remote figures against a landscape of river and trees. Thomas Nelson finds that the pervasiveness of the zoom allows Kubrick to combine an intimacy not usually seen in historical dramas with the distancing effect that such films usually achieve: "The aesthetic of the zoom allows him to capture close-up the triviality, absurdity, and tragedy of various human entanglements, some of which collectively add up to history, while from a distance it stimulates, through an integration of spatial form and temporal content, a release made possible by the perspectives of art."[30]

Their different styles, however, go hand in hand with Richardson's and Kubrick's mutual obsession for getting historical details right. Ken Adam recalls he and Kubrick doing "research on the toothbrushes of the period, on the contraceptives, on a mass of things which finally didn't appear on the screen."[31] Stemware, however, did appear in *Barry Lyndon*. "The variety of glasses changes from scene to scene, character to character," observes C. S. Tashiro, "but none violates norms of eighteenth-century design or shows the surface perfection of machine-turned stemware."[32] Richardson surpassed even this attention to detail in *Joseph Andrews* when he rented "authentic eighteenth-century varieties of sheep and cows from the Rare Breeds Survival Center."[33] It is difficult to say whether this fetishism with detail has an impact on the audience. Condoms of dried goat intestines steeping in a water jar might elicit a certain frisson and a sharp eye might notice anachronistic stemware, but only a very specialized few would recognize eighteenth-century sheep.

The problems of designing the past, furthermore, raise questions about how much strangeness the non-specialized audience is willing to tolerate. As we have seen, Hollywood productions negotiate subtly between rendering the past and adjusting the look towards the present. Makeup is more contentious in this regard. The heavily powdered look of the upper classes in the eighteenth century is not at all attractive to contemporary audiences, and, indeed, heightens the sense of alienation. If we are looking for authenticity this is all to the good. But films modify makeup for a variety of reasons. The camera will not necessarily give the greatest viewing pleasure through mere authenticity. Edward Maeder criticizes *Tom Jones* and *Barry Lyndon* on account of makeup; he points to the 1960s-style frosted lipstick sported by Diane Cilento as Molly in *Tom Jones*, and while praising the makeup in *Barry Lyndon* for being "historically accurate in the gambling scene where the performers wear mouches and white powder," notes that elsewhere in the film the women's makeup is "very much in the style of the seventies."[34] Lassally's remarks on makeup in Richardson's movie point to another reason for inaccuracy besides the desire to render the past more palatable. The "colours in common use . . . were much too pink . . . a tendency accentuated even further by the duping stage [the process of duplicating the negatives] needed to make a large number of release prints." To compensate he tried "an ordinary street makeup by Dr. Payot . . . a liquid makeup more yellowy-brown than the 'Pan-stick type.'"[35] As this account reveals, Lassally at no point considered using period makeup, but even had it been a consideration, the requirements of the film stock would still have militated against cosmetic authenticity.

In the distribution of authentic and inauthentic makeup, furthermore, we find ourselves compelled by the storyline to an odd complicity with the filmmakers' own tendency to view history as slightly repulsive. More authentic makeup is assigned to minor or villainous characters: the grotesque eighteenth-century face paint of Sir Charles Lyndon renders his heart attack at the gaming table ludicrous, and the risibility of both the young gambler whom the Chevalier de Balibari cheats at the gaming table and the Chevalier himself is mostly due to their period makeup, enhanced in Balibari's case by an eyepatch. This tendency is notable also in other historical movies. Maeder mentions the foppish makeup and wigs for the villain of MGM's 1938 *Marie Antoinette*, the Count d'Orleans, and a still photograph shows Joseph Schildkraut with beauty patches and heavy powder.[36] In this scheme, authentic details are not so much a glimpse into the past as a guide to theme and character that mobilizes the viewer's sense of unsympathetic otherness. Narrative and theme are among those features of filmmaking that deflect the goal of authentication. Yet we may still catch in the cinematic images a glimpse of something not necessarily real but sufficiently illusionary as to induce us to suspend our critical faculties. If we look past the narrative codes that mark Sir Charles Lyndon as a cuckold or the young gambler in *Barry Lyndon* as a swindler's mark, we will be delighted by examples of eighteenth-century styles in motion. The cinema of attractions can still hold out the possibility of transcending the limitations of the narrative.

The tradition of using paintings to guide the restoration of the past has a more pointed application to another fetish of Hollywood design, the costume department. *Barry Lyndon* and *Tom Jones* are distinctly different from previous historical movies in either Hollywood or England. Yet the fetish of clothing authenticity goes back almost to the beginning of cinema. Maeder tells us that many of the fabrics used for *Marie Antoinette* were specially woven in Lyons, France. Though *Tom Jones* does not display the lavishness of costume to the same extent as either the Hollywood studio productions or *Barry Lyndon*, Richardson gives us some hint of his dedication to authenticity when he refers to "Jocelyn [Herbert] working tirelessly, trying to perfect everything from the tint and texture of paneling to the detail of every extra."[37] Kubrick in true Hollywood fashion went out of his way to achieve authenticity of the sort that LoBrutto describes: "They purchased eighteenth-century clothes, which were still available in England. On the average, people were smaller in the eighteenth century, so the clothes had to be opened up and new costumes created using the same patterns. The production operated a factory at Radlett to produce the many costumes needed to populate Kubrick's time machine visit to the eighteenth century."[38] But costume authenticity will succumb to pressures ranging from the convenience of modern sewing techniques to the need to flatter the star's silhouette. Maeder points out that at the music recital where Barry assaults his son-in-law, Lord Bullingdon, "[Marisa] Berenson wears a dress that is laced up the back – a method that was not used in European dress of the period."[39] Yet Kubrick does achieve some nice effects when he indicates the passage of time from the Seven Years War to the French Revolution through Barry's switch of headgear from the tricorne early in the film to the tam in the scene where Bullingdon challenges him to the climactic duel.

The burden on costume of conveying the period feel of a film is complicated by many other factors. Costume must appeal to the camera lens: in *The Four Feathers* the dog-carts and tents used by the British in the Sudan in the 1880s are resolutely authentic, but the uniforms of the regiment have been changed from blue to red to accommodate a better color contrast with the desert exterior. Costume also must subserve the narrative hierarchy and support themes and characters by indicating states of mind, social status, and ethical dispositions (black hat, white hat). Jane Gaines, however, understands costume as intensifying the detail almost to compete with the direction and editing – "The costume plot," she says, "often exceeds the narrative line."[40] In some responses to costume we can see how viewers other than historians can magnify the image at the expense of the narrative. Clothes designers, as might be expected, have a feel for visual flair that ignores the storyline in much the same way as do aficionados of the historical period. It is not unusual, as a recent *New York Times* fashion magazine puts it, for "the wardrobe to wear the movie." In a feature on the favorite films of contemporary designers, Anna Sui shows her eclectic taste by picking two gypsy movies and *Barry Lyndon* as appealing to her on the grounds of costume alone.[41] In 1963, the impact of costume was observable in the popularity of Tom Jones shirts – for women rather than men. *Vogue* gushed: "We have a thousand delicious memories of the movie, but what we came away with was a really insatiable craving for: the Tom Jones shirt... the thinnest handkerchief linen... those marvelously full sleeves, tight and ruffled around the wrist... entrancingly in character."[42] These film versions of the eighteenth century, in addition to being literary critics' movies and historians' movies, are also couturiers' movies.

These are some of the restrictions on "being there" in the terms of what the past might have looked like. We will only not be disillusioned because it would have been too naive to have had illusions in the first place. The filmmaker's authentic detail is contaminated by contemporary norms and cinematographic styles that have far more to do with technical developments than authentic reconstruction. Yet the power of mimesis makes this hybrid compelling, more compelling often than the narrative as a whole. The sets and costume inhabited by people engaged in an occupation identified by the film sequence as real life evoke a sense of immediacy, or, to put it another way, the mimetic effect of the "attraction" lends visual credence to the pseudo-historical mise-en-scène.

The cinema of attractions has its own topoi: images that recur across the whole line of movie genres and in the work of all directors. Some of the more obvious are the spectacular explosions typical of the action-adventure film, Western shoot-outs on Main Street, balls and bedrooms, storms at sea, nature scenes, cityscapes, monuments, and architecture. Two of the "attractions" of the historical film are the hunt and the duel. Both Richardson and Kubrick have taken advantage of their popularity to stage some of the best the cinema has known, sequences that are worth discussing a little in depth to test whether or not they can hold the viewer's attention above and beyond the plot. Both sequences have some relevance to the plot, Kubrick's more than Richardson's. Barry, overcome possibly by the recollection of his own son's death, surrenders his hard-won social status when he cannot bring himself to shoot his stepson after the other's pistol misfires. But we do not need an extended depiction of a meet and a hunt for Tom's rescue of Sophia from her runaway horse to seal their bond to each other. Both sequences, significantly, are vastly in excess of the story and drawn out to the point where the viewer might even forget the plot or be irritated by its intrusiveness.

The final duel in Kubrick's *Barry Lyndon* is perhaps the best duel ever filmed, with the possible exception of Danny Kaye's spectacular duel scene in the 1956 *Court Jester*. It is intensely dramatic though it lasts almost nine minutes and is remarkably devoid of action. Kubrick took great risks since it is the third duel in a movie that begins with a duel. Indeed, he seems to invite us to compare the cinematic genres of dueling, from the burlesque of Barry's pistol duel with Captain Quin through the highly choreographed sword-fight between Barry and an aggrieved losing gambler. The confrontation between Barry and Lord Bullingdon, then, must be seen in terms of Kubrick's abiding concern with technical formalism, familiar to viewers of all his films. It illustrates how the deliberate prolongation of the scene entices the viewer to forgo the narrative in favor of the image. The ratio of time spent on the duel is notably out of proportion to the time of exposition; in the mechanics of the confrontation the viewer eventually loses a sense of the story and even the reasons for the duel in the first place. Kubrick here uses some techniques that seem designed to give us a sense of the presentness of history. Foremost among these is the matching of the filmic scene to actual time. Though Kubrick does edit this scene, he does so with reverse angles rather than with omissions that would abbreviate the time of the action; furthermore, the takes are unusually long. Kubrick's slowing of the drama to foreground the image allows the viewer more time to set aside the narrative and process the visual excess. We are not, consequently, obliged to suspend the contemplation

2. The duel between Barry (Ryan O'Neal) and Bullingdon (Leon Vitali) in *Barry Lyndon*

of the spectacle in order to keep up with the narrative, but have leisure to meditate on the ruins, as it were, of the past.

Kubrick cleverly matches the strange formality of this life-and-death struggle to the formality that the movie as a whole attributes to the historical period itself. Real time here, however, is not an analog for a real past, like some modern version of the dramatic unities. Its function is precisely the opposite: by keying the tempo to the protraction of the image in putative real time it reverses the convention of narrative progress. The director relies on a strategy of delay, which, though consonant with our daily experience, is inimical to our expectations from the screen. The juxtaposition of the real and the formal is the mode of the scene as a whole. The formalism of the composition of the shots – the striking framing of the actors against the arch of the ruined chapel – avoids the kind of realistic documentary effects that Lassally works for, and it is matched by the extreme formalism of the event: the action is subject to the intense formality of the rules of engagement, reiterated in the maddeningly precise instructions to the duelists by the stony-faced seconds. The fetishism of the spectacle is enhanced by the sparseness of the dialogue and the extreme deliberateness of the actors' motions and delivery (the two seconds who register disapproval of Bullingdon's vomiting fit exchange impassive glances only after a perceptible time lapse). This formalism is balanced or even counteracted by the aleatory elements of the scene, the sounds of the feet shuffling on the straw, and above all by the cries of the doves and their unpredictable fluttering around the set, elements of composition most likely not very firmly under directorial control. This aleatory element brings real time into conflict with the formal structure. The artificial mise-en-scène compounding real time, aleatory elements, and severe composition manages to distance viewers from, as well as involving them in, the scene. The "description," as Kubrick himself refers to his reenactment of the past, engages the viewer in a kind of pattern-recognition stimulated by mutually trespassing channels of visual codes in a spatial format not available to the written word.

The equivalent scene in *Tom Jones* is the stag hunt. This scene could hardly be more different from Kubrick's duel, yet in the prolonged presentation and the sense of immediacy imparted by Lassally's filming techniques as well as through the participation of experienced hunters, the hunt too exceeds the tyranny of plot and theme. The duration of the sequence is not only out of proportion to the narrative but stands as an instance of the difference in emphasis between the two mediums. Fielding's reference to the hunt is a short one-sentence paragraph satirizing Squire Western's preference for his hounds over his daughter that acts as a mere prelude to the incident of Tom breaking his arm while saving Sophia from a fall from her horse.[43] Richardson, however, seizes upon this fleeting reference to provide a vibrant cinematic experience that yields much more to the audience than a device for furthering the love plot between Tom and Sophia. The vertiginous rush of the galloping horses is an instance of that cinema of attractions where the viewer is invited to participate in "the realistic illusion of motion" that Gunning describes as being the stock in trade of early movies.[44] The hunt in *Tom Jones* is simply a fairground sideshow inserted into the storyline, but an extremely exciting one to which the viewer returns when the storyline has been exhausted.

Richardson's hunt, moreover, is the site of a sustained clash between thematic notes and cinematic values. One of the most severe restrictions on the power of the attraction is the supposed satire on hunting, what George Perry thinks of as "a crude piece of anti-blood-sport propaganda."[45] Many viewers recall the bleeding horse, the broken-necked goose, and the grotesque juxtaposition of the bleeding stag's head with Griffith's inflamed toper's visage. The blood sport issue is rather vexed from the point of view of historical accuracy: it is hard to believe that the intensity of this issue in contemporary Britain is appropriate to the eighteenth century, even though we can recall Pope's lines against killing animals in the *Essay on Man* and Thomson's similar views in *The Seasons*. What background we have about the director's intentions on this issue is somewhat contradictory. Richardson "had permission to cull venison from an overstocked herd," and in his anxiety to get "a viable image" of dogs tearing into a deer he "stuffed the deer with expensive beef liver." Not the actions of a dedicated animal-rights activist. Richardson did, however, have trouble with some local members of the "hunting fraternity" who heard that the sequence was to be a slur on their activities; they broke into his kennels and overfed his dogs the night before the first shoot so "the dogs were too bloated to do more than sniff at [the deer's] carcass and back away."[46] Nevertheless, Peter Bull, who played Thwackum, attributes the success of the sequence to the participation of the "distinguished Hunting Set": "members of the county," he remarks, "rode at full gallop to give the scenes verisimilitude." In particular, Lady Cranborne, "as an expert horsewoman (very spectacular she looked riding side-saddle) ... much embellished the picture."[47] Indeed some of the images that combine the quotidian and the historical most effectively are the marvelous glimpses of a woman careening over the countryside at full speed, sidesaddle, in antique hunting costume. In effect the visual components of the spectacle clash in a way that prevents them from being easily subordinated to a theme: the anti-blood-sport insertions contend with rather than complement or subordinate the intensity of the motion of the galloping horses.

The sequence finally owes its power to that most cinematic of formulas, the chase, whether on horseback or in automobiles, which, of course, is always part of the cinema of attractions. Richardson furthermore struggles to make the past more concrete by first filming the meet: a horseback-riding crowd of actors and extras in period costume mills around in a village street, snacking, drinking, and joking while Lassally's cameras roll. Lassally differentiates the camerawork of the meet from that of the hunt. "We staged the meet that precedes the hunt as an event to be covered by three hand-held cameras, newsreel fashion."[48] Astonishingly they got this sequence with a minimum of retakes. Lassally says that "the scene was shot in half a morning," not much longer than a meet itself would take. The hunt by contrast is a sequence of dizzying speed achieved, Lassally believes, "by the intercutting of low-angle ground and low-angle helicopter shots."[49] It is the intense activity of the chase that differentiates this scene from the duel. The sequence is by no means in real time: a hunt, after all, that could go for fifty miles would by no means take three to five minutes. Yet, though we recognize the shaping presence of the cutting room, we are drawn into the event by the dynamic visual experience. Both the mundaneness of the meet and the action of the chase familiarize the alienation of history and foster the illusion that we are peering into the past. Even the bloodiness translates rather into a representation of more barbaric times than into propaganda. The compulsiveness of the non-narrative image that *Barry Lyndon* achieves by formal composition *Tom Jones* achieves by the oldest topos in Hollywood. Those moments when we almost cease to recognize the deviousness of the director and the art director and lose ourselves in the illusion of the past may be when the cinema's power of display overwhelms all those little unsatisfactory adjustments of character and theme that pertain to the narrative.

The history of film is for a large part the history of the development of narrative techniques, and there is no doubt that even the films discussed here would be less watchable if they lacked a plot – indeed in the case of *Tom Jones*, a plot brilliantly rendered by the director, Tony Richardson. I set out, however, to amend in some slight degree an overemphasis in discussions of film adaptations from novels on finding the pictorial equivalent of theme and narrative. Whether in condemnation or praise, this practice is anti-ocularist insofar as the visual image is always, in the words of Norman Bryson with regard to a similar problem in the history of art, "curtail[ed] . . . through its conversion into a site of meaning." The thought processes that went into the creation of these two films, no less concentrated and powerful than those that went into the creation of the novels, were directed primarily at visual effects. It is up to us to direct our attention to a time when, as Bryson says, "the image [has] been granted full independence – allowed simply to exist, with all the plenary autonomy enjoyed by the objects of the world."[50]

NOTES

1 Roland Barthes, *The Pleasure of the Text*, trans. Richard Miller (New York: Hill and Wang, 1975), p. 11.
2 Barbara Stafford, *Good Looking: Essays on the Virtues of Images* (Cambridge, MA: MIT Press, 1966), pp. 61, 65.
3 Tom Gunning, *D. W. Griffith and the Origins of American Narrative Film* (Urbana and Chicago: University of Illinois Press, 1991), p. 17.
4 Gunning, *Griffith*, p. 41.
5 Harold Rosenberg, *The Case of the Baffled Radical* (Chicago and London: University of Chicago Press, 1985), p. 91.
6 Vincent LoBrutto, *Stanley Kubrick: A Biography* (New York: Da Capo Press, 1999), p. 390.
7 Leonard Maltin, *Movie and Video Guide: 2000 Edition* (New York: NAL; London: Penguin, 1999), p. 254.
8 C. S. Tashiro, *Pretty Pictures: Production Design and the History Film* (Austin: University of Texas Press, 1998), p. 64.
9 Simon Schama, "Visualizing History," *Harper's Magazine*, February 2000, 37.
10 Henry Home, Lord Kames, *Elements of Criticism* (New York and Chicago: A. S. Barnes and Company, 1874), p. 67.
11 Pierre Sorlin, *The Film in History: Restaging the Past* (Totowa, NJ: Barnes and Noble Books, 1980), pp. x–xi.

12 Sorlin, *Film in History*, pp. x–xi.
13 Michael Ciment, *Kubrick*, trans. Gilbert Adair (New York: Holt Rinehart and Winston, 1983), p. 167.
14 Tashiro, *Pretty Pictures*, p. 7.
15 William L. Horne, "'Greatest Pleasures': *A Taste of Honey*, 1961 and *The Loneliness of the Long-Distance Runner*, 1962," in *The Cinema of Tony Richardson*, ed. James M. Welsh and John C. Tibbetts (New York: SUNY, 1999), p. 105.
16 Tony Richardson, *The Long-Distance Runner: A Memoir* (New York: William Morrow and Co., 1993), p. 159.
17 Richardson, *Runner*, p. 158.
18 Richardson, *Runner*, p. 159.
19 Ciment, *Kubrick*, p. 205.
20 LoBrutto, *Kubrick*, p. 386.
21 John C. Tibbetts, "Breaking the Proscenium," in *Tony Richardson*, ed. Welsh and Tibbetts, p. 77.
22 Alan Spiegel, "Kubrick's *Barry Lyndon*," *Salmagundi*, 38–9 (Summer–Fall 1977), 194–208, 199.
23 Walter Lassally, *Itinerant Cameraman* (London: John Murray, 1989), p. 73.
24 Richardson, *Runner*, p. 159.
25 George Perry, *The Great British Picture Show* (Boston, Toronto: Little, Brown and Company, 1974, revised 1985), p. 219.
26 Lassally, *Cameraman*, p. 81.
27 Spiegel, "Kubrick's *Barry Lyndon*," 199.
28 LoBrutto, *Kubrick*, p. 300.
29 LoBrutto, *Kubrick*, p. 390.
30 Thomas Allen Nelson, *Kubrick: Inside a Film Artist's Maze* (Bloomington: Indiana University Press, 1982), p. 185.
31 Ciment, *Kubrick*, p. 205.
32 Tashiro, *Pretty Pictures*, p. 13.
33 Don Radovich, *Tony Richardson: A Bio-Bibliography* (Westport, CT and London: Greenwood Press, 1995), p. 143.
34 Edward Maeder, "The Celluloid Image: Historical Dress in Film," in *Hollywood and History: Costume Design in Film*, ed. Edward Maeder (London: Thames and Hudson; Los Angeles: Los Angeles County Museum of Art 1987), pp. 16, 209.
35 Lassally, *Cameraman*, p. 76.
36 Maeder, "Celluloid Image," pp. 73–4.
37 Richardson, *Runner*, p. 167.
38 LoBrutto, *Kubrick*, p. 381.
39 Edward Maeder and David Ehrenstein, "Filmography," in *Hollywood and History*, ed. Maeder, p. 209.
40 Jane Gaines, "Costume and Narrative: How Dress Tells the Woman's Story," in *Fabrications: Costume and the Female Body*, ed. Jane Gaines and Charlotte Herzog (New York: Routledge, 1990), p. 205.
41 Amy Calabrese, "They Lost it at the Movies," *Fashions of the Times*, Part 2, Spring 2000, *New York Times*, February 20, 2000, 116.
42 Quoted in Satch LaValley, "Hollywood and Seventh Avenue: The Impact of Period Films on Fashion," in *Hollywood and History*, ed. Maeder, p. 94.

43 Henry Fielding, *The History of Tom Jones, A Foundling,* ed. Fredson Bowers (Middletown, CT: Wesleyan University Press, 1975), IV: 13.

44 Gunning, *Griffith,* p. 41.

45 Perry, *Picture Show,* p. 219.

46 Richardson, *Runner,* p. 166.

47 Peter Bull, *Bull's Eyes,* ed. Sheridan Morley (London: Robin Clark Ltd., 1985), p. 155.

48 Lassally, *Cameraman,* p. 76.

49 Lassally, *Cameraman,* p. 77.

50 Norman Bryson, *Word and Image: French Painting of the Ancien Regime,* (Cambridge: Cambridge University Press, 1981), p. xvi.

2   Three cinematic Robinsonades

Robert Mayer

Robert Zemeckis's *Cast Away* (2000) has recently reminded us that Daniel Defoe's *Robinson Crusoe* is a novel with great cinematic potential. The text offers filmmakers a rich set of images to be realized: great voyages, a storm at sea, a solitary individual's difficult journey to a desert island, a lonely life on that island in which the protagonist "discovers" various crucial tools and techniques, the physical transformation of the hero, and encounters with strange and frightening creatures. Zemeckis's picture, however, succeeds as a retelling of the Crusoe story not because it is a faithful realization of Defoe's novel but because it is a visually stunning and at times harrowing representation of an important part of that mythic ordeal: the physical and psychic torment resulting from a long period of isolation in the wilderness.[1] That Zemeckis's film also heavily rewrites the story by placing it in the twentieth century and tailoring it to a con-temporary movie audience's expectations – adding a love story, making the contemporary "Crusoe" (Tom Hanks) an employee of a multina-tional corporation – is nothing particularly noteworthy. As Pat Rogers observes, *Robinson Crusoe* was copied, imitated, abridged, and rewritten almost from the moment it first appeared, so much so that the rework-ings of the Crusoe story came to be classified as "an entire sub-branch of continental literature," the Robinsonade.[2] For most of the history of this little-noticed genre, Robinsonades have revised Defoe's story but embraced the values that are generally associated with the book: indi-vidualism, spiritual and moral seriousness, inventiveness and proficiency in matters of technique and human economy.[3] Tom Sullivan discusses conventions that have endured through many modifications: "reduced to its most minimal attributes, the Robinsonade tells the story of a castaway, or of a group of castaways, who, separated from their native society, must survive in a limited area isolated from the rest of the world and create there a viable society." According to Sullivan, these narratives depict an abundant nature that allows castaways to thrive in isolation and assure readers that European man, faced with the challenges of life in such a set-ting, would "domesticate a world full of wonders." Sullivan demonstrates, moreover, that the Victorian Robinsonades were even more triumphalist and optimistic than earlier works of this sort; in the nineteenth century, the Robinsonade was "adapted . . . to the demands of an audience which wanted to be reassured that God, nature, and his fellow man were all benevolent" and which believed unquestioningly in "the technical and moral superiority of a proper group of Englishmen" confronted with antagonists that included pirates and "savages."[4]

The tradition of the Robinsonade has endured down to our own day, not only in works of fiction by writers like Michel Tournier and J. M. Coetzee but also in a number of film versions of the text.[5] The filmic Robinsonades have included such oddities as *Mr. Robinson Crusoe* (1932), Douglas Fairbanks's last picture in America; *Robinson Crusoe-Land* (1952), a lesser effort by Laurel and Hardy; and *Robinson Crusoe on Mars* (1964).[6] Many recent Robinsonades, however, whether cinematic or literary, have departed from the pattern set from the eighteenth down to the early twentieth century not only by reworking Defoe's narrative but also by breaking with the beliefs and values held by many readers to be embodied in that text. This essay focuses on three such cinematic Robinsonades from the second half of the twentieth century: Luis Buñuel's joint Mexican–American production, *The Adventures of Robinson Crusoe* (1952); Jack Gold's British film, *Man Friday* (1975); and *Crusoe* (1989) by the American cinematographer-turned-director, Caleb Deschanel.[7]

Most Robinsonades are, of course, deeply fascinated by the spectacle of a man who recreates civilization by himself on a desert island and makes himself the "Master of every mechanick Art," and cinematic Robinsonades generally revel in the visual possibilities of the text as well as the opportunity the book presents for telling a story of endurance and even triumph over nature, hardship, and time.[8] But *Robinson Crusoe* also clearly presents certain problems to contemporary filmmakers (as to fiction writers like Tournier and Coetzee). While one often finds in these adaptations some treatment of the religious side of Crusoe's experience, most of the films either are skeptical about the piety of Defoe's protagonist or simply ignore it.[9] They also often embody a critical view of the colonial enterprise that has been linked with Defoe's novel. Most important, the works treated in this essay focus in one way or another on race, and on the confrontation between European and non-European man, and in the process make it clear that race is *the* dilemma presented to twentieth-century artists who appropriate Defoe's text for their own purposes. Earlier films referring to the novel, such as *Mr. Robinson Crusoe* and *Robinson Crusoe-Land*, unintentionally highlight the racial problematic simply by being egregiously racist.[10] The films by Buñuel, Gold, and Deschanel, however, focus on the Crusoe–Friday relationship by transforming it and, in the process, critiquing Defoe's version of that mythic encounter. I shall argue that these cinematic Robinsonades move beyond the novel in a way that is described by Homi K. Bhabha, who describes the post-colonial as a maneuver that "locate[s] the question of culture in the realm of the *beyond*," somewhere that is "neither a new horizon, nor a leaving behind of the past" but is, instead, a "moment of transit." This moment involves not only "repetition" but also "displacement and disjunction." The colonial work of art or form of discourse, that is, is not obliterated in the post-colonial text; rather the latter "renews the past, refiguring it as a contingent 'in-between' space, that innovates and interrupts the performance of the present." The post-colonial, Bhabha's work suggests, may both refer to the colonial and in important ways revitalize it even as it criticizes and transforms the earlier formulation. Bhabha describes the "beyond" or "the 'in-between' spaces" that constitute the locus of the post-colonial as "sites of collaboration, and contestation."[11] The films discussed in this essay differ from each other in the ways that they emphasize either collaboration or contestation as a means of post-colonial transformation. The films by Buñuel and Deschanel both reconceive the Crusoe–Friday relationship by casting Crusoe as a figure reformed by his encounter by Friday, even though Deschanel goes much further than Buñuel in making a case against Defoe's hero. Gold's film, however, differs from the other two cinematic Robinsonades by representing Crusoe as beyond redemption; *Man Friday* effectively rejects both Crusoe the hero and *Robinson Crusoe* the novel as unreclaimable.

The British director Tony Richardson observed that Buñuel's *Adventures of Robinson Crusoe* (1952) is "as remarkable in its fidelity to Defoe as in its transmutation," and indeed the film positions itself somewhere between a straightforward retelling of the novel and a thorough reworking of the original narrative that functions as a rejection of its values.[12] In his memoirs, Buñuel acknowledges that the project was not one about which he was initially very enthusiastic, and one can easily see why. Again in his memoirs, the former Roman Catholic declares himself "Still an Atheist . . . Thank God!" and elsewhere he rejects the tenets of Italian neorealism in favor of a cinema that has the quality of dreams.[13] Throughout his career, furthermore, Buñuel made films like *L'Age d'Or* (1930), *The Exterminating Angel* (1962), and *That Obscure Object of Desire* (1974) that Gillian Parker rightly describes as "ferocious raiding parties on the dignity of the acquisitive bourgeoisie."[14] Defoe's novel, then, with its celebration of "the middle Station of Life" and its debt to Puritan spiritual autobiography, not to mention its position as one of the constitutive works of the realist novel in English, was not a work ready-made for the attentions of the one surrealist director who also had a major career making feature films (5). Nevertheless, *The Adventures of Robinson Crusoe* was an important picture for its director: his first color film (and, he reports in his memoirs, "the first Eastmancolor film in America") and one of his two English-language features. The film garnered an Academy Award nomination for Dan O'Herlihy, the actor who plays Crusoe, and despite his initial misgivings, Buñuel declares himself "very fond" of the film, no doubt because he made *Robinson Crusoe* very much his own.[15] Parker comments: "Defoe used the experience of the island shipwreck to tell one story, Buñuel to tell another."[16]

Nevertheless, in important ways Buñuel's film *is* faithful to Defoe's novel. The use of voice-over narration in the film helps suggest the different levels of storytelling in the book, both the first-person narrative and the journal contained within it. The film also depicts Crusoe's life on the island as described in the novel more amply than any other film version discussed here. Much attention is paid, for example, to Crusoe's bringing ashore supplies from the wreck of his ship, and the film represents the protagonist raising crops, exploring his island, identifying flora and fauna, building a raft, and making pots. Buñuel, who observed "what interested me in the story was the solitude of Robinson," also represents Crusoe's isolation and loneliness in rich detail.[17] However, whereas Buñuel's account of Crusoe mastering "everything in my island" is very like a transcription of aspects of Defoe's novel, the filmmaker's treatment of Crusoe's psychic torment – his experience on *"the Island of Despair"* (italics in original) – features many striking Buñuelian inventions (70). In one, a drunken waking dream, a desperate Crusoe (O'Herlihy) hears the voices of former companions singing in a tavern. The song they sing reflects Crusoe's own state of mind: "Down among the dead men, down among the dead men . . . down among the dead men, let them lie." When the singing abruptly stops, Crusoe looks stupefied, and then he weeps. Later, he runs into the ocean in a frenzy, crying "Help! Help!" and then we see him talking to insects, calling two of them "my little friends," offering them an ant to lure them out of the sand into which they have burrowed, and then relishing their eating of it.

Buñuel also departs from Defoe's narrative when he shows Crusoe tormented by sexual desire. In the novel, Crusoe observes that one of the advantages of being on the island is that he is free from "the Lust of the Flesh" (128), and James Joyce once observed that "the sexual apathy" of Crusoe was one of the ways in which "the whole Anglo-Saxon spirit" is in Defoe's character.[18] Buñuel's Crusoe, by contrast, is a notably sexual being. At one point, he looks stricken when he catches sight of a scarecrow he has unthinkingly covered with a woman's dress. Later, when Friday

(Jaime Fernandez) innocently dons a dress and wears a "necklace" made of coins that he has fashioned for himself, Crusoe angrily orders him to remove the costume. It is too strong to say, as Richardson does, that in Buñuel's film Crusoe's "torment is above all sexual," but one of the ways that Buñuel breaks with Defoe's version of the story is to insist upon a sexual component of Crusoe's loneliness.[19]

What is more, although religion figures importantly in this film, it provides Buñuel's Crusoe no real solace. Crusoe's religious awakening is treated, but perfunctorily. When the protagonist is tormented by loneliness and is close to becoming unbalanced, the film represents him as running to his "valley of the echo" to listen to the reverberation of his own voice. There he recites the 23rd Psalm, repeating the declaration "He restoreth my soul" and then exclaiming, "My soul!" although the echoing lines, along with Crusoe's anguished expression, make it evident that the Biblical passage is devoid of meaning for the speaker. In the next scene, Crusoe again reads the same Psalm, stopping at "green pastures" and repeating that phrase as if he cannot comprehend the words. He then comments in a voice-over narration: "the scriptures came meaningless to my eyes. The world seemed but a whirling ball – its oceans and continents a green scum, and my soul of no purpose, no meaning." Buñuel seems here to be declaring of Crusoe: "Thank God! An atheist – at last!" Later, in a conversation with Friday that is quite close to one in the novel, Crusoe attempts to explain why God allows the devil to tempt men, but the Englishman is confounded by Friday's line of questioning in which the latter asks: "is God not much more strong as devil?" and then "why not God kill devil, so make him no more wicked?" Finally there is this exchange:

FRIDAY: Is God let devil tempt us?
CRUSOE: Yes.
FRIDAY: Then why God mad when we sin?

At this point Crusoe gives up, declaring to his nearby parrot: "Friday can't get these things into his head." But although the novel describes a similar colloquy, it returns to the matter and assures the reader that in the end Friday was convinced, and Crusoe relates in the text that his companion became "a good Christian, a much better than I" (218–19, 220). Buñuel's film, however, provides no follow-up to this conversation and in fact the failed attempt on Crusoe's part to justify the ways of God to Friday is the last mention of religion in the film.

Finally, in a dream sequence that is his most striking revision of Defoe's narrative, Buñuel also recasts Crusoe's relationship with his family. The admonition of Crusoe's father before the young man goes to sea in which the father enjoins his son to be content with "the middle Station

3. Friday (Jaime Fernandez) and Crusoe (Dan O'Herlihy) in Luis Buñuel's *Adventures of Robinson Crusoe*

of Life" and to avoid "the Passion of Envy, or secret burning Lust of Ambition," which Defoe's hero tells us was delivered by his father "in the most affectionate manner," becomes in the film the warning of a cold and seemingly cruel father (5). The father's admonishing remarks occur not at the beginning of the film, not, that is, before Crusoe has arrived on the island, but in the midst of his island experience, and it comes to him as a tormenting nightmare.[20] As the father delivers his advice in the film, he washes a pig, in Crusoe's dream, standing in water himself and knocking over large beakers of water, all as the feverishly ill Crusoe pleads for a drink: "Water, father, give me water!" The father laughs to himself, seemingly enjoying his son's torment, and tells Crusoe:

Why did you fling yourself into this stupid adventure? Did you not know that your mother and I were praying that God would not separate us from you? But you were always wayward. Your mother and I will forgive you. But remember God will not forgive you . . . Remember! He will not forgive you! You will die!

Thus, the novel's celebration of "the middle Station" becomes in Buñuel's film an outrage committed by a cold, judgmental, and unloving father against his son. Admittedly, this takes place in a dream in the film and in that dream sequence the role of the father is played by O'Herlihy, who is also the son, but even though the vision of the father is, therefore, the son's projection, the dream sequence is nevertheless Buñuel's only glimpse of Crusoe's familial relations and it is not a happy one. The filmmaker turns Crusoe's father's "serious and excellent Counsel," extolling "the middle State" as "the best State in the World," into a typically Buñuelian attack on the bourgeois family (4).

One also sees this tendency on Buñuel's part to repeat important features of the novel and simultaneously disrupt them in the film's rendering of the relationship between Crusoe and Friday. Friday's experience as Crusoe's servant is presented in the film in a relatively untroubled way; for example, the movie contains the scene from the novel in which Friday lays his head on the ground and places Crusoe's foot upon it, which in the book is taken as a sign "of Subjection, Servitude, and Submission . . . to let me know, how he would serve me as long as he liv'd" (206). At the end of the film, furthermore, Crusoe leaves the island dressed as an English gentleman, and Friday leaves with him, but the latter is dressed in home-spun and is prepared to follow his "master" to England. At the same time, however, Buñuel's film represents Crusoe as a suspicious, brutal, and arrogant master. Whereas in the novel, Crusoe almost immediately entrusts Friday with weapons ("giving him the Sword in his Hand, with the Bow and Arrow at his Back, which I found he could use very dextrously" [207]), in the film Crusoe does so only after he has treated Friday quite savagely. One night Friday enters Crusoe's supposedly secure inner sanctum in pursuit of tobacco, and Crusoe shackles him. When Friday asks why Crusoe is treating him in this fashion, the Englishman replies: "I'm your master; I'll do as pleases me," and in the voice-over narration Crusoe recalls that many years earlier he had intended the shackles for the African slaves he was in search of when his ship foundered. In this scene, Friday's frenzy is represented with an intensity that underlines Crusoe's inhumanity; Friday implores his master to kill him.[21] Faced with Friday's grief, however, Crusoe relents and undergoes a major transformation, begging Friday to forgive him and declaring: "I want you to be my friend." In the voice-over, Crusoe declares that "Friday was as loyal a friend as ever man could want," and in the next scene the two men are shown hunting, each with his own gun. Later, Crusoe observes, as Friday is shown fishing with a spear, "with his many different skills, he enriched my life on the island." In Buñuel's film, as Virginia Higginbotham observes, "it is Crusoe, not Friday, who is growing in humanity."[22]

Buñuel's transformation of Defoe's novel, therefore, entails a clear critique of many of the book's presuppositions: Puritan religiosity, sexual repression, bourgeois family values, and a belief in the natural division of European and non-European man into the roles of master and slave. The film also features a sympathetic portrayal of Friday that suggests that the latter is, in important respects, Crusoe's moral superior. Yet, this *Robinson Crusoe* also reproduces important features of the Crusoe–Friday relationship as represented in the novel and thereby demonstrates that fidelity to Defoe's text entails, to some degree at least, an acceptance of the novel's colonial vision.

Jack Gold's *Man Friday*, by contrast, is much more single-minded about breaking with the novel. The 1975 film, based on Adrian Mitchell's 1973 play of the same name, makes essentially no use of Crusoe's individual experience at sea or on the island. Like Buñuel's film, *Man Friday* represents nothing of Crusoe's experience before the shipwreck, but, in addition, in Gold's film the island itself is represented almost claustrophobically whereas Buñuel (like Deschanel later) takes full advantage of the opportunity presented to him by color cinematography to convey a sense of the beauty and grandeur of Crusoe's island. (Richardson observes: "The film was shot in the soft green mountains of Manzanillo . . . and the Technicolor has great delicacy."[23]) Except on a few occasions when the film focuses on Friday, there are essentially no vistas of the sea or of verdant nature in *Man Friday*, and frequently the island seems bathed in a cruel white light. The only real reference to Crusoe's technical mastery, moreover, is his use of an elaborate and vaguely absurd contraption worthy of Rube Goldberg that functions as a ladder into his stockade. Crusoe's dwelling, furthermore, is so elaborate as to seem somehow suburban and as a result similarly ridiculous.

Gold's film goes much further than Buñuel's in rejecting the values associated with Defoe's novel and in its critical treatment of the Crusoe–Friday relationship. *Man Friday*, like Deschanel's film after it, emphasizes the importance of race in that relationship by casting an African-American actor, Richard Roundtree, in the role.[24] *Man Friday* relates the encounter between Crusoe and Friday from the latter's point of view, and in fact the only part of Crusoe's island experience that is represented is his relationship with Friday. In a framing narrative, Friday (Roundtree) addresses a tribal assembly after he has returned to his own people. The purpose of the assembly is to consider Crusoe's request that he be taken in by the tribe. Describing his life with Crusoe in support of his contention that his people must not accept the Englishman into their midst, Friday begins by telling of the occasion when he and three others prepared to eat one of their own, "so we could take some of the spirit of that man whom we loved into the future with us." Thus, of Crusoe's "rescue" of Friday, the latter relates that he and the others had just started eating their old friend "when death visited us again," death this time being Crusoe himself, who, misapprehending everything, tells Friday: "I have come to rescue you from these foul cannibals . . . [and] save your benighted soul." The film thus refigures cannibalism, which Markman Ellis argues is, in the book, an occasion for Crusoe to "creatively dehumanise" Friday and his kind. Ellis points out that the very existence of this practice is at issue, citing William Arens who questions what he calls "the man-eating myth" and argues "that the description by one group of people of another people as cannibals is an ideological and rhetorical device to establish moral superiority."[25] *Man Friday* accepts the existence of cannibalism but suggests that anthropophagy might well be a loving act and thus not a sign of degeneration making colonization with its putative "civilizing" effect almost inevitable. In this way, the film announces its intention of transvaluing the givens traditionally located in *Robinson Crusoe*.

Not surprisingly, therefore, when Crusoe, who relishes his possessions, tries to explain to Friday the principle of ownership, Friday is simply mystified by the idea that anything "can be for one person only." At the tribal meeting Friday describes the English as "a tribe of people who go about saying 'this is mine; this is yours,'" and his comment evokes general hilarity. Similarly, Crusoe explains sport as "war without weapons" and "cutthroat competition in which no throat is cut," but Friday prefers to emphasize the beauty of a man running or the pleasure of swimming. Sex is at least momentarily important in this film as well; in *Man Friday* the two men talk about sex because Friday finds Crusoe engaged in self-flagellation, certain that God is angry with him because he has had an erotic dream. Friday, however, argues "God would not send you a love dream if he were angry with you," and then offers to help Crusoe satisfy his sexual needs: "if you had told me you needed loving, I would have helped you . . . I have a body too. I am a loving man." Crusoe denounces Friday ("you have offered me a poisonous gift"), but the film endorses Friday's point of view – his pleasure in the body, his untroubled view of sexuality, and his refusal to accept the idea of an angry, vengeful god. At the end of the scene in which Friday and Crusoe discuss the latter's sexual needs, Crusoe's parrot chimes in: "Poor Robinson Crusoe!" Earlier, during the tribe's discussion of Crusoe's view of sport as a symbolic pitched battle, one young man speaks in favor of competition, and the tribe's elder declares, "this boy is not well," and sends him off with a young woman who is meant to cure him by having sex with him.

The film unfolds through a series of discussions between the two men in which Crusoe acts rather like Gulliver in Book Four of *Gulliver's Travels*, explaining Western culture and values to Friday, who functions a bit like a Houyhnhnm master and becomes increasingly dismayed by what he hears. These always contentious discussions are punctuated by moments when Crusoe uses a gun or manacles to insist upon his mastery and the rightness of his views. (The most sustained dispute between the two men results from Friday's declaration that he "will not live as a slave," and his subsequent refusal to work "until all the work is shared.") At the end of the film Friday brings his former master into the tribal assembly and Crusoe declares: "I would very much like to stay. I know I have wronged your tribe in the past... [but] it was simply because I didn't understand." He offers, in return for being allowed to live with Friday's people, to teach them "about the world beyond the ocean." Friday strenuously objects, however, arguing: "I think he would destroy our tribe like a great sickness." When the tribe's leader argues they should allow Crusoe to stay in order to cure him, Friday warns that Crusoe "is sickness itself" and declares that the only thing Crusoe teaches is fear; Friday insists above all else that Crusoe must be kept away from the tribe's children. His arguments clearly convince the tribe's elders because in the last scene of the film, the Englishman is back on his island, reading from his Bible, seated in a blinding light on the beach: "in the image of God created He him... And God blessed them, and said to them be fruitful and multiply and replenish the earth and subdue it." Crusoe is again alone, and his final desolation is represented as the result of his attempt at achieving a kind of monstrous mastery over everything around him. Crusoe's God and his Bible are associated with the hero's egotism, willfulness, greed, sexual repression, and self-hatred. In the cut of the film that was shown at the 1975 Cannes Film Festival – later recut and softened – the film ended with Crusoe holding a gun to his own head, prepared to commit suicide.[26] But in the film that was finally shown in theaters, Crusoe's situation is only marginally less bleak: he is alone, bathed in a cruel white light, and likely to stay that way. Using Friday's discussion of his island experience to represent Robinson Crusoe as a pathological racist and imperialist, a representative of exploitative, destructive European man, the film anticipates the arguments of later critics who focus on colonialist features of Defoe's novel, such as, for example, Edward Said, who links the rise of the novel and the European imperial project and declares: "The protoypical modern realistic novel is *Robinson Crusoe*, and certainly not accidentally it is about a European who creates a fiefdom for himself on a distant, non-European island."[27]

Thus, Gold's film is more an exercise in *anti*-colonial rhetoric than a post-colonial reappropriation of Defoe's narrative. *Man Friday* does not so much refigure the Crusoe myth as discard the figure of Crusoe, identifying the character as one that cannot be reformed or recuperated but that instead has to be rejected. Given the importance of the Crusoe myth – Watt identifies Defoe's narrative as one of four "myths of modern individualism" – casting Robinson Crusoe in this light was bound to be problematic at best, and the fact that the filmmaker took such a radically critical stance in respect to Defoe's narrative and hero may help explain why the film was a failure, both critically and commercially.[28] Penelope Houston observed in *Sight and Sound* that *Man Friday* "stacks the cards for the noble savage," and Hugh James similarly objected that "the Englishman...is left alone on his island to read about his dreary God while Friday returns to his tribe to sing and dance and make love."[29] The film, in truth, makes it virtually impossible to sympathize or identify with Crusoe. Peter O'Toole's performance renders the character strident and, finally, odious. The audience is denied all opportunities to take any pleasure from either Crusoe's island or his mastery of various skills and techniques. Instead, the film focuses our attention relentlessly on Crusoe's attempt to subject Friday to his will and force him to embrace views and beliefs that the latter rejects as irrational and destructive. One might argue that the film's refusal to luxuriate in exotic locales and "surprising adventures" constitutes its most resolute rejection of the objectionable politics of Defoe's novel, but it is also emblematic of its essential rejection – rather than its refiguring – of the figure of Crusoe. Gold's Robinsonade constricts Crusoe's world and confines the protagonist to a harsh and impoverished version of his mythic island. *Man Friday* refuses to "collaborate" with *Robinson Crusoe*; it refigures Defoe's protagonist in a wholly negative way.[30]

Crusoe also makes a very strong case against both novel and hero but the treatment of the Friday–Crusoe relationship in Deschanel's film is, finally, profoundly different from what one finds in *Man Friday*. *Crusoe* opens not in England and not in the seventeenth century but in Tidewater Virginia in 1808. Crusoe (Aidan Quinn) is an American, then, and he is, seemingly, a slave trader by profession. He makes a perilous journey to Africa late in the season because he has heard that "the pens in Guinea are crammed" and estimates that he can buy slaves at "twenty-five dollars for a buck, ten dollars for a girl." His ship goes down at sea, of course, and Deschanel thus implicitly raises the issue of ambition thwarted and greed and inhumanity punished. But *Crusoe* does not focus on its protagonist's corruption as relentlessly as does *Man Friday*. Deschanel first distinguished himself as the cinematographer on Carroll Ballard's *The Black Stallion* of 1979, a film particularly notable for its nature photography, and he clearly relished the opportunities the Crusoe narrative presents to the filmmaker.[31] Like Buñuel's film before it, furthermore, Deschanel's *Crusoe* both undermines important elements of the Crusoe myth and at the same time "celebrates Crusoe's achievements."[32] The shipwreck is visually memorable, and the film shows Crusoe exploring his island, making fire, building a boat, raising crops, enduring illness, and, at one point, descending toward madness. Yet the second half of the film focuses almost exclusively on encounters between Crusoe and two black men, each of whom functions as a version of Friday in this Robinsonade. In the process *Crusoe* identifies race as the prime issue forced upon the filmmaker transforming Defoe's novel but also represents Crusoe's encounter with the two Fridays as a "spiritual retreat" that reforms the erstwhile dealer in slaves.[33]

In this telling of the Crusoe tale, there is no footprint. Although Crusoe sees signs of cannibalism early in the film, the first sense he gets that there are visitors on the island who might be dangerous is when he encounters blacks bringing a deceased king to the island for a burial ceremony. When the body is placed on a funeral pyre, two other black men have their throats cut and their blood is poured on the fire. Crusoe fires his musket at the group, enabling a third man who is about to be similarly sacrificed to escape. This man Crusoe dubs "Lucky" because, as Crusoe explains to him, there is no one to whom the slave trader can sell the black man. Crusoe tries to teach Lucky (Hepburn Graham) table manners at the point of a gun; later, he manacles his captive for the night and at that point, Lucky escapes. The next morning Crusoe finds Lucky's severed head, and then immediately encounters another black man – "the Warrior" (Ade Sapara) – who captures Crusoe with a booby trap that hoists him in the air and leaves him dangling upside down from a palm tree.

With his capture, Crusoe's moral education begins. Somewhat inexplicably set free by his African captor (although the release does have the effect of suggesting the greater humanity of the latter), Crusoe nevertheless attacks him. After the white man fails to kill the Warrior with his pistol, they fight hand to hand and eventually they wrestle in a muddy bog. The fight ends with both men sinking into quicksand.[34] The Warrior manages to pull himself to safety and then watches as Crusoe sinks, spreading the mud that covers his body over his limbs with a satisfied air until he rescues Crusoe at the last possible moment. *Crusoe*, therefore, like the films of both Gold and Buñuel, represents Friday as Crusoe's (actual or potential) savior and argues that it is the non-European who has much to teach the white man. In a later scene, the two men achieve a kind of rough equality on the terrain of language. When Crusoe attempts to teach the Warrior English, the latter instantly strikes his would-be instructor who nevertheless defiantly continues the lesson, naming several things in the immediate vicinity of the two: "fire," "tree," "leaves," "ocean," "sand," "meat." (The Warrior has cooked and is eating one of the geese that Crusoe has carefully raised and tended during his stay on the island.)

4. Colloquy between Crusoe (Aidan Quinn) and the Warrior (Ade Sapara) in Caleb Deschanel's *Crusoe*

The black man then introduces Crusoe to his word for meat: "jala," but Crusoe insistently repeats the English word. He strikes the Warrior and then retreats after receiving an answering blow. Many commentators on *Robinson Crusoe* have noted the protagonist's unstated assumption that Friday will and should learn Crusoe's language but that Crusoe himself need pay no heed to any language that Friday speaks. Fakrul Alam observes that "Crusoe almost suggests that Friday had no language of his own," and Maximillian Novak shows that Crusoe cannot learn Friday's language because the Englishman "uses language as a form of dominance."[35] In Deschanel's film, however, Crusoe gives way; he accepts some of the cooked meat from the Warrior and uses the other man's word – "jala" – as he eats it.[36] Only then does the Warrior relent and repeat Crusoe's word: "meat." In Deschanel's retelling of the Crusoe story, therefore, Crusoe is not only nourished by the Warrior but also accepts instruction from him.

At the end of the film, however, it is Crusoe, clearly transformed by his interaction with the black man, who saves the Warrior. The latter man has been taken captive by men aboard an English ship that has landed on the island. (Interestingly, the Warrior's captors are not slave traders or military men but anthropologists.) Apparently no longer inclined to view all Africans as potential slaves, Crusoe frees the Warrior at night and allows him to escape. In the last scene of the film, Crusoe is seen at sea the next morning, clean-shaven, clear-eyed, a bit stunned, and, we are meant to see, spiritually renewed. Thus, unlike *Man Friday*, Deschanel's *Crusoe*, although it represents the protagonist of its narrative as a slave trader and a would-be imperialist, nevertheless also sees Crusoe as redeemable and indeed as redeemed by his encounter with the African with whom he shares his island for a time. Pauline Kael characterizes the film as a "stripped down search for values" and "a late-sixties fable made in the late eighties." Deschanel's film is fascinated with Crusoe's experience at sea and on the island, which it represents in rich detail, but it is mainly concerned with the fate of these two representative men: "it's all images of entrapment and freedom," Kael comments.[37] In the end, Deschanel's film, like Gold's, resolves the problems that arise from the Friday–Crusoe encounter, by separating the two characters, but in *Crusoe* each man is represented at the end as free in his own world.

What these filmic Robinsonades suggest, finally, is that the Crusoe story is indeed a central myth of modern Western civilization but also a myth that is so vexed that it must be disrupted as it is retold. The many filmic versions of *Robinson Crusoe* make it clear not only that Crusoe and Friday are inescapably part of the received images of Western culture but also that they are figures that haunt us. Drawn to the Crusoe myth for whatever reasons, Buñuel, Gold, and Deschanel produced films that suggest a fundamental antipathy to important features of Defoe's famous narrative. The films by Buñuel and Deschanel, however, make a kind of post-colonial peace, or at least a truce, with Defoe's text whereas Gold's *Man Friday* adopts a rejectionist position vis-à-vis the Crusoe myth.

Interestingly, these films also serve as striking illustrations of the very process of the cinematic adaptation of novels. Béla Balázs declares that novels can be no more than "raw material" for films and even argues that although "the subject, or story, of both works (film and novel) is identical, their *content* is nevertheless different."[38] Films make use of novels, then, but can have no debt to them; the film is a distinct work of art, with both a different manner or technique and, as a result, a wholly different content, and supersedes the literary text as it reworks it. Similarly, Bhabha argues that the truly post-colonial work necessarily contains the past and yet rewrites it as the present, disrupting the earlier work as it refigures it. His analysis of the "'post'-ness" of post-colonial works argues that such texts by definition cannot obliterate but instead must productively reimagine the original narrative. Post-colonial texts, then, have much in common with cinematic "adaptations" of novels. Discussing the boundary or borderline that he argues *is* the post-colonial perspective, Bhabha declares:

if the jargon of our times – postmodernity, postcoloniality, post-feminism – has any meaning at all, it does not lie in the popular use of the "post" to indicate sequentiality – after-feminism – or polarity – anti-modernism. These terms that insistently gesture to the beyond, only embody its restless and revisionary energy if they transform the present into an expanded and ex-centric site of experience and empowerment.[39]

Bhabha's point seems to be that "'post'-ness" both begins from and thus appropriates, and yet also supersedes or passes beyond that which it succeeds. Certainly, the filmic Robinsonades treated in this essay are works of art that simultaneously contribute to the perpetuation and elaboration of the Crusoe myth and also to its fundamental transformation, even, in one case, to the point of rejecting the figure of Crusoe. Both as "post"-colonial works of art and as cinematic "adaptations," therefore, these films bespeak a similar idea of "fidelity" to the past – one that entails both repetition and metamorphosis.

NOTES

1 For the Crusoe story as myth, see Ian Watt, *Myths of Modern Individualism: Faust, Don Quixote, Don Juan, Robinson* (Cambridge: Cambridge University Press, 1996), pp. 141–92. I discuss *Cast Away* at greater length in "Robinson Crusoe in Hollywood," in *Approaches to Teaching Robinson Crusoe,* ed. Maximillian Novak and Carl Fisher, forthcoming from MLA.

2 Pat Rogers, *Defoe: The Critical Heritage* (New York: Barnes and Noble, 1972), p. 23.

3 Tom R. Sullivan, "The Uses of a Fictional Formula: The Selkirk Mother Lode," *Journal of Popular Culture* 8 (1974–5), 36.

4 Sullivan, "Uses of a Fictional Formula," 36, 38, 43; see also J. H. Scholte, "Robinsonades," *Neophilologus* 35 (1951), 137–8.

5 J. M. Coetzee, *Foe* (New York: Viking Press, 1987); Michel Tournier, *Friday,* trans. Norman Denny (New York: Pantheon, 1985). For discussions of these two novels in respect to Defoe's, see, among others, Sullivan, "Uses of a Fictional Formula," 48–50; and Victoria Carchidi, "At Sea on a Desert Island: Defoe, Tournier and Coetzee," in *Literature and Quest,* ed. Christine Arkinstall (Amsterdam and Atlanta: Rodopi, 1993), pp. 75–88; Susan Naramore Maher, "Confronting Authority: J. M. Coetzee's *Foe* and the Remaking of *Robinson Crusoe,*" *International Fiction Review* 18 (1991), 34–40; and Anthony Purdy, "From Defoe's 'Crusoe' to Tournier's 'Vendredi,'" *Canadian Review of Comparative Literature* 11 (1984), 216–35.

6 The Laurel and Hardy film was released in the UK as *Utopia.*

7 While the Buñuel film is seemingly a straightforward rendering of Defoe's narrative, it in fact merits the label Robinsonade because of the many transformations (discussed below) worked by the director on the original narrative.

8 Daniel Defoe, *Robinson Crusoe*, ed. J. Donald Crowley (Oxford and New York: Oxford University Press, 1972), p. 68; hereafter cited in the text.

9 In *Cast Away* Tom Nolan (Hanks) briefly considers praying over the dead body of a man who has washed ashore on his island and then evidently dismisses the idea as pointless; Crusoe makes no reference to religion whatsoever.

10 For example, in *Mr. Robinson Crusoe*, directed by Edward Sutherland, the "natives" the Crusoe character, Steve Drewell (Fairbanks), encounters are of the Hollywood bone-in-the-nose variety; Drewell ties Friday up and tells him: "when you're house-broken... I'm going to untie you."

11 Homi K. Bhabha, *The Location of Culture* (London and New York: Routledge, 1994), pp. 1, 4, 5, 7, 2.

12 Tony Richardson, "The Films of Luis Buñuel," in *The World of Luis Buñuel: Essays in Criticism*, ed. Joan Mellen (New York: Oxford University Press, 1978), p. 134.

13 Luis Buñuel, *My Last Sigh*, trans. Abigail Israel (New York: Alfred A. Knopf, 1983), pp. 191, 171; Buñuel, "Poetry and Cinema," in *World of Buñuel*, ed. Mellen, pp. 105–10. David Thomson declares that "the realism of his films ... should not lead us into thinking that Buñuel believed in reality"; *A Biographical Dictionary of Film*, 3rd edn. (New York: Alfred A. Knopf, 1994), p. 98.

14 Gillian Parker, "Crusoe Through the Looking-Glass," in *The English Novel and the Movies*, ed. Michael Klein and Parker (New York: Frederick Ungar, 1981), p. 15.

15 Buñuel, *My Last Sigh*, p. 191.

16 Parker, "Looking-Glass," p. 16.

17 Buñuel is quoted in Francisco Aranda, *Luis Buñuel: A Critical Biography* (New York: Da Capo Press, 1976), p. 156.

18 Quoted in Watt, *Myths*, p. 171.

19 Richardson, "Films of Buñuel," p. 134.

20 The film begins with Crusoe coming ashore and ends with him leaving the island.

21 In the novel, Friday says that Crusoe should kill him rather than send him away (226).

22 Virginia Higginbotham, *Luis Buñuel* (Boston: Twayne, 1979), p. 74; see also Richardson, "Films of Buñuel," p. 135, and Parker, "Looking-Glass," p. 24.

23 Richardson, "Films of Buñuel," p. 35.

24 Timothy C. Blackburn observes: "Friday is, of course, an Indian, not a black, though confusion about this arises because Friday calls Crusoe 'master' and because of the common view that Crusoe treats Friday 'in the manner of a benevolent slave owner.'" The films under discussion here suggest that the treatment of Friday's ethnicity or race results not so much from "confusion" as from a tendency to see Friday as a representative of the primary racial or ethnic "Other" in a given society. The Anglo-American films present Friday or his equivalent as an African; in Buñuel's Mexican-American production, Friday is an Indian. Blackburn, "Friday's Religion: Its Nature and Importance in *Robinson Crusoe*," *Eighteenth-Century Studies* 18 (1984–5), 361–2.

25 Markman Ellis, "Crusoe, Cannibalism and Empire," in *Robinson Crusoe: Myths and Metamorphoses*, ed. Lieve Spaas and Brian Stimpson (London: Macmillan; New York: St. Martin's, 1996), pp. 47, 46. At pp. 47–8, Ellis

acknowledges that Crusoe questions his own right "to be Judge and Executioner upon these Men as Criminals" because of their cannibalism, but he
also observes that later Crusoe concludes that "the Usage they thus gave one
another, was thus brutish and inhuman," even though he also observes that
"it was really nothing to me."

26 Leonard Maltin, *Movies and Video Guide 1999 Edition* (New York: Signet,
1998), p. 848.

27 Edward Said, *Culture and Imperialism* (New York: Alfred A. Knopf, 1993),
p. xii. Also, in addition to Blackburn and Ellis, cited above, see, among
others, J. A. Downie, "Defoe, Imperialism, and the Travel Book Recon-
sidered," *Yearbook of English Studies* 13 (1983), 66–83; Roxann Wheeler, "'My
Savage,' 'My Man': Racial Multiplicity in *Robinson Crusoe*," *ELH* 62 (1995),
821–61.

28 Watt, *Myths*, p. 141–92.

29 Penelope Houston, "Cannes 75," *Sight and Sound* 44 (1975), 159; see also
Hugh James, "*Man Friday*," *Films in Review* 26 (1975), 635.

30 *Cast Away*, conversely, solves the problem of the Crusoe–Friday relationship
by eliminating Friday, refiguring him as "Wilson," a volleyball with an exotic
head "drawn" upon it, "who" is the sole companion of Noland–Crusoe during
his ordeal on the island, a move that is far from being politically neutral.

31 "If Crusoe has an antecedent in Deschanel's work...it is undoubtedly the
mesmerically beautiful *Black Stallion*, another tale of shipwreck and self-
discovery"; John Pym, "Crusoe," *Sight and Sound* 57 (1987), 81.

32 Parker, "Looking-Glass," p. 19.

33 Pauline Kael, "The Current Cinema," *The New Yorker*, April 17, 1989, 115.

34 There is a vaguely homoerotic aspect to this combat, echoed briefly by a slow-
motion view of the Warrior's beautifully muscled body as he runs that may
be seen as a shot representing Crusoe's point of view, but these are virtually
the only suggestions of a sexual component to Crusoe's island experience in
Crusoe, and they are slight.

35 Fakrul Alam, "Religious and Linguistic Colonialism in Defoe's Fiction," *North
Dakota Quarterly* 55 (1987), 120; Maximillian E. Novak, "Friday: or, the Power
of Naming," in *Augustan Subjects: Essays in Honor of Martin Battestin*, ed.
Albert J. Rivero (Newark: University of Delaware Press; London: Associated
University Presses, 1997), p. 117.

36 There is a similar contest later in the film over song. Each man assertively
sings his own song, attempting to drown out the other. Moments later each
man sings the other's song, with the Warrior taking the lead.

37 Kael, "Current Cinema," 114–15.

38 Béla Balázs, *Theory of the Film* (New York: Arno Press; New York Times,
1972), p. 260.

39 Bhabha, *Location of Culture*, p. 4.

3   Adaptations of Defoe's *Moll Flanders*

Catherine N. Parke

My purpose in this essay is to examine how Defoe's *Moll Flanders* has been recreated in three screen adaptations (Terence Young's *Amorous Adventures of Moll Flanders* [1965], Pen Densham's *Moll Flanders* [1995], and David Attwood's *Fortunes and Misfortunes of Moll Flanders* [1996][1]) as female, feminine, and feminist, as site of commodified identity, and as both locus of and object lesson in beauty's exchange value. These several interpretations of the first *Moll Flanders*, in the words of Virginia Woolf, might "well have puzzled [Defoe]" who was "careful to disguise" some of these meanings "even from his own eye."[2] But one suspects that this complex of interpretations might also have pleased him as a significant measure of his protagonist's enduring and adaptable vitality as a container for many meanings over many years.

Defoe, of all the writers included in this volume, is arguably the one whose body of work, mind, and temperament are best suited to the business, technology, and mythos of screen media. These three suitabilities, the first formal/aesthetic, the second and third biographical – and, though admittedly imaginative, also grounded in empirical fact – help explain why this novel and its writer remain distinctively, if paradoxically, untouched by screen adaptations. This explanation, in turn, foregrounds by disjunction perennial issues of screen adaptation and how it is authorized. Let me pause briefly over these two matters, first Defoe the person, then his novel, before proceeding to discuss these adaptations.

Throughout his various careers, including merchant, soldier, government agent, and writer of prose fiction, Defoe's signature commitment and style were characterized by a "practical bias toward schemes for modernizing and improving the life of his own day and for keeping his country in the forefront of contemporary developments."[3] If the motion picture camera had existed when he wrote his *Essay upon Projects* (1697), with its diverse practical proposals for improving Great Britain (a national road system, pensions, insurance, and academies for military studies and the education of women, among them), one can readily imagine a national motion picture studio numbering among his proposals.

Thus Defoe's characteristic affinity for his era's distinctive new technologies, financial venues and opportunities, emerging modern values and infrastructures of commerce, trade, production, and consumption, and nation-building, which his fiction and nonfiction helped define and dramatize, would surely have drawn him to explore the screen's resources. Rhetorical strains of his practical enthusiasm resound in early twentieth-century writings about the new movie industry, such as W. L. Gordon's description of this business as a "delightful, magical fairy tale of commerce, finance, and human interest."[4] Furthermore, in creating his two most popular characters – Moll Flanders, foremother of the first wave of modern Western feminism, and Robinson Crusoe, embodiment and agent of the newly developing imperialistic market economy – Defoe produced durable topoi of the social, economic, and political values of Western modernity, not without their implicit internal contradictions. In so doing, he also produced the kind of material loved by screen media.

Defoe's realism, the "amazing, powerful, unflagging verisimilitude" of his novels,[5] appears to hindsight as if written in precocious appreciation of the screen's love affair with realism, in general, and the complex appetite for recording truth, identifying artifice, and inducing fantasy that the camera, in particular, was invented to satisfy. Readers of Defoe in the realist tradition have noted that he "does not so much portray his heroine's character as assume its reality in every action, and carry his reader with him."[6] They have praised him as master of "personations . . . disguises, [and] cross-dressings,"[7] who prompts us to "accede to the reality of the deed," after which "it is difficult to challenge the reality of the doer" (Watt, 8). These evaluations implicitly identify Moll's verbal reality as being similar to film's distinctive ontology of creating character through the compelling realism of visual action. Thus Moll's first creator, Defoe, provides an inferable logic and paradoxical authorization for screen adaptations of his work.

As critics have often noted, *Moll Flanders*, the verbal narrative, is not in line with the novel's subsequent direction after Defoe, a fact which her compatibility with film and the novel's near dispensability in two of the adaptations may, in turn, help to explain. Specifically Defoe's novel is not in line with the way narrative fiction's subsequent contract with readers has typically placed increasing emphasis on authorial presence manifest in notions of creativity, originality, and control. He presents Moll's story as a redacted version of an authentic first-person document. Many readers have found this personation successful and satisfying. Willa Cather, in her preface to *Roxana*, which may be extended legitimately to Moll, has observed: "From the first paragraph one never doubts that this is a woman's actual story, told by a woman. The author never gets outside his character, never insinuates anything through her, has no feelings about her beyond those she has about herself" (Cather, 83). This praise of Defoe's successful disappearance into his female protagonist has been strongly contested by some scholars of the late twentieth-century gendered revisionist history of the novel. I will return to this matter in the final section of this essay, which imagines Moll in the company of female, not male, creators. But in discussing the three screen adaptations by male directors I will take as my informing analysis of these three Molls, different though they are in many ways from one another, the observation by Ian Watt, another of her male creators: she is a woman who accepts none of the liabilities of her sex, struggles persistently against "any involuntary involvement in the feminine role" (Watt, 113), and exerts power not in spite of but because of her guiding ethic of middle-class gentility.[8] This Moll has proved to be responsively adaptable to the screen.

Moll Flanders who is (not) Tom Jones: Terence Young's *Amorous Adventures of Moll Flanders* (1965)

Terence Young's *Amorous Adventures of Moll Flanders* is a glossy romantic comedy in period costume. The credits generally indicate a debt to "the works of Daniel Defoe," not to *Moll Flanders* in particular. The latter part of the credit sequence, however, suggests the influence of Tony Richardson's *Tom Jones* (1963), the commercially successful film adaptation of Henry Fielding's *History of Tom Jones, a Foundling* (1749). This relationship, acknowledged in a witty disclaimer that shares the frame with the director's name, reads as follows: "Any similarity between this film and any other film is purely coincidental." Young, in the way he allies his film with its successful predecessor, promises movie-goers who enjoyed *Tom Jones* a similar enjoyment in *Moll Flanders*. Movie Moll is thus introduced as a female twin of the libidinous, liberated, good-hearted Movie Tom. In addition to tapping into the popularity of its predecessor film, the director, by the end of the credits, has doubly dispensed with Defoe's novel, thereby repositioning his Moll completely within the visual realm of film and implicitly dispensing with any obligation to be faithful to the verbal narrative.

Young's heroine, in keeping with this movie's cheerfully revised title, *The Amorous Adventures of Moll Flanders*, is worlds apart from Defoe's ghastly résumé of crime and perversion: *The Fortunes and Misfortunes of the Famous Moll Flanders, &c. Who was Born in Newgate, and during a Life of continu'd Variety for Threescore Years, besides her Childhood, was Twelve Year a Whore, five times a Wife (whereof once to her own Brother) Twelve Year a Thief, Eight Year a Transported Felon in Virginia, at last grew*

Rich, liv'd Honest, and died a Penitent, Written from her own Memorandums. Young, popularly known for three of the early James Bond films (*Dr. No*, 1962; *From Russia With Love*, 1963; and *Thunderball*, 1965), introduces a Moll for the 1960s sexual revolution. His female protagonist, though in eighteenth-century dress and spiced with elements of 1960s liberal feminism, seems also to have been cast in the mold of one of Bond's fantasy playmates: beautiful, buxom, savvy, tough, yet also compliant to male desire.

Kim Novak plays Moll. Columbia Pictures groomed Novak for sex-symbol stardom in the mid-1950s after she was discovered touring the country as "Miss Deep Freeze." By this stage of her career Novak had played a series of roles that drew upon and developed a forceful complex of seeming opposites in her screen presence, namely an aggressive eroticism, sexual submission, and a desire for conservative femininity. This complex is exemplified in her roles as a witch who yearns to become a mortal woman, in *Bell, Book and Candle* (1958); a working-class woman hired to impersonate (and subsequently all but become) a murdered rich woman, in *Vertigo* (1958); a sympathetically conflicted divorcee, in *Strangers When We Meet* (1960); and a sociology graduate student, mistaken for a prostitute, who then takes on this persona to conduct research on male sexual fantasies, in *Boys' Night Out* (1962).[9]

This adaptation of Defoe's documentary moral melodrama into a romantic comedy spares Moll most of the life-threatening, degrading liabilities of being female explored by Defoe. Movie Moll, like Movie Tom, has a good heart, robust body, and appetites to match. She lives a relatively carefree sexual life, exchanging sex for money or gifts, never loathing and rarely failing to enjoy nearly all aspects of these transactions. Moll's sexual liaisons are reduced to three, her marriages to two, her criminal acts to a few acts of slapstick thievery, and her children to none. Thus all events become motivated by and finally converge on her reunion with her one true love, Jemmy, the highwayman.

Two comic subplots forward the principal plot line of romantic comedy. Jemmy the highwayman works in league with a bumbling but good-hearted assistant and a long-time female partner-in-crime and paramour. Moll enters service with an impecunious British noblewoman and her lower-class Italian lover, disguised as an aristocrat. These two pairs of characters serve conventional comic ends first as impediments to and finally as agents of the beautiful young couple's union. Intersecting conservative forces of eugenics, marriage, and money that conventionally define comedy dictate the film's final scene. Moll and Jemmy, setting sail for Virginia while still young and beautiful, are married by the ship's captain. Pictured as deserving lovers on a honeymoon rather than convicted

5. Moll Flanders (Kim Novak) savoring her first gift of jewelry in Terence Young's *The Amorous Adventures of Moll Flanders*

felons suffering transportation, the happy couple, enfolded in one another's arms, gazes toward the New World.

Although this Moll is a heroine of comic romance, not Defoe's victim of circumstance and the accidental revolution of fortune's wheel, she embodies fascinating, if unintentional, parallels with Defoe's character, while the sanitized differences serve, at least for those who compare film and novel, to underscore Defoe's grittily disturbing details. Young's Moll arguably "accepts none of the disabilities of her sex [and] fully realise[s] one of the ideals of feminism: freedom from any involuntary involvement in the feminine role" (Watt, 117). Her sex is scarcely a liability and its principal female and feminine social markers, childbearing and motherhood, are deleted. Experiencing only one interlude of poverty that motivates her turning briefly to theft, this Moll endures few anxious pressures of brutal want and insecurity. Her dirtiness consists chiefly of smudges on her face. Her strong yet wholesome and untainted sexuality makes her the quintessential embodiment of Defoe's "Honest Projector," who, but by dint of unfortunate circumstance, could have lived "by fair and plain principles of Sense, Honesty, and Ingenuity... [and] contents himself with the real Produce, as the profit of his Invention."[10] Young does not follow Moll into old age, as does Defoe – nor does either of her other two directors. There may be a number of reasons for this decision, including temporal compression, typical of screen adaptations, and the desire to remain focused on a single, unified, and unchanging adult Moll. Yet one suspects that twentieth-century Western culture's age-phobia – our loathing of women's aging, in particular – was the chief factor dictating a camera fade-out while the heroine is still young.

This film develops its comedy of romance, pursuing the intertextual relation to *Tom Jones* through a number of visual citations from the preceding film, including accelerated-motion photography, quick panning, and light-hearted harpsichord music. This visual grammar assures viewers that sex will never become rape, nor will family arguments produce irreversibly sinister consequences. The contract with the audience promises that benevolence will out. The sequence of establishing shots at the film's outset dramatizes Moll's desire to be a gentlewoman and promises from the beginning that this desire is practicable in a orderly world so long as the female protagonist thinks strategically for herself and on her own behalf. A full shot depicts several older, well-dressed men and women walking toward a line of well, if simply, dressed young girls who await inspection. The camera tracks backward to position the viewer with the orphans so that we see from their perspective as they are quizzed by this delegation of civic and religious figures charged with the children's welfare. Medium close-up shots of the first two girls who dutifully answer questions about the Bible and aim no higher than to become dairy maids prepare for an extreme close-up of Moll's sensuous face. Red curls peep out from her cap; blue-shadowed eyelids flirt coyly with her male observers. Moll's face is brightly lighted, perhaps also using filler light in addition to a pale shade of pancake makeup, so that lighting is keyed to her face. Whenever Novak is shot in close-up, throughout the rest of the film, these lighting and makeup techniques recur to reduce shadows and emphasize the regularity and sensuous good health of her face. Moll quotes provocatively from the *Song of Solomon* ("I am my beloved's") as prologue to announcing to her inquisitors her immodestly radical aim to become "a gentlewoman." Her words evoke knowing laughter from the visitors, motivate one woman to comment that a child of such beauty might well succeed in her wish, and prompt the gift of a coin, foreshadowing the function of Moll's beauty as commodity, from an admiring city official who promptly adopts Moll.

Beginning with the protagonist as a school-age child, the film narrative then condenses several intervening years, rejoining Moll in young womanhood, and thereafter proceeding linearly but without precise reference to time. By contrast, the other two film adaptations develop Moll's story through flashback in order to underscore the protagonist's self-reflexive interior dramas of anxious self-awareness and analysis. Young's adaptation depicts a consistent, unchanging Moll who begins life as a confident, beautiful, self-directed child and succeeds in reaching adulthood with all these qualities intact.

Thus the film's opening scene illustrates a transactional world of commodified identity and establishes beauty's exchange value. In the way Moll savors her first gift of money, rubbing it between her fingers, touching it to her lips with a knowing look that invites inference about this young girl's dawning insight about how to rise in the world, she embodies pragmatic confidence. This first image of Moll, focusing on her beautiful face, to be sure, yet more so on the confident thought process inferable from her facial expression, is developed throughout the film in the protagonist's first-person voice-over narration. This narration allies the viewer with Moll sympathetically and appreciatively from the outset. Beginning with this close-up, viewers are cast as the heroine's rational, admiring, and confident allies who are along for the ride in this lightweight romp.

Moll, motherhood, and minority rights: Pen Densham's *Moll Flanders* (1995)

Pen Densham, co-founder with John Watson and Richard Lewis of Trilogy Entertainment (1986), known as the "new moguls" of TV horror–fantasy–sci-fi (*The New Outer Limits*) and action movie blockbusters (*Backdraft*, *Blown Away*), had made other contemporizing adaptations before turning to *Moll Flanders*. Trilogy produced *Robin Hood: Prince of Thieves* (1991), based on another legendary criminal, a television movie remake of *Poltergeist*, and an updated version of the popular 1960s series *Outer Limits*, financed in an MGM/Showtime TV syndication mega-deal typical of late twentieth-century multimedia corporate high finance. Trilogy's founders identify themselves as "a maverick independent company that likes to do films that are not copies of last year's hits,"[11] develops strong relationships with its casts, and works as a team of on-set, hands-on writer–producers.

Densham remarks that his idea to write and direct *Moll Flanders* developed "after helping his wife through the birth of their first child." Inspired by this experience, he wanted to make "a film about a woman who undergoes extraordinary life changes after having a baby ... 'a mother who had made mistakes, who had lost her direction, and then regained it'."[12] He chose the Moll Flanders topos to dramatize this story of female insight and transformation. Densham expands these remarks about the autobiographical origins of his project in another interview that identifies the pivotal theme of gender: "After *Robin Hood*, I wanted to attempt to create a film that was as positive for a female character as Robin had been for a male. I think I was influenced by the fact that I had been lucky enough to have a daughter, as well as a son" and grew up in a house where "[William] Hogarth engravings filled the walls."[13] Densham's comments about his personally inspired agenda to make a female companion piece to *Robin Hood* express Trilogy's agenda of producing character-driven action films, however oxymoronic such a designation may be, and the company's self-described commitment to combine, without compromise, a corporate big budget and a director's personal passion.

Densham's Moll is played by Robin Wright, who identifies a "theme of conviction, a certain independence of spirit"[14] both within herself and throughout her film roles: feminist under siege in *Moll Flanders*; Jenny, ally of the eccentric protagonist in *Forrest Gump*; and sensitive artist in *The Crossing Guard*. By contrast with Novak's voluptuous body and classical features, Wright is an eccentric beauty of waifish slimness. These qualities are emphasized throughout this film by backlighting, available-light photography and/or filters which, by contouring shadows on her face, portray a kind of ravaged regality, midway on the visual spectrum between her first starring role as the ethereal princess in *The Princess Bride* (1987) and her role, after Moll, as an abused woman/faithful wife in *She's So Lovely* (1997). This Moll for the 1990s, announced in the credits as being "based on a character from the novel by Daniel Defoe," is reconceived as a victim of aggressively corrupt, sadistic, and exploitative social and cultural institutions, including family, church, and class. Densham, in developing this pattern of narrative departures from Defoe, rewrites Moll as radical feminist who combines being a courageous, gender-neutral human being, inspired by a noble passion for living in the truth of personal emotion and political justice, with her roles of faithful, self-sacrificing wife and tenaciously committed good mother.

Densham makes several key narrative revisions in order to reconceive Moll's character as abused woman, angry feminist, and good wife and mother: (1) her mother is hanged, rather than transported, so that Moll may become the story's preeminent mother with no subsequent competition or diversion; (2) she marries only once, the love of her life, an artist not a highwayman, who renounces his tyrannically heartless family, marries Moll, and dies soon thereafter; (3) this good male figure is replaced by an African, who becomes Moll's ally and intimate friend; (4) Moll is exploited and sadistically victimized by the female owner of the brothel where she is imprisoned, rather than supported by this woman, as in the novel; and (5) she bears only one child, not five, a daughter, whom she adores, loses, and commits herself to finding, whereas, in Defoe's novel, Moll's only beloved child is the son fathered by her own brother, with whom she eventually reunites. These many revisions are organized into a new narrative by a master visual trope that, from the outset, generates mystery, suspense, and passion. The opening sequence of establishing shots begins Moll's story at the penultimate episode of a long search. A wide-angle, full-screen shot of the ocean is followed by a close-up of spy-glass, then a pan to a man looking through a spy-glass, a continuing pan to include a blurred background figure of a woman, and a final pan to a three-masted ship. These visual clues to a mystery that subsequently unfolds in flashback and concludes successfully in the film's final scene initiate our curiosity. At the outset the viewer does not know the identities or relationship of the white woman and black man, both of whom are looking out to sea through spy-glasses. But clearly one is intended to infer that a passionately difficult search is entering its final phase and to wish to know the story behind these mysteriously motivated but visually self-evident emotions.

A cut from this exterior mise-en-scène and extreme aerial long shot of the ship transfers the viewer to a shadowy interior scene with close-up of a flickering, moving candle, followed by a mid-torso shot of a habited nun, keys dangling heavily and noisily from her waistband as she walks toward a sinister locked door. When opened, this door reveals a scene of sleeping ragamuffin girls in chiaroscuro lighting. One of these children, scrappy and rebellious even in the presence of sinister authority, is dragged roughly to an interview with the black man previously shown beginning his sea voyage. The viewer learns that this man, Hibble (Morgan Freeman), has been charged to bring Moll Flanders' daughter, Flora, to a wealthy benefactor and, during the course of their journey, to read aloud to her the memoirs of her criminal mother.

Defoe's convention of Moll's memoranda, revised and edited by another writer, is adapted visually and orally into this film's first-person account written by Moll herself. Moll's handwritten memoir is an angry discourse against injustice and oppression combined with a powerful expression of anguish over lost love. Carried across the sea and read by a second mistreated, heroic minority figure to a third such figure, this memoir thus triples the discourse of oppression and doubles the film's point of view. Hibble reads Moll's life in her own words to her beloved daughter. This reading, in turn, motivates the film's flashback narrative account of Moll's life, which comes full circle when mother and daughter are reunited in Virginia and the shadowy woman looking through the spy-glass in the opening sequence is revealed to be Moll herself.

Densham's Moll is thus a feminist variation on the Victorian angel of the house. She combines rebellious individualism with traditional womanly faithfulness to her daughter and the memory of her adored, dead husband. Throughout the film she allies herself with similarly mistreated minority figures: exploited prostitutes, an exiled artist, and the African participant-narrator, played by the same actor (Freeman) who had played an analogous partner-of-color to Densham's Robin Hood. Defoe's lifelong commitment to women's education, in both his writing and personal life as husband and father,[15] exists as a subtext in this film, perhaps more by accident than design, inscribed in the fable of a young girl's instruction by two heroically successful fugitives, Moll's mother and her African ally, about the dangers of living in a patriarchal world.

This biracial couple, so the final frames suggest, will raise this female child to be the new woman for a new age. Moll's voice-over identifies this screen adaptation's twin themes of personal passion and political justice: "We fluttered and glided on the currents of our emotions. We celebrated in the great truth that we had learned from her father – that all men and women are created equal." The film's closing sequence begins with a full shot of mother and daughter dancing on the beach, soon joined by Hibble. This group portrait in motion alludes to the oil portrait of Moll and her husband, which Moll, in the scene just preceding, has shown to her daughter. It serves as visual metaphor of this threesome's newly found joy and freedom while also making punning reference to the ontology of film as moving/motion picture. A tracking long shot that pulls the viewer back from this threesome then dissolves into an image of the ocean with which the film began.

Faithful to the novel: David Attwood's *Fortunes and Misfortunes of Moll Flanders* (1996)

The Fortunes and Misfortunes of Moll Flanders, directed by David Attwood, and aired in the US on Masterpiece Theater, was advertised on the PBS web site as "faithfully follow[ing] the bawdy, often unpredictable plot of Defoe's book" and presenting an authentic version of Moll who "walks out of the pages of Defoe's novel into your home" unlike "the recent Hollywood film by the same name."[16] The aesthetic value that underwrites this promotion, namely that screen adaptations of novels should be true to their original texts, also informs reviews of the other two screen Molls. Brendan Gill faulted Young's Moll for looking like "a grown-up Brownie, much more likely to be found baking tollhouse cookies than picking pockets and bargaining over the price of her body,"[17] while Stacey Richter criticized Densham's Moll for "bear[ing] only a superficial resemblance to the novel you read in Freshman English."[18] This legislating aesthetic of remaining faithful to the original has served as Masterpiece Theater's signature promotional identity, forwarding its educational agenda and ideology of Anglo-American cultural continuity since the series' inception in 1971. Actors and actresses chosen for leading roles typically have had prestigious legitimate stage experience, another mark of cultural seriousness. Alex Kingston, who plays this Moll, trained at the Royal Academy of Dramatic Arts and acted in repertory theater, including the Royal Shakespeare Company, before appearing on screen.

This adaptation's relation to Defoe and his novel is, by contrast with the other two versions, more than briefly acknowledged or alluded to in the credits. In order to underscore both the existence and legislating importance of the literary source, the novel's short title appears in a frame preceding the opening credits in a typeface conventionally associated with the printed book. The novel's time-frame is suggestively imitated in the four-hour two-part format, more than twice as long as conventional feature-length films. The manner and place of consumption of this Moll – on television at home rather than in a movie theater – also reproduce defining aspects of the scene of novel reading: domesticity, privacy, and duration.

Russell Baker, journalist and author, who introduced the US airing of *Moll Flanders* on Masterpiece Theater, recited Defoe's complete title in order both to locate this adaptation in direct genealogical line with the novel and warn parents that themes of bigamy, prostitution, and incest might make this program unsuitable for children. With this remark Baker also energized and updated a nearly three-hundred-year-old book by identifying it as a lively, current media event about which viewers must make moral, psychological, and educational choices. While director Young essentially dispensed with Defoe and his novel, allying his *Moll Flanders* with another film adaptation in order to bring it vitally into the present, this screen adaptation revitalizes the novel, in Baker's R-rating warning, and thereby dispels, at least by indirection, any sense that the drama we are about to watch is a dusty, schoolroom classic.

This screen treatment retains most of Defoe's subject matter. Chief departures include: (1) omission of one dead child; (2) development of an explicitly sexual lesbian relationship with Moll's partner in crime; (3) Moll's reprieve from the gallows not through confession but by the threat of blackmail against a judge with whom she has had a lurid sexual encounter; and (4) her departure for Virginia with her Lancashire husband while both are still young and beautiful (as in the other two *Moll*s). Thus this adaptation, with its self-announced faithfulness to its literary source and preservation of most of Defoe's narrative, serves as a particularly useful concluding case study in techniques of adaptation.

Attwood's Moll is both a credible individual – characterized by a distinctive complex of emotions, behaviors, and drives: gullibility, insecurity, aggressiveness, intelligence, and erotic force – and a conceptualized site of cultural construction. This production's techniques converge on the project of believably creating this doubleness so that Moll is a figure, both particular and general, self-made and socially constructed, individual and symbolic. The audience is introduced into Moll's world by a Newgate Prison guard who leads a group of upper-class Londoners on a tour to see the frightening yet also pitiable inmates of this chiaroscuro-lighted chamber of horrors. Conventions of handheld camera documentary film making – jerky and apparently unscripted motion, producing a ragged and unbalanced visual composition – situate viewers perilously and unpredictably within, rather than reassuringly outside of and in control of the frame.

This unsteady but searchingly inquisitive and all but prurient camera seeks out and eventually finds Moll, huddled indistinctly, looking less like a human being than a pile of rags and matted hair. As the camera moves to close-up, Moll turns toward the camera eye in direct address to the viewer. She threateningly cross-examines the visitors' curiosity by remarking that we, too, could suffer her plight. Throughout the subsequent four hours, narrative flashbacks of Moll's life are repeatedly punctuated by this convention of direct address at moments of moral crisis and decision. This translation of the novel's first-person point of view into visual direct address positions the audience uneasily, self-consciously, and emphatically with Moll. This visual technique forbids condescending pity and positions us to believe that we are experiencing an unmediated empathy with the heroine. She asks repeatedly, in various tones ranging from comic to melodramatic, "What would you do?" Toward the end of her account, she tells us fiercely twice to go away, to leave her alone, gesturing angrily, moving her hand into the plane of the lens, once seeming almost to touch the camera, like a celebrity fending off invasive, exploitative paparazzi.

This narrative unfolds as flashback, like Densham's, but without Densham's device of visual and oral reference to Moll's memoirs, to recount how Moll came full circle to her birthplace in Newgate Prison. Abandoned to the gypsies, she is adopted by the Mayor of Colchester with whom she comes to live "almost as one of the family." The riddling ambiguity of this phrase, repeated in Moll's voice-over and contrasting with the 1965 Moll's remark, "For though only a servant, I was treated as *one of the family*" (my italics), is developed by the mise-en-scène of crowded and duplicitously coded family life. Two long scenes at the dinner table, for instance, are mediated by medium and full shots of small groups of characters (first Moll's adoptive family, later an additional party of four invited guests) with whom she is sometimes seated, from whom she is sometimes separated, and among whom she threads closely in and out, while she serves food before she sits down to dine (with the family but not with the subsequent guests). Such scenes are emblematic of Moll's formative early challenge to comprehend and survive within ambiguous and precarious circumstances.

Like Attwood's earlier *Wild West* (1992), the story of another struggling outsider, a young street-smart Pakistani, living with his widowed mother in class-ghettoized London, this adaptation of *Moll Flanders* recasts Defoe's analysis of early-stage capitalism's class struggle from an explicitly Marxist–feminist perspective. Material objects, forms of art, behavior, and communication are dramatized as functioning with oppressive, cumulative logic in this narrative of class exploitation and struggle. Attwood's Moll is an embodied Marxist feminist. Her existential anger and acumen combine to make her daily life a narrative critique of the society in which she lives.

To the degree that Attwood's Moll is a construction of class, it is her sexual awakening and the various plots that her body incorporates and participates in over time (trust, betrayal, power, business, exile, fantasies of self-love and self-loathing) that become this adaptation's visual metonymy for the meaning of her life. Kingston combines aspects of the voluptuousness and classical beauty of Novak with the haggard and eccentric beauty of Wright. Kingston's variety of appearances is developed systematically by photographic and lighting/makeup techniques, their cumulative effect being to depict something like a decline into multiple personalities, one of the classic pathologies resulting from abuse. As Moll declines in station and opportunity and subsequently turns to prostitution and theft, she takes on the visual conventions of the mad woman (a glitteringly fixed gaze, wild hair, dirty face) that, in retrospect, make the smudge marks on Novak's face look like just so many swipes with a piece of burned cork. She is, however, a woman for whom the decline into madness seems to be paradoxically the only legitimately rational response to the double bind of gender-based inequality and class-based oppression.

6. Moll Flanders (Alex Kingston) being sentenced to be hanged for theft in David Attwood's *Moll Flanders*.

Moll among women; or the director Moll hasn't had

Moll began as a male author's invention and has remained, in her screen adaptations to date, the invention, if not the property, of men, the latter being a point on which readers and viewers may reasonably disagree. Young's Moll is a sexually liberated, honestly pleasure-seeking, and romantically idealistic woman. She activates the viewer's fantasy of all-encompassing, safe, innocent, and prosperous pleasure. Densham's Moll is a rebellious, victimized member of a gender minority who allies herself with other abused minority figures: an African servant, a disabled artist-husband, and a child. Motherhood first and heterosexual romance second redeem, provide opportunity for, and give meaning to her otherwise alienated existence. She activates the viewer's fantasy that radical feminist politics and traditional womanly values are compatible. Attwood's Moll is a satirist. Of the three Molls she is the one who most actively communicates with viewers by examining herself and them simultaneously. This Moll's combination of socio-political analysis and eros activates a powerfully paradoxical fantasy of satire being morally energized by voyeurism – a vision worthy of Jonathan Swift. Moll's four male creators have depicted four women quite different from one another, together accumulating into an intertextual multiple identity. This collective Moll elicits from her audience a varied mix of responses and engagement (fear, apprehension, comprehension, empathy, sympathy, admiration, self-analysis) that disallows condoning her, precludes smug self-congratulation, and makes repulsion inadequate and pity irrelevant.

Though, in their respective development of Moll's and her daughter's bond of feminist education and of Moll's female-centered phase of alienated criminality, Densham and Attwood have briefly explored Moll from a woman-centered perspective, women on the Internet have made Moll their own more thoroughly. On "www" Moll has entered a virtual community of women, or at least self-identified women, who have appropriated her personally and adapted her pragmatically in a format that echoes and replicates aspects of Defoe's Moll's memoranda. A woman identified as "Mollflanders/wouldbe" remarks on the origin of her email penname: "We're not identical twins, but we have the same dragged through a hedge after shagging all afternoon hairstyle and at the same time I was struggling to survive with my mind, heart & soul intact." Moll became this woman's "therapeutic persona" to use as her public face at a time when "the real me had difficulty just dressing myself in the morning. And it worked! Moll is the bright & breezy, flirty side of my character & she always has fun." "Mollflanders/wouldbe" is Moll with an education, a doctoral student in history at the University of Nottingham. She is the woman whom Defoe argues implicitly Moll could have become under different circumstances of non-gender-biased educational opportunity. She loves to read autobiographies of working-class women, ride classic motorcycles, and drink a "nice Caber[n]et Sauvignon."[19]

The Moll Flanders web page, created by "Julie, Candice, Kristin, and Agnies," offers a summary of the novel, a fictive interview with Daniel Defoe, essays, analysis, bibliography, and a Moll Flanders quiz.[20] "A Moll Flander's [sic] Guide to Historic Women" notes that, though fictional, she is important in the "historic sense . . . that she accurately represents the experience of multitudes of women struggling to survive in Early Modern Europe. Regardless of class, women were dependent on men for food, protection and shelter."[21] Moll on the Internet is placed in the company of actual historical women: Mary Wollstonecraft, Elizabeth I, Eleanor Marx, Rosa Luxemburg, and Nell Gwynne, a varied group but united by their accomplishments and enduring fame. Moll's fictional reality as a perceptual entity on screen is transformed into a virtual reality among a community of historical women in cyberspace, blurring the boundary between fiction and history in a manner not unlike Defoe. Here Moll is united with a female society that, actively engaged and intercommunicative with their own times, has remained adaptively comprehensible to subsequent generations.

So why has Moll attracted no female director? Why has no Dorothy Arzner (*Working Girls*, 1931), Lizzie Borden (*Working Girls*, 1987), Martha Coolidge (*Valley Girl*, 1983), Amy Heckerling (*Clueless*, 1995), Patricia Rozema (*Mansfield Park*, 1999), or Emma Thompson (screenplay for *Sense and Sensibility*, 1995) made Moll her own by conceiving of this character from women's perspectives? This absence might surprise some of Defoe's feminist critics who read him as a strong supporter of women's rights from a gender-democratic perspective. Virginia Woolf admired Defoe for the degree to which he "thought deeply and much in advance of his age upon the capacities of women, which he rated very high, and the injustice done to them, which he rated very harsh" and rendered accurately Moll's identity as "a woman on her own account" (Woolf, 102 and 101). Miriam Leranbaum has argued that it is inaccurate to put gender identity first in discussions of the character Moll Flanders. Katharine M. Rogers has assessed Defoe's demonstrated "recognition of [women's] full humanity and his wish to free them from sexual as well as economic dependence on men" and the strength of his pursuit of "feminism beyond the bounds of respectable thought."[22] Paula Backscheider has remarked that Defoe wrote to be useful, practiced what he preached about women's education, "took an interest in every thing that might better individuals, [and] society," and was invigorated in all of his projects by a "wide-ranging sympathy and tireless sense of justice" (Backscheider, 502, 491, 530).

But this lack to date of a female director to interpret Moll would probably not surprise scholars of the 1990s gendered cultural history of the novel who have revised Watt's and his heirs' story of the rise of the novel. These critics have read Defoe, in general, and his female protagonists, in particular, as exploitatively manipulative. These insights, though contesting Watt's masculine/patriarchal history of the novel, also draw directly, if unself-consciously, upon his analysis of Moll being "suspiciously like her author" (Watt, 113), as contestation frequently does. Madeleine Kahn has examined the transvestite structure of Defoe's narrative, particularly in *Roxana*, though also briefly in *Moll*, by recasting the familiar gender question from "Did he create a believable woman?" to "What did he have to gain from the attempt?"[23] In Margaret Anne Doody's and William Beatty Warner's critical histories of the novel, Defoe is either all but removed or significantly displaced.[24]

One can, perhaps, infer speculatively from Moll on the Internet what a future female/feminine/feminist-directed Moll on screen might be, namely an exemplary figure for engaging issues of women-centered

politics, therapy, and advice for safe living. A pre-teen female audience –
the target group for many current big-budget films – could mock-
encounter through Moll with how to be safe in an unsafe world.[25] A post-
teen female audience could engage with Moll in a variety of age-specific
ways in order both to analyze past experiences of violence and victimage,
specifically associated with their sex, and prepare for future challenges.
One suspects that a feminist director would not cut short Moll's story
while the protagonist is still young and beautiful, but rather would follow
her into old age, as did Defoe. Market factors associated with the demo-
graphic bulge of women aged fifty-plus, increasing female longevity, and
the continued popularity of self-help and therapeutic literature, would
suggest that the time is ripe for another Moll on screen.

NOTES

1 A fourth screen adaptation of *Moll Flanders* (BBC, 1975) was apparently aired
   only in the UK: Part 1, "Mother and Daughter," 102 minutes; Part 2, "Mother
   and Son," 100 minutes. It is housed at BBC Archives, Brentford, and available
   only to BBC personnel.
2 Virginia Woolf, "Defoe," *The Essays of Virginia Woolf*, ed. Andrew McNeillie,
   4 vols. (London: The Hogarth Press, 1994), vol. IV, p. 102. Hereafter cited in
   text by author name and page number.
3 James Sutherland, *Daniel Defoe: A Critical Study* (Cambridge, MA: Harvard
   University Press, 1971), p. 7.
4 W. L. Gordon, *How to Write Photoplays* (Cincinnati: The Writer's Digest,
   1925), p. 2.
5 Willa Cather, *On Writing: Critical Studies on Writing as an Art* (Lincoln and
   London: University of Nebraska Press, 1988), p. 82. Hereafter cited in text by
   author name and page number.
6 Ian Watt, *The Rise of the Novel: Studies in Defoe, Richardson and Fielding*
   (Berkeley and Los Angeles: University of California Press, 1967), p. 108. Hereafter cited in text by author name and page number.
7 J. Paul Hunter, "Serious Reflections on Daniel Defoe (with an Excursus on
   the Farther Adventures of Ian Watt and Two Notes on the Present State of
   Literary Studies)," *Eighteenth-Century Fiction*, "Reconsidering the Rise of the
   Novel," 12 (1999–2000), 234.
8 See Michael Shinagel, *Daniel Defoe and Middle-Class Gentility* (Cambridge,
   MA: Harvard University Press, 1968), pp. 43–7 and 155, who has developed
   Watt's analysis.
9 See David Thomson, *A Biographical Dictionary of Film*, third edition (New
   York: Alfred A. Knopf, 1995), p. 531.
10 Daniel Defoe, *An Essay upon Projects* (Menston, England: Scolar Press, 1969),
   p. 35.
11 *emedia* (Omni Publications International, 1997), Interview with Pen Densham,
   May 5, 1997. http://www.omnimag.com/archives/chats/emo50597.html.

12 Ted Fry, "The Mr. Showbiz Interview," June 4, 1999.

13 *emedia*, May 5, 1997.

14 Jeanne Wolf, "Art imitates life for rising star Robin Wright," *The Detroit News*, June 14, 1996.

15 See Paula Backscheider, *Daniel Defoe: His Life* (Baltimore and London: Johns Hopkins University Press, 1989), pp. 501–2. Hereafter cited in text by author name and page number.

16 "'Moll Flanders' Charms PBS Viewers," PBS online, June 7, 1999, http://www. pbs.org/insidepbs/news/moll.html.

17 John C. Tibbets and James M. Welsh, *The Encyclopedia of Novels into Film* (New York: Facts on File, 1998), p. 126.

18 Stacey Richter, "*Moll Flanders*," *Tucson Weekly*, June 20, 1996.

19 "Why Moll Flanders?" and "The Woman Pulling Mollie's Strings," http:// www. hyperchat.co.uk/u/mollflanders/wouldbe.html.

20 "All About Moll Flanders," http://www.argo217.k12.il.us/apeng/flander/ mollanaly.html.

21 "A Moll Flander's [sic] Guide to Historic Women," http://www.hyperchat.co. uk/u/mollflanders/hist.html.

22 Miriam Leranbaum, "Moll Flanders: A Woman on Her Own Account," in *The Authority of Experience: Essays in Feminist Criticism*, ed. Arlyn Diamond and Lee R. Edwards (Amherst: University of Massachusetts Press, 1977) pp. 101–17. Katharine M. Rogers, *Feminism in Eighteenth-Century England* (Urbana: University of Illinois Press, 1982), pp. 70, 66.

23 Madeleine Kahn, *Narrative Transvestism: Rhetoric and Gender in the Eighteenth-Century English Novel* (Ithaca: Cornell University Press, 1991), pp. 9–10 and 62–5.

24 Margaret Anne Doody, in *The True Story of the Novel* (New Brunswick, NJ: Rutgers University Press, 1996), refers only once to Moll Flanders (p. 503). William Beatty Warner, in *Licensing Entertainment: The Elevation of Novel Reading in Britain, 1684–1750* (Berkeley: University of California Press, 1998), does not refer to this novel. See also the informative discussion of this critical phenomenon in Maximillian E. Novak's "Gendered Cultural Criticism and the Rise of the Novel: The Case of Defoe," *Eighteenth-Century Fiction*, "Reconsidering the Rise of the Novel," 12 (1999–2000), 239–52.

25 There is a large body of literature on this subject directed toward women readers as, for instance, Harold H. Bloomfield and Robert K. Cooper, *How to Stay Safe in an Unsafe World* (New York: Crown Publishers, 1997), which also has a substantial bibliography.

4   Film, censorship, and the "corrupt original" of *Gulliver's Travels*[1]

Alan D. Chalmers

Fair LIBERTY was all his cry;
For her he stood prepared to die;
For her he boldly stood alone;
For her he oft exposed his own.

> Jonathan Swift, "Verses on the Death of Dr. Swift" (1731)

... you have either omitted some material Circumstances, or minced and changed them in such a Manner, that I do hardly know mine own Work.

> 'A Letter from Capt. Gulliver to his Cousin Sympson"
> *Gulliver's Travels* (1726)

Any would-be adapter to the screen of Jonathan Swift's *Gulliver's Travels* (1726) should notice, among other more obvious discouragements, those elements of the book that reflect upon such a process, sometimes obliquely, sometimes prophetically. During Gulliver's third voyage, for example, a professor, knowing "how laborious the usual Method is of attaining to the Arts and Sciences," invents a machine for producing books "without the least Assistance from Genius or Study." This brave new technology consists of a frame, "about the Sides whereof all his Pupils stood in Ranks," each in charge of an iron handle. Within the frame was a system of wires and bits of wood with paper pasted upon each face, "and on these Papers were written all the Words of their Language in their several Moods, Tenses and Declensions, but without any Order." Turning the handles on command, the pupils would record "any three or four Words together that might make Part of a Sentence," repeating the exercise for six hours a day, so that the professor had "several Volumes in large Folio already collected, of broken Sentences," out of which he intended to "give the World a compleat Body of all Arts and Sciences."[2] This model of cultural production, in which large numbers of technicians routinely produce – or rather, fail to produce – what was once the province of individual genius and study might sound, to the hostile, akin to the business of commercial film adaptations of literary works. In goes the language of writers, and out comes inchoate trash. The professor's students perhaps anticipate Pierre Bourdieu's description of those working in large-scale media production in general and television in particular as "cultural producers – who are more or less locked into the role of pure technicians."[3]

Similarly suggestive is the expedient, offered by other projectors in the Academy at Lagado, that, "since Words are only names for Things, it would be more convenient for all men to carry about them, such Things as were necessary to express the particular Business they are to discourse on." Despite the fact that many subscribers to this new system are to be seen "almost sinking under the Weight of their Packs, like Pedlars among us," one of its great advantages is to "serve as an universal Language to be understood in all civilized Nations" (185–6). Film offers to fulfil the desire that generates such a fantasy, since as Alain Robbe-Grillet points out, "the essential characteristic of the image is its presentness. Whereas literature has a whole gamut of grammatical tense . . . by its nature what we see on the screen is in the act of happening, we are given the gesture itself, not an account of it."[4] Such moments in Swift are cautionary not least because they present collective efforts at enhanced communication via new media as both preposterous and degenerative. Thus filmmakers, perhaps especially television filmmakers, must run Swift's gauntlet as they adapt his book.

Does the latest adaptation – the 1996 television two-part mini-series *Gulliver's Travels*, directed by Charles Sturridge and produced by RHI Entertainment Inc. and Channel Four Television – emerge unscathed? Certainly it raises the hopes of anyone interested in seeing Jonathan Swift's original text adapted successfully to the screen. Sturridge, a British director whose career began in television, has directed the television adaptations of *Brideshead Revisited* (1981), *A Handful of Dust* (1987), and *Where Angels Fear to Tread* (1991), and so appears in his element. This expensive (twenty-eight million dollars), long (over three hours), beautifully crafted, well-acted film is much more attentive to its literary source than earlier productions, which have often had junior audiences in mind and regularly have eliminated the less approachable second half of the book. Such productions include Dave Fleischer's well-animated children's *Gulliver's Travels* (1939); Jack Sher's musically memorable, otherwise unremarkable *The Three Worlds of Gulliver* (USA/UK/Spain, 1960); a partly animated, action-filled version directed by Peter Hunt, starring Richard Harris, and containing, as one reviewer puts it, "treacly sentiment" and a "pasteboard Lilliput" (UK, 1977);[5] *Gulliver in Lilliput* (1981), made for the BBC, capturing the spirit of Swift's political satire in Part 1 of the *Travels* but departing freely from the letter; *Los Viages de Gulliver*, also known as

Land of the Giants: Gulliver's Travel Part II (Cruz Delgado, director, Spain, 1983), which as its English title declares is concerned only with the voyage to Brobdingnag.[6] The recent TV version compares favorably with all these predecessors in that it contains no such radical curtailments – it is the first film to depict all four voyages – and is more faithful to much of the detail of the original book.

Here, for example, Lemuel Gulliver (played by Ted Danson) extinguishes the fire at the Lilliputian Empress's apartment by urinating upon it. Gulliver describes European civilization for his Brobdingnaggian masters so revealingly as to elicit the famous judgment: "I cannot but conclude the bulk of your Natives, to be the most pernicious Race of little odious Vermin that Nature ever suffered to crawl upon the Surface of the Earth" (132). The flying island of Laputa is rendered with beautiful special effects. Flappers serve their intensely speculative masters with blows to "the organs of Speech and Hearing" (159). The preposterous experimenters at the Academy of Lagado are represented by Sir John Gielgud, in a wonderful cameo as the dotty scientist devoting his life to the extraction of sunlight from cucumbers. Real horses play the parts of the Houyhnhnms, with whom Lemuel Gulliver converses quite convincingly. The Yahoos are fairly repugnant. Danson, as Gulliver, pursues successfully some of the flexibility of Swift's original character, looking in various scenes appropriately gullible, or pompous, or zealous, or abject, or bemused. Some of these Swiftian features, among others, coupled with the film's special-effects-enhanced realism, prompt reviewers to warn that the film is unsuitable for young children. One reviewer even complains cryptically that the film "has perhaps been too faithful to the original."[7] Such a production, then, would seem to have taken comparatively Brobdingnaggian steps in the direction of fidelity in its adaptation.

However, and perhaps inevitably, this film 'screens' *Gulliver's Travels* not only in the sense that it visually projects it, but also in the sense that it subjects it to ideological scrutiny, and in key respects suppresses it. Indeed, this essay's central claim about the film is that its elisions, evasions, and commercial accommodations commit tacitly a kind of censorship of Swift's *Gulliver's Travels*. Further, while the film mutes Swift's original in certain key respects, paradoxically it adds material that affirms the principle of free speech. It is upon this paradox that this essay focuses its attention.

To construe creative adaptation as a kind of censorship begs several questions, of course. Indeed, the problems of using the term in such a context appear acute. Do not those who adapt original works to another medium enjoy creative license? To accuse them of censoring the original is perhaps to apply normative standards for adaptation that are themselves potentially a form of censorship. Indeed some critics in this arena have claimed "that filmmakers, TV classical serial makers and all the rest of them, have their own goals and imperatives, and that the cry of being 'true to the text' is not defensible, and need not be defended."[8] So perhaps to talk of adaptation as censorship is an extreme instance of the kind of judgment Brian McFarlane finds all too ubiquitous among critics of adaptations of novels to film. Referring to "those many accounts of how films reduce great novels," McFarlane finds in them "words like 'tampering' and 'interference,' and even 'violation' [which] give the whole process an air of deeply sinister molestation."[9] At the root of such responses, writes McFarlane, is the absence of a theoretical framework for approaching adaptation – a framework that "could deflect reviewers and critics from pointlessly chastising a film for not reproducing their sense of the original text."[10] Taking up another line of argument, one might ask whether an adaptation can be said to transgress or censor the original while that original remains freely available, as *Gulliver's Travels* does in homes, libraries, and bookstores. And finally, does not every adaptation, whether skilful or inept, return us to the original with renewed interest and appreciation?

One negative answer to this last question is provided by John Ellis, who asks whether an adaptation of novel to film trades "upon the memory of the novel, a memory that can derive from an actual reading or . . . a generally circulated cultural memory . . . [so that] . . . The adaptation consumes this memory, aiming to efface it with the presence of its own images."[11] Such a process of effacement as Ellis describes is illustrated vividly by Sturridge's *Gulliver's Travels*, not least because of the film's own foregrounding of censorship as a theme. This theme marks a departure from Swift's original, enacting an effacement of the original, on Ellis's terms, yet serves to reassure the audience that the film upholds respect for free expression and, more particularly, the integrity of author and text alike.

The theme of censorship emerges as part of the film's approach to the difficult challenge of adapting Gulliver's first-person perspective on his adventure. Gulliver's point of view is integral to the strongest effects of Swift's book, and some earlier film versions simply ignore it. This movie opens with Gulliver's final return home after his voyage to Houyhnhnmland, and his adventures are then depicted as he recalls them. In between these recollections, the returned Gulliver tries desperately to reorient himself, and to convince those around him of the veracity of his stories, and ultimately of his sanity. The film is thus structured as a chronological sequence of flashbacks to the travels themselves, between which we return to Gulliver recalling and narrating his travels in a way that unifies them, and that avoids the repetition involved in depicting each of his journeys home.

This narrative economy would not necessarily compromise Swift's text very much, if it were not that the filmmakers, basing the main action in the days and weeks after Gulliver's final homecoming, have written a new plot to facilitate this new focus. It is in this un-Swiftian material that the theme of censorship arises. Having returned to pick up his life in England, Gulliver is pitted against Dr. Bates (James Fox) who in Gulliver's protracted absence has become his wife's suitor. While the physician's professional judgment might urge him to commit the ranting Gulliver to an asylum, his own amorous plans determine him to do so. Dr. Bates's medical colleagues support him – they can only deduce from Gulliver's extravagant ranting that he is mad, despite his protestations. So Gulliver finds himself in something like the position enunciated famously by Nathaniel Lee: "They called me mad, and I called them mad, and damn them, they outvoted me."[12]

Indeed, as in Swift's original, Gulliver is living in two worlds after his return, suffering a kind of post-traumatic stress disorder, and is often delusional, confusing memories with present actualities. For Roy Porter, Swiftian narrators like Lemuel Gulliver exemplify the dangers of auto-biographical writing: "For the form itself demands a solipsism which might be seen as inherently pathological. To tell one's story: what could better establish one's veracity, or provide more conclusive symptoms of utter self-delusion?"[13] Institutional treatment of the mad historically has included various methods of silencing this "pathological" self-telling, and perhaps the Hallmark film is informed by this history. Certainly Simon Moore, who wrote the screenplay, "was inspired by research that showed Swift had visited England's first mental hospital."[14] Porter records the case of one asylum inmate whose "lifeline to sanity . . . was often a stub-end of pencil secreted away somewhere in his cell." He tells of another who complained of "his isolation from his fellow men and the unremitting destruction or censorship of letters written by or sent to him."[15] The Gulliver of the film has just these forms of deprivation inflicted upon him. He is committed to Bethlehem Hospital, where he is forbidden visits, and in this situation is censored at every turn. Bates destroys the bulging, leather-bound journal that is Gulliver's record of all his adventures, and does so with a certain grim relish – he tears it methodically page by page, and consigns it to the fire. A close-up shows a drawing of the box in which Glumdalclitch had kept Gulliver during his sojourn in Brobdingnag being consumed by flames. Bates also intercepts, reads, and then secretes all correspondence between Gulliver and Mary. Thrown into solitary confinement as a result of an assault upon Bates, Gulliver is denied the audience of inmates he has been entertaining with his tales. In his confinement Gulliver asks Bates "Will you bring me paper and ink? – I'm going to write down everything that's happened to me." Denied these, he writes his entire story on the walls in chalk. The film returns to Gulliver at work on this improvised text no less than five times, in images incidentally reminiscent of Hogarth's depiction of a graffiti-scribbling Bedlamite, in the eighth plate of *A Rake's Progress*. The moment Gulliver is released from this cell, however, Bates with consistent ruthlessness instructs the warders to "wash this rubbish off" the walls. Thus Swift's narrative is interwoven with a new strand of plot which gives prominence to censorship. Indeed, the climactic scene of the film centers on the moment when the authenticity of Gulliver's account is at last publicly established (on the empirical evidence of a Lilliputian sheep, released in the courtroom), and so his judges grant him his liberty – Dr. Bates now powerless to silence him.

Perhaps it could be said, in defense of this adaptation's striking narrative departure from its original, that Swift's political and satirical writings are generated and shaped at different levels by a contention between censorship and liberty of expression. More persuasive, as a defense of the film's new theme of censorship, is the possibility that it signals and internalizes the censorious responses *Gulliver's Travels* has elicited since its first publication. Such responses have been so ubiquitous throughout the history of the book's reception that Swift's work can be regarded as a kind of "corrupt original." Michael Holquist uses this apparently contradictory phrase in quite a different context, but one that is particularly germane here. Holquist illustrates its meaning by recalling Fray Luis de Leon (1527–91), who was jailed for translating the Song of Songs into Spanish from the original Hebrew. The Inquisition's objection was not only that Spanish was a vernacular, but also that his source language, Hebrew, was vernacular too, as opposed to the authoritative Latin. Thus the Hebrew text constituted "a corrupt original." On the basis of this and other examples, Holquist concludes that "the censor must assume that all originals are corrupt":

"Corrupt original" goes to the heart of any attempt to understand censorship if only because the concept's surface contradiction points to the frangibility of all claims to authority made on the basis of originality. If all originals are open to corruption in the sense that their authority is hostage to the contexts in which they are consumed rather than to the ones in which they were produced, censorship is inescapable as well as arbitrary.[16]

Thus, Holquist suggests, just as the Inquisition could declare a translation more authoritative or "purer" than the original, so all original works – particularly one as provocative as *Gulliver's Travels*, no doubt – are at risk of being held "hostage" later, not only in translations but in other forms of adaptation that knowingly or unknowingly censor the original, usurping its textual authority.

Swift and his Scriblerian friends, especially Pope, were highly sensitive to this distinction between the author's and the reader's contexts and to the crisis of authority implicit in any literary transaction between them. Swift wrote often, for example, of the vanity of presuming anything about the persistence of cultural values over time, noting that "It is pleasant to observe, how free the present Age is, in laying Taxes on the next. 'Future Ages shall observe this: This shall be famous to all Posterity.' Whereas, their Time and Thoughts will be taken up about present Things, as ours are now."[17] For Swift, human beings seemed diminished by their cultural parochialism, their preoccupation with the present. Literary posterity seemed a vain hope. Such perceptions, and the apparent arbitrariness of readers' authority, fuelled Swift's antagonism towards, his desire to vex his own readers. And this satiric intention to vex gives the term "corrupt original" a particular resonance in Swift's case. His most powerful satires, including *Gulliver's Travels* and especially Part IV, have a notoriously sullying or corrosive force, in response to which some critics' censure has implicitly or explicitly included a call for censorship. Clearly, Swift himself thought it likely the book would arouse a hostile reception when he wrote to Pope on September 25, 1725 that he was "finishing, correcting, amending and Transcribing my Travells ... intended for the press when the world shall deserve them, or rather when a Printer shall be found brave enough to venture his Eares."[18] It remains a matter of critical debate whether Swift's printer John Motte altered Swift's manuscript before publication, and if so, how much. And whether it was censored at the source or not, it later provoked critical outcry from some quarters, often expressing a barely concealed desire for censorship. The earl of Orrery's *Remarks on the Life And Writings of Dr. Jonathan Swift* (1752) exclaims against "a misanthropy that is intolerable. The representation which [Swift] has given us of human nature, must terrify, and even debase the mind of the reader who views it."[19] Translating *Gulliver's Travels* into French, the Abbé Desfontaines "believed it proper to take the course of suppressing [allegorical elements] entirely," and admits that "there were passages at which his pen escaped his hand, from actual horror and astonishment at the daring violations of all critical decorum," but reassures his readers that he has undertaken to censor the book on their behalf: "not only has he changed many of the incidents, to accommodate them to the French taste, but moreover, they will not be annoyed, in his translation, with the nautical details, and minute particulars, so offensive in the original."[20] James Harris writes, in 1781, "MISANTHROPY is so dangerous a thing that I esteem the last part of Swift's Gulliver [to be] a worse Book to peruse, than those which we forbid, as the most flagitious and obscene."[21] Even a more tolerant reader of Swift like Sir Walter Scott never fully disengages Swift's originality, which Scott claims even his severest detractors cannot deny, from his corruption. But for Scott Swift also reflects his times. Scott writes complacently of the righteous censoriousness of his own age, compared to the regrettable freedoms of Swift's: "we should do great injustice to the present day, by comparing our manners with those of the reign of George I. The writings even of the most esteemed poets of that period, contain passages which, in modern times, would be accounted to deserve the pillory."[22] Such commentary, which has subsided in our own time, demonstrates how Swift's book regularly elicits censorious impulses, because of the difficulty of confronting the view (if not the smell) of ourselves upon which Swift's satire insists.

That the film adaptation incorporates and thematizes this legacy of hostile reception is made clear when, in the climactic scene, Dr. Bates condemns Gulliver's testimony in terms that are lifted verbatim from William Makepeace Thackeray's famous response to Part IV of the *Travels*: "It is Yahoo language: a monster jibbering shrieks, and gnashing imprecations against mankind – tearing down all shreds of modesty, past all sense of manliness and shame; filthy in thought, furious, raging, obscene."[23] Dr. Bates also refers more than once to Gulliver's affront to Christian values, a charge quite frequently leveled against Swift by his later moralizing detractors.

To incorporate into a film adaptation something of the reception history of the original work appears encouragingly literate and ambitious. But does such occasional allusiveness indicate any deeper intuitions on the part of the filmmakers about the abiding provocations to censorship offered by Swift's text? It is hard to see the movie's treatment of censorship as an adaptation of either Jonathan Swift's attitudes toward censorship or his relations with censors or would-be censors. A fundamental strategy of Swift's book is to offer readers liberty through imaginative fantasy, and then to return them abruptly to themselves through satire. So in a broad sense the book hinges on a dialectic between imaginative liberty and censoriousness. In the screen adaptation this dialectic is reduced to a simplistic scheme, with Ted Danson's Gulliver as conquering hero pitted against institutionalized hypocrisy and conformism. The original Gulliver ends up perplexed and ultimately profoundly alienated by his exposure to other strange worlds, forced to see himself in the bestial Yahoos, identifying hopelessly with a society of horses. As Denis Donoghue puts it, "Gulliver's sense of life differs from ours and is palpably inadequate to the reality it negotiates."[24] Beginning in comic adventure, Swift's book finally turns downwards and inwards, toward outrage and madness, leaving Gulliver to behold in his species "a Lump of Deformity, and diseases both of Body and Mind, smitten with Pride." This, he tells us, "immediately breaks all the Measures of my Patience; neither shall I be ever able to comprehend how such an Animal and such a Vice could tally together" (296). By contrast the narrative trajectory of the movie turns up and outwards. Gulliver, confused and exhausted in the early scenes, proves his sanity in the end in a formal hearing – replete with most of the cliches of the courtroom climax – and returns from Bedlam to "life and freedom," as his wife puts it. So the conclusion does not portray Gulliver, as Swift's does, stopping his nostrils with "Rue, Lavender or Tobacco-Leaves" in order to brook others' human smell, nor Gulliver considering "with the utmost Shame, Confusion, and Horror," "that by copulating with one of the Yahoo-Species, I had become a Parent of more" (295, 289). The conclusion is, rather, of Gulliver and his wife kissing passionately amid a beautiful Dorset landscape. Here the singularities of Swift's satire are effaced by a trite commonplace of period romance: the costumed couple (here with child) receding into an English pastoral scene. While in the book readers are left within the deranged contradictions of Gulliver's consciousness, here a helicopter shot widens viewers' distance from him in slow ascending loops, accompanied by sweeping orchestration. In this last scene of the movie Gulliver's voice-over, which is bereft of irony, is the most risibly un-Swiftian feature of the entire production: "You see, when night falls and you close your eyes to sleep and dream, I have seen the things that you can only dream about . . . I have been there. Oh yes. All the way. And back."

This devolution into romance is of course one more example of a ubiquitous feature of adaptations of novels to the screen, and especially the television screen. One reviewer points to it when he refers to the presence of "all the usual appurtenances of the [TV mini-series] genre."[25] Deborah Kaplan points to it while discussing screen adaptations of Jane Austen. Kaplan observes that "to put Austen's novels on film by means of corporations (Columbia and Miramax) that produce what is now a global culture informed by American tastes is to enter a medium shaped by powerful generic conventions of romance."[26] If, as Kaplan believes, these conventions result in the distortion of Austen's art, then the way they shape the conclusion of the televised *Gulliver's Travels* is obviously less a distortion than a travesty.

Some strain between the originality of the literary text and the evolving conventions of the literary adaptation genre seems endemic. Roger Sales demonstrates the crucial biographical and historical misconceptions shaping our "consumption" of Jane Austen, including film productions of her novels.[27] Andrew Higson gives an acute account of such strain among what he calls the "heritage films" of the 1980s, a group that includes examples of Sturridge's earlier work (*Brideshead Revisited, A Handful of Dust*). Exploring these films for their representation of a national heritage, Higson argues that in them "the past is displayed as visually spectacular pastiche, inviting a nostalgic gaze that resists the ironies and social critiques so often suggested narratively by these films" and by the novels upon which they are based.[28] Sturridge's *Gulliver's Travels* falls outside Higson's purview on many counts: it is not exclusively British, and was made in the 1990s; most significantly, it cannot be seen clearly as responsive to contemporary politics, in the way that Higson's heritage films can. The Thatcher administration was itself responsible for rhetorical and legislative strategies that linked the concepts of heritage and enterprise in radical new ways, as Higson points out. The 'packaging' of the past for profit, the desire for nostalgic refuge from the economic realities of Thatcher's Britain – these forces shaped many British screen adaptations. The film *Gulliver's Travels* was made internationally, and in the less polarized political atmosphere (at least from a British perspective) of the 1990s. The action of *Gulliver's Travels* takes place largely in imaginary foreign lands, which of course reflect English life in Swift's time, but not directly in a way that lends itself to nostalgic visual exploitation. Nonetheless, Higson's terms often resonate accidentally with the film *Gulliver's Travels*:

The self-conscious visual perfectionism of these films and their fetishization of period details create a fascinating but self-enclosed world. They render history as spectacle, as separate from the viewer in the present, as something over and done with, complete, achieved. Hence the sense of timelessness rather than historicity in relation to a national past which is "purged of political tension" and so available for appreciation as visual display.[29]

Gulliver's Travels, like Higson's chosen films, is visually sumptuous, a spectacle that leads us away from its historicity, particularly since that spectacle is already in Swift's text one of fantasy rather than realism. More problematically, this movie, too, is "purged of all political tension." Higson finds elements of the novels' plots and characters remaining at odds with the construction of nostalgic spectacle (*Brideshead Revisited* being a case in point). The newly enhanced plot of *Gulliver's Travels*

achieves the opposite, easing tensions further by enacting emphatic romantic closure, creating a very strong sense of something over and done
with, "and refusing the possibility of a dialogue or confrontation with the
present."[30]

In this way, and with an irony of which the filmmakers may not have
been fully conscious, but which Swift of all writers would have understood, the theme of freedom in this film constitutes a form of censorship
of the original text. The television Gulliver's ultimately triumphant struggle for truth, justice, and liberty belongs to a very large family of popular
narratives – that to which Kaplan refers – whose familiar form renders
familiar results: comfortable, sympathetic audience involvement of a not
necessarily thoughtful kind. One recalls George Orwell's claim that in
Part III of *Gulliver's Travels*, "there is a perception that one of the aims of
totalitarianism is not merely to make sure that people will think the right
thoughts, but actually to make them less conscious."[31] This is Swift's
perception – one of his many uncannily prophetic intuitions. And one
feature of his book that makes us more conscious, not less, is the suscep-
tibility of Gulliver's consciousness to modification from without, from
his immediate social environment. As Denis Donoghue writes, *Gulliver's
Travels* "touches us . . . in our sense of imprisonment – not necessarily imprisonment in a concentration camp, but in any imposed system of ideas
and values." Claiming that the book "is only superficially about big men
and little men: it is really about entrapment," Donoghue notes Gulliver's
inability to resist ideology of any stamp: "As long as he is inside the system, he doesn't bring any irony to bear on it. Irony is the counter-force
to brainwashing: it brings to bear upon a given system values antithetical to those in place; it holds out against the system's blandishments.
Gulliver doesn't."[32] Swift's Gulliver, in other words, gullibly internalizes
both the prevailing ideology of his hosts and the censorship integral to
its constitution, and in the process becomes the butt of Swift's irony. Ted
Danson's earlier work in comedy demonstrates how well he can appear
gullible, but this movie dignifies him instead, and makes him the reliable
center of a story that eschews irony while rehearsing a familiar system of
ideas and values.

Thus, while Gulliver's struggle for free and authentic self-expression
is central to, and ostensibly morally endorsed by, the film, covertly the
film is in league with this Gulliver's oppressors, the Bedlam Doctors who
would suppress the subversive potential of his tale. Swift, like the film's
protagonist, has been doctored. The film's infidelities counterbalance
and finally outweigh the fidelities to Swift's book described at the beginning of this essay. Remarkably, but in keeping with American television's
restrictive standards of decency, the physicality so prominent in Swift's

7. Mary (Mary Steenburgen) attempts to vindicate Gulliver (Ted Danson) in the climactic scene of Charles Sturridge's *Gulliver's Travels*

book – the way in which human aspirations and pretensions are so often pricked by reference to our bodies – is systematically suppressed. Ironically, Swift's interest in purgation is itself purged here. In Lilliput for example, we are spared Gulliver's embarrassment over the removal of his excrement in wheelbarrows. The matter of his worn-out breeches as he stands Colossus-like over the Lilliputian army, and his painstaking vindication of the reputation of the six-inch tall treasurer's wife, with whom he vehemently denies engaging in any adulterous improprieties – these matters are also omitted from the film. In the adaptation of the second voyage, Brobdingnaggians become beautiful, not grotesque, and the magnified skins of these giant people never appear as Gulliver sees them: "coarse and uneven, so variously coloured when I saw them near, with a Mole here and there as broad as a Trencher, and Hairs hanging from it thicker than Packthreads" (119). Neither do we see huge cancers and wens on this magnified skin, nor "the most hateful Sight of all [which] was the Lice crawling upon their Cloaths" (112–13). No maids of honor sexually abuse the protagonist. We do not hear, with the horrible amplification that Swift imagined, a giant head, severed by a giant executioner, as it hits the ground. In the third part, at the Academy of Lagado, no dogs are destroyed in cruel experiments, nor landscapes laid waste in the name of scientific progress. No government agents root around in political

8. The Yahoos in Sturridge's *Gulliver's Travels*

suspects' waste in search of incriminating evidence. No brain surgery
is undertaken to eliminate political dissidence. The Struldbruggs are not
old and repugnant – their representative, the "Immortal Gatekeeper," is
the actress Kristin Scott Thomas, the glamorous female lead in the Oscar-
winning film *The English Patient* (1996). Gulliver defers to, but never pros-
trates himself before authority in the way that Swift's protagonist is compelled to in Laputa, "crawl[ing] upon my Belly, and lick[ing] the Floor as I
advanced" (204). Yahoos are not naked – the feature upon which Swift's
Gulliver bases his vital but tenuous distinction from them – and their
dung-flinging is glimpsed almost too briefly for perception, and relegated
to a verbal reference by Gulliver at his hearing. Most importantly, we are
not affronted by Gulliver's insistence upon our sub-bestial moral status;
rather, we are amused at the prim discomfiture of Gulliver's antagonists
as he confronts them with a toned-down version of Swift's message. We
might smile, for instance, at the shocked reaction in the public gallery
when Gulliver challenges the prevalent association between clothing and
civilized society, and asks them why they might not go about naked and
unashamed. Yet in covering the Yahoos' privates, for example, the film
surely shares the prudery it depicts as risible. At his clinical hearing,
Gulliver addresses many of his most unpalatable observations to the public gallery, which the camera usually shoots from Gulliver's position, or
from behind Gulliver to include him in the frame. Either way the audience

is visually aligned with Gulliver, not those to whom he addresses himself. A camera positioned in the public gallery would have created a small measure of the unease created by the conclusion of Swift's book, since Gulliver would then have appeared to be addressing us directly. Indeed, camera work throughout the movie misses opportunities to catch many key features and effects of the book – not least those of scale, which even the small screen of television could much more thoroughly exploit.

Such "softening" by omission and alteration compounds the effect of the movie's development of a family melodrama in which the hero's wife and son play important roles. Mary Gulliver (Mary Steenburgen), with a lachrymose helplessness bordering on masochism, at last stands up in Gulliver's defense, proclaiming that he is "a good man, an honest man, he's returned a better man." Tom Gulliver (Thomas Sturridge), referred to by one reviewer as a "pretty sop to sentimental viewers,"[33] remains faithful to his father – "I want him to come home," he declares – and steadfastly pursues the evidence that will free him. Their patrimonial reunion seems a particularly conservative "enhancement" of the dubious reconciliation described by Swift.

This adaptation of *Gulliver's Travels* is after all, then, a commercial product, made under the auspices of Hallmark Entertainment Inc., part of a corporate empire built in part upon the mass distribution of bland and sentimental imagery. It has designs upon the desires of large numbers, and is designed for interruption by commercials offering their own incitements to desire. In such a context, Swift's satiric exposure and excoriation of the role of desire in human life, most memorably embodied in the Yahoos, seems doomed. Such a pessimistic conclusion is confirmed by Sue Curry Jansen, a recent theorist of censorship. She cautions us that, "In capitalist economies the organizational structure of television production, like other forms of production, is formally totalitarian. It is under the hierarchical control of a corporate elite." She notes, no more cheerfully, that "the consciousness industry [is] the linchpin of the new monolithic market system."[34] So trying to rescue Swift from such an overtly corporate project might seem uncomfortably akin to the work of the scientists in the Academy of Lagado, who attempt to extract "Sun-beams out of Cucumbers," and "reduce . . . Excrement to its original Food" (179, 180). Yet the film's often scrupulous attention to Swift's words, its sometimes powerful realization of Swift's fantasy, make it important to resist the perception that it faithfully "adapts" Swift's original, on whatever terms such fidelity is established. Indeed, the film betrays Swift's complex, often contradictory understanding of liberty (inextricable as it is from his own strong censorious tendencies), erasing it under a cruder, more dominant ideological discourse in which the transcendent role of "freedom" obscures the presence, within such discourse, of censorship. As Jansen says, "the absence of an adequate vocabulary of resistance ... permits the corporate state to use the language of liberty to deny liberty."[35]

One special irony of this process is that the movie version of *Gulliver's Travels* resembles in its narrative structure what Roy Porter refers to as "the great heroic myths of the New World [which] were secularized optimistic recensions of the protestant ethos of individual salvation."[36] The television Gulliver, more like the heroes of such myths than like his Swiftian namesake, remains steadfast through his trials and tribulations until the climactic moment of his just reward. This new narrative relationship seems a sort of belated revenge on Swift, for whom the dissenting protestant ethos was anathema, as several of his best-known works, and his attitude to Daniel Defoe, for example, make clear.

This affinity of the movie to a large family of hackneyed narratives is itself a betrayal of what Sir Walter Scott called the "distinguished attribute of ORIGINALITY ... [which] cannot be refused to Swift by the most severe critic."[37] Swift's book's relationship to other literary modes is usually self-conscious and parodic – in its imitation of popular travel narratives, for example. It never falls unwittingly into a predictable narrative groove, and indeed part of its creative energy derives paradoxically from its tendency to undermine its own narrative stability wherever it threatens to develop – not least in the character of the narrator. Gulliver is a collapsible satiric device in Swift's hands, absurdly impervious to the enormity of his experiences, inhumanly adaptable, simultaneously the recorder and embodiment of all human folly and vice. To give flesh to this textual phenomenon is inevitably to impose upon it the consistency of character, a more or less stable identity, which Swift's man unnervingly lacks.

Finally, this new narrative element of the film, which casts Gulliver as entirely sympathetic and trustworthy, and culminates in his triumph over corrupt oppressors, emplots what Holquist refers to as a persistent, "crude axiology ... an absolute choice between prohibition and freedom." The idea of such a choice dissolves under Holquist's sophisticated scrutiny, informed as it is by a post-structural understanding of language and a post-Freudian understanding of the mind, so that even the sequential relationship between writing and censorship is challenged, as we have seen. For Holquist, censorship seems everywhere already there, so that the simple opposition of censorship and freedom

denies the reality of interdiction, and masks the necessity of choosing between the myriad specific conditions that embody censorship's fatedness. To be for or against censorship as such is to assume a freedom no one has. Censorship is. One can only discriminate among its more and less repressive effects.[38]

The 1996 film of *Gulliver's Travels* fails or refuses to acknowledge its own acts of interdiction, its simultaneous revival and suppression of Swift's original. One might modify an assertion made by Dallas Smythe, that "the act of modern censorship is essentially a decision as to what is to be mass-produced in the cultural area,"[39] and stress rather the importance of how cultural artifacts are produced once they have been selected. Certainly the closer the proximity between Swift's writing and its adaptation to the screen, the more suspicious the process seems. The unparalleled astringency of Swift's satire, its ability to entrap readers within its scathing ironies, derives in part from its medium: writing is solitary, undertaken in privacy, and in its vital stages relatively cost-free. Filmmaking is from the outset a collective enterprise, more vulnerable to compromise, and payment of its costs depends upon the anticipated satisfaction of its audience. Independent filmmakers may achieve relative creative independence, but *Gulliver's Travels* would be almost impossible to produce on most independents' budgets. So Swift's book is perhaps doomed to an adaptation that suppresses its satiric wrath.

Nonetheless, there are degrees of suppression. Paul Giles observes that "in America the typical television movie appears as an inexpensive B movie program" and contains "the most conventional narrative forms of romance and melodrama," while in Britain during the 1980s the medium sometimes rose above such mediocre fare. Indeed it "offered space to many of the country's best writers and directors, whose films for the small screen surpassed most 'British Cinema' during the period."[40] This kind of national difference is too often overlooked by theories of television, John Caughie argues, claiming that such theories (those of Raymond Williams, Marshall McLuhan, and Jean Baudrillard, for example) universalize a local, national experience – the US experience – as "the essence of television."[41] Might this television *Gulliver's Travels*, with its part-British production, have resisted its own descent into American narrative pap? Or would certain conventions of British television period drama, such as those analyzed by Roger Sales and Andrew Higson, have muted Swift in more subtle (and therefore insidious) ways? (*Gulliver in Lilliput*, made by the BBC in 1981, is not especially encouraging.) In either case, the heart of Swift's *Gulliver's Travels*, its excoriation of contemporary vice and folly, seems unlikely to flourish.

When, at the end of Swift's book, Gulliver writes, "I am not a little pleased that this Work of mine can possibly meet with no Censurers" (292), the irony of the double register is obvious: Gulliver, comically oblivious to the implications of his words; Swift fully aware of their provocations. Swift's habitation within or between the words of his narrator exemplifies a part of Holquist's notion of the corrupt original. Indeed

Holquist talks broadly (at what he calls an "overabstracted level") of the necessity of "reading between the lines" as evidence "that all originals are indeed corrupt."[42] And the frequent resistance of Swift's ironies to firm measurement elicits, as we have seen, what Holquist describes as "the monologic terror of indeterminacy that is the essence of all censorship."[43] When Ted Danson's voice-over at the end of the movie version proclaims "I see myself for what I truly am," its monologic narrative function is thus also that of the censor; any ironic potential resides exclusively with the viewer, alas. Thus, while Swift's avowed intent was to vex his reader, this film vexes admirers of Swift by vexing us too little. In another context, Sue Curry Jansen claims, hopefully, that "We can use parables of persecution to secure a new talisman against censorship."[44] Viewers of the recent *Gulliver's Travels* will discover censorship already at work within those very parables.

NOTES

1 Title phrase derived from Michael Holquist, "Corrupt Originals: The Paradox of Censorship," *PMLA* 109 (1994), 14–25. I am indebted to Holquist for ideas that have become central to this essay.
2 Herbert Davis, ed., *The Prose Works of Jonathan Swift*, 14 volumes (Oxford: Basil Blackwell, 1939–68), XI: 182–4. All subsequent references to *Gulliver's Travels* will be to this edition and volume and will be cited in parentheses in the body of the essay.
3 "The Market of Symbolic Goods," in *The Critical Tradition: Classic Texts and Contemporary Trends*, 2nd edn., ed. David Richter (Boston: Bedford Books, 1998), p. 1242.
4 Cited in Robert Giddings, Keith Selby, and Chris Wensley, *Screening the Novel: The Theory and Practice of Literary Dramatization* (New York: St. Martin's Press, 1990), pp. 15–16.
5 John Pym, *The Time Out Film Guide* (London: Penguin, 1993), p. 285.
6 A Soviet adaptation, *Novyj Gulliver (The New Gulliver)*, 1935, directed by Aleksandr Ptushko, has proved unavailable to date.
7 Andy Wickstrom, *Video*, 20: 6 (October 1996), 87–8.
8 Giddings et al., *Screening the Novel*, p. xix.
9 Brian McFarlane, *Novel into Film: An Introduction to the Theory of Adaptation* (Oxford: Clarendon Press, 1996), p. 12.
10 McFarlane, *Novel into Film*, p. 196.
11 Cited in Giddings et al., *Screening the Novel*, p. 21.
12 Cited in Roy Porter, *A Social History of Madness* (New York: E. P. Dutton, 1987), p. 3.
13 Porter, *Madness*, p. 29.
14 John P. McCarthy, *Variety*, February 5, 1996, 36.
15 Porter, *Madness*, pp. 30, 31.
16 Holquist, "Corrupt Originals," 8.

17 Davis, ed., *Prose Works*, I: 243. See also Swift's *A Tale of a Tub*, whose radically unreliable narrator brings to a comic crisis the precarious terms of textual transmission.

18 Harold Williams, ed., *The Correspondence of Jonathan Swift*, 5 volumes (Oxford: Clarendon Press, 1963–65), III: 102.

19 Christopher Fox, ed., *Gulliver's Travels: Case Studies in Contemporary Criticism* (New York: Bedford/St. Martin's, 1995), p. 273.

20 Kathleen Williams, ed., *Swift: The Critical Heritage* (New York: Barnes and Noble, 1970), pp. 79–80.

21 Fox, *Gulliver's Travels*, p. 275.

22 Williams, *Critical Heritage*, pp. 295–6.

23 Denis Donoghue, ed., *Penguin Critical Anthologies: Jonathan Swift* (Harmondsworth, Middlesex: Penguin, 1971), p. 117.

24 Donoghue, "The Brainwashing of Lemuel Gulliver," *Southern Review* 32:1 (1996), 128–46.

25 Robert S. Rothenberg, "Gulliver's Travels," *USA Today*, March 1997, 97.

26 Deborah Kaplan, "Mass Marketing Jane Austen: Men, Women, and Courtship in Two Film Adaptations," in *Jane Austen in Hollywood*, ed. Linda Troost and Sayre Greenfield (Lexington: University Press of Kentucky, 1998), p. 180.

27 Roger Sales, *Jane Austen and Representations of Regency England* (New York: Routledge, 1994).

28 Andrew Higson, "Re-presenting the National Past: Nostalgia and Pastiche in the Heritage Film," in *Fires Were Started: British Cinema and Thatcherism*, ed. Lester Friedman (Minneapolis: University of Minnesota Press, 1993), p. 109.

29 Higson, "Re-presenting the National Past," p. 113.

30 Higson, "Re-presenting the National Past," p. 119.

31 "Politics v. Literature: An Examination of Gulliver's Travels," (1946) cited in Donoghue, *Jonathan Swift*, p. 352.

32 Donoghue, "Brainwashing," 141.

33 Steven Poole, "In a Stable Condition," *The Times Literary Supplement*, April 19, 1996, 20–1.

34 Sue Curry Jansen, *Censorship: The Knot That Binds Power and Knowledge* (London: Oxford University Press, 1988), pp. 162, 138.

35 Jansen, *Censorship*, p. 15.

36 Porter, *Madness*, p. 189.

37 Williams, *Critical Heritage*, p. 296.

38 Holquist, "Corrupt Originals," 16.

39 Cited in Jansen, *Censorship*, p. 65.

40 Paul Giles, "History With Holes: Channel Four Television Films of the 1980s," in *Fires Were Started*, ed. Friedman, p. 70.

41 Cited in Giles, "History With Holes," p. 70.

42 Holquist, "Corrupt Originals," 23.

43 Holquist, "Corrupt Originals," 21.

44 Jansen, *Censorship*, p. 191.

5   Adapting Fielding for film and television

Martin C. Battestin

Some time ago in an essay on the film of Fielding's *Tom Jones* (1963), I made what remains for me the essential point about adapting novels for the screen: analogy is the key.[1] Since it is impossible to duplicate in visual images in the course of two hours (or five, as in the case of a television series) the substance of a novel of a thousand pages whose effects depend entirely on the written word, the makers of the film, while recalling the movement of the plot, must find ways of capturing the essential spirit of the work of fiction, of striking analogous attitudes and finding analogous rhetorical techniques. To borrow terms preferred by Brian McFarlane,[2] the narrative of the novel – its storyline, characters, setting – is rather easily "transferable" to film; far more challenging is the art of "adaptation," of finding the means, from among the distinctive technical resources of cinematography, to evoke the essential character of the original: the intangible elements of tone and value that constitute its meaning.

In considering the problem of turning the words of Fielding's fiction into pictures, it is worth remembering that Fielding himself endorsed in his novels the Horatian concept *ut pictura poësis*, the idea that poetry and painting are "sister arts." In the Preface to *Joseph Andrews* (1742) he distinguished at some length between "the Comic and the Burlesque" (4),[3] invoking the example of his friend William Hogarth to illustrate the difference – a compliment Hogarth returned the following year when he referred purchasers of his print *Characters and Caricaturas* to the passage in question. Hogarth, with regard to the relation of novels and movies, seems particularly apt; for Fielding, who called him "a Comic History-Painter" (6) and himself the author of "a Comic Epic-Poem in Prose" (4), had in mind Hogarth's picture-narratives, *A Harlot's Progress* (1732) and *A Rake's Progress* (1735) – the former depicting in six "frames," as it were, the story of Kate Hackabout's descent from innocence to a vile death from venereal disease; the latter, in eight frames, depicting the story of Tom Rakewell, prodigal heir to his miserly father's riches, whose indulgence in the vices of the town brings him to debtors' prison, and at last to Bedlam. In these two popular series, Fielding declared in *The Champion*

(June 10, 1740), Hogarth had shown himself to be "one of the most useful Satyrists any Age hath produced." In the story of Wilson in *Joseph Andrews* (III: iii–iv) Fielding would produce his own prose version of Tom Rakewell's progress, though giving it a happy ending. And Hogarth, for his part, attempted in his own way to bring the two art forms closer together by filling each picture of his "histories" with emblematic details that reveal the moral he meant to inculcate; his pictures, as art historians have remarked, must be "read" as well as viewed.[4]

Fielding in his novels often renders popular subjects of the visual arts. Besides the Wilson story, an example from *Joseph Andrews* is the chapter in which the hero resists the blandishments of Lady Booby (I: v), a scene duplicating that between Joseph and Potiphar's wife in Christian art; another is the comic redaction of the parable of the Good Samaritan (I: xii), a subject that Hogarth had painted in 1737. In *Tom Jones* (V: xi) Fielding directs the reader to plate 6 of Charles LeBrun's series depicting the victories of Alexander. In mock-heroic style, he "freezes" the action, presenting "the Aspect of the bloody Field" after Tom and Squire Western have beaten Blifil and Thwackum in a punch-up: Thwackum, "like King *Porus*," stands "sullenly submitting to the Conqueror," as the "last Figure in the Piece . . . *Western the Great*" looks on, "most gloriously forbearing the vanquished Foe."[5]

Yet if, in these ways, Fielding saw the possibilities of a reciprocal relationship between the verbal and visual arts, he well understood the limits of the analogy: that one cannot do in prose what the artist can do graphically, and vice versa. In the Preface to *Joseph Andrews* he thus remarks: "Now what *Caricatura* is in Painting, Burlesque is in Writing; and in the same manner the Comic Writer and Painter correlate to each other. And here I shall observe, that as in the former, the Painter seems to have the Advantage; so it is in the latter infinitely on the side of the Writer: for the *Monstrous* is much easier to paint than describe, and the *Ridiculous* to describe than paint" (6). What he has intuited here is the epistemological distinction later articulated by the pioneering theorist of film, George Bluestone, and adopted ever since by his successors: "between the percept of the visual image and the concept of the mental image lies the root difference between the two media," between movie and novel.[6]

In *Tom Jones* Fielding thus despairs of conveying to his reader an adequate idea of the attitude and appearance of the messenger who, on the morning of her betrothal to the odious Blifil, brings Western the news that Sophia has fled: "O, *Hogarth*, had I thy Pencil! then would I draw the Picture of the poor Serving-Man, who, with pale Countenance, staring Eyes, chattering Teeth, faultering Tongue, and trembling Limbs . . . entered the Room, and declared, – *That Madam* Sophia *was not to be found"* (x: viii). Fielding, moreover, preferring not to attempt the impossible task of rendering in prose exact images of his characters, on three occasions refers the reader to Hogarth's graphic works: we may *see* Bridget Allworthy in Hogarth's "Morning" (from his *Four Times of the Day* [1738]) (I: xi); Mrs. Partridge, he informs us, "exactly resembled the young Woman who is pouring out her Mistress's Tea in the third Picture of the Harlot's Progress" (II: iii); and for Thwackum's "Countenance" he refers us to "that Gentleman, who in the Harlot's Progress [Plate 4] is seen correcting the Ladies in *Bridewel"* (III: vi). Introducing Sophia, he struggles in vain to give the reader "an exact Idea" of her, at last directing us to Kneller's portrait of Lady Ranelagh, or still better, to Lely's portrait of the Duchess of Mazarine (IV: ii).

Fielding, however, while recognizing ways in which visual representations of scenes and characters could, on occasion, serve a useful function in his narratives, never supposed that pictures could substitute for the mental pleasures of his prose or that they could adequately express the complexities of the moral and philosophical issues he wished to explore. In our own time three picture-narratives have been made of Fielding's novels: films of *Tom Jones* and *Joseph Andrews*, both directed by Tony Richardson, were released in 1963 and 1976, respectively; and in 1997 appeared the BBC's television production of Fielding's masterpiece. How well, we may ask, do these three works succeed in meeting the challenge of reconciling the two media – one verbal, the other visual – which are in every essential respect disparate? How well do they succeed in adapting Fielding's novels to the screen?

When *Tom Jones* opened at Cinema 1 in New York on October 7, 1963, the reviews it elicited from two of the principal critics of the time could not have been more at odds. Bosley Crowther in the *New York Times* (October 8) was rhapsodic in praising every feature of the film: the cinematography of Walter Lassally, the editing of Anthony Gibbs,[7] the music of John Addison, the acting; and praising most of all John Osborne, who wrote the screenplay, and Tony Richardson, for having together "worked out a structure and a rhythm that constitute a major creative achievement."[8] In *The New Republic* (October 19) Stanley Kauffmann was no less fervid in execrating the film, which he found to be "the product of uncertainty, nervousness, muddled method." In a postscript written some time later he acknowledged that his was a "minority report": "*Tom Jones* [he conceded] is one of the outstanding successes, financially and to a large extent critically, of recent years." He remained, however, unconvinced of its merits: "Fielding seems further away than ever. In my view, to argue that the film tries to reflect qualities in the novel is merely to emphasize how those qualities have been whooped-up and vulgarized, rather than artistically adapted and directed."[9] In critics as well informed as Kauffmann and Crowther, differences of opinion as irreconcilable as these may be discounted as chiefly subjective; they are colored by the personal taste and sensibilities of the reviewer. The filmmaker must equally be allowed his own "reading" of the novel, so long as the work he creates faithfully reflects essential qualities of the original that are recognizably there. What is missing from the film of *Tom Jones* is owing chiefly to the gulf that separates the philosophical assumptions of Fielding's age and our own: missing are Fielding's confidence in the underlying order of things and the moral seriousness of purpose that informs his comedy.

But if Osborne and Richardson missed, or perhaps deliberately ignored, the didactic intent of Fielding's novel, they fully grasped and brilliantly recreated its essential spirit and manner. They succeeded in this by striking attitudes consonant with Fielding's comic vision and his ridicule of the malevolent and hypocritical, and by adopting in their own medium a narrative point of view and rhetorical techniques that are analogous to Fielding's own. The genius of the film as an adaptation of Fielding's masterpiece is its imaginative imitation of the art of the novel. The now famously ostentatious tricks of the camera that Kauffmann scorned, but which delighted audiences, are technically analogous to Fielding's stylistic mannerisms and his own distinctive narrational devices.

Consider, for example, the opening sequence of the film. Before the title and credits we are presented with a rapid succession of scenes done in mimicry of the silent movies, with subtitles supplying both commentary and dialogue (even Mrs. Wilkins's "aaah!" as she sees Allworthy in his nightshirt),[10] and with John Addison's spirited harpsichord setting the mood in the manner of the upright of the "flicker" days. The device serves practical purposes, of course: exposition that required two books in the novel is presented here swiftly and economically, and a playful comic tone is at once established. What is more, the reminiscence of the earliest era of the cinema (when in 1917 Edwin Collins directed the first film of *Tom Jones*) also serves to remind us that Fielding's book appeared at a comparable moment in the history of that other peculiarly modern genre, the novel. Less obviously, in the exaggerated reactions and posturing of the actors, and in the use of subtitles, Richardson and Osborne translate into the medium of cinema two aspects of Fielding's technique that contribute to the comic effect. The overstated acting of the silent-film era is analogous to what may be called the "Hogarthian" manner (we recall that Fielding himself made the comparison) of characterization in the novel. Even after spoken dialogue has been introduced (after the credits) and the need for pantomime is no longer present, Richardson continues to elicit hyperbolic performances from his actors – a style which, as in Hogarth and Fielding, serves not only to amuse, as caricature does, but also to accentuate the essential natures of the characters. Fielding declared in *Joseph Andrews* (III: i) that he described "not Men, but Manners; not an Individual, but a Species." His characters, like Hogarth's, verge on caricature: they do not ask, as Moll Flanders or Clarissa Harlowe ask, to be accepted as real people, but rather as types of human nature; they have the reality of symbol rather than of fact. So, in Richardson's production, the actors rarely behave in the understated, naturalistic manner of the conventional film: smiles become leers, glances become ogles, gestures are heightened into posturings.

Just as the miming of the actors during the opening sequence establishes the hyperbolic style of the performances throughout, so Osborne's initial use of subtitles prepares us for the spoken commentary of the narrator, whose voice is the first we hear in the film and who will accompany us throughout as an invisible guide. Osborne's commentator is a clever adaptation of Fielding's "omniscient" narrator, whose presence is constantly felt in *Tom Jones*, describing the action, remarking on the characters' motives and deeds, entertaining us with his wit and learning, controlling our attitudes and responses. It has been remarked that the most important "character" in Fielding's novel is the author–narrator himself,[11] whose genial and judicious spirit pervades the work, presiding providentially over the world of the novel, reminding us that the creation we behold is his own. He it is who more than any character in the story – more than Tom, more even than Allworthy – provides the moral center of the book. Osborne's commentator functions correspondingly: when we first see Tom, now a full-grown young scamp prowling for nocturnal sport in the woods, the voice-over of the commentator informs us that Tom is "far happier in the woods than in the study," that he is "as bad a hero as may be." Like Fielding's, Osborne's commentator presents his fallible hero while, by his tone of wry amusement and affection for the character, controlling our attitude toward him, establishing that tolerant morality which makes Tom's peccadilloes seem less important than his honesty and zest for life. Though Fielding's narrator has the advantage of being continually present, Osborne's commentator is heard often enough that his own relationship with the audience is sustained, and with each intrusion his own "personality" becomes more sharply defined: in matters of morality he is tolerant of everything but hypocrisy and inhumanity; he knows his Bible and his Ovid; he can recite a verse or apply an adage; and he has a becoming sense of decorum in turning the camera away from a bawdy tumble in the bushes. Though necessarily a faint echo, he is the film's counterpart of Fielding's authorial voice.

A further effect of the intrusion of the narrator in both novel and film is to ensure that the audience remains aloof, detached from the drama. We are never allowed to forget that this is not a slice of life, but only a tale told, or depicted on screen. The narrator is always between us and the images on the screen, preventing that empathic involvement with the characters which generally occurs in movies, or in fiction. Such detachment is part of Fielding's comic purpose: his fictional world is not offered to us as an imitation of life in any "realistic" sense, but rather as a consciously contrived and universalized representation of human nature and society. We are asked to behold it from a distance, at arm's length, as it were, to enjoy it and to learn from it.

The use of type characters and of a self-conscious narrator are, moreover, only two of the means by which Fielding achieves this comic distance. The style of *Tom Jones* is itself highly mannered and often deliberately "rhetorical." To reproduce this feature of Fielding's book, Richardson flaunts every device in the rhetoric of his own medium. Just as Fielding indulges in amplifications, ironies, similes, mock-heroics, and parodies, so the film similarly exploits for comic effect a circusful of "wipes," "freezes," "flips," "speed-ups," "irises" – in short, the entire battery of camera tricks.[12] The effect of this is again to call attention to the skill of the artist, to the intelligence manipulating the pen or the camera, as the case may be. Particularly remarkable in this respect is the most celebrated of Richardson's stunts: his deliberate violation of the rule that actors must never take notice of the camera, because to do so is to dispel the illusion of "life" on the screen. Richardson's actors are constantly winking at us, appealing to us to settle their disputes, thrusting their hats before our eyes. The effect, paradoxically, is not to involve us more intimately in their drama: reminded of the presence of the camera, we are prevented from seriously entering the vicarious world unfolding on the screen. In just this way Fielding's rhetorical somersaults keep us aware that his own fictional world is being supervised and manipulated by a controlling and ultimately benign intelligence resembling the providence his contemporaries believed in.

The brilliance of Osborne and Richardson's adaptation may be seen not only in the general handling of character, narrator, and rhetoric, but also in the treatment of particular scenes from the novel. With regard to Fielding's theory of comedy, the most significant of these is the sequence in which Tom, concerned that he has got Molly Seagrim with child, pays an unexpected visit to her in her garret bedroom only to find he has been sharing her favors with the philosopher Square.[13] When a curtain falls, the prim metaphysician – who has made a career of denouncing the body – is revealed in his hiding place, clad only in a blush and Molly's nightcap.

9. Tom Jones (Albert Finney) and Mrs. Waters (Joyce Redman) in the "eating scene" in Tony Richardson's *Tom Jones*

In both novel and film this scene dramatizes Fielding's satiric theory and practice: "the true Ridiculous," as he defines it in the Preface to *Joseph Andrews*, has its source in the affectations of those whose deeds do not match their professions. As a graphic enactment of this comic theory – the hilarious revelation of the naked truth behind the drapery of pretense – the exposure of Square is the quintessential scene in all Fielding's fiction.

But the most impressive instance of Osborne and Richardson's genius in translating Fielding's manner, attitudes, and intentions into their own medium is the famous "eating scene" at the inn at Upton.[14] Virtually every gesture and every grimace in the film sequence – as well as its basic metaphorical equation of lust and appetite – originated with Fielding in the chapter entitled *An Apology for all Heroes who have good Stomachs, with a Description of a Battle of the amorous Kind.*" The chapter opens with the narrator's reluctant admission (echoed by the voice of the film's commentator) that even the most accomplished of heroes have more of the mortal than the divine about them: even Ulysses must eat. When Jones and Mrs. Waters sit down to satisfy their appetites – he by devouring three pounds of beef to break a fast of twenty-four hours, she by feasting her eyes on her companion's handsome face – the narrator proceeds to define love, according to the modern understanding of the word, as "that Preference which we give to one Kind of Food rather than to another." Jones loves his steak and ale; Mrs. Waters loves Jones. During the course of the meal the temptress brings to bear on her companion "*The whole Artillery of Love*," with an efficacy increasing in direct proportion to Jones's progress in appeasing his hunger. The narrator, invoking the Graces, describes the lady's artful seduction of the hero in the amplified, hyperbolic language of a mock-epic battle:

First, from two lovely blue Eyes, whose bright Orbs flashed Lightning at their Discharge, flew forth two pointed Ogles. But happily for our Heroe, hit only a vast Piece of Beef which he was then conveying into his Plate, and harmless spent their Force.

Mrs. Waters heaves a sigh, but this is lost in "the coarse Bubbling of some bottled Ale." The assault continues as, "having planted her Right Eye side-ways against Mr. *Jones*, she shot from its Corner a most penetrating Glance." Perceiving the effect of this ogle, she coyly lowers her glance and then, having made her meaning clear even to the unassuming Jones, she lifts her eyes again and "discharged a Volley of small Charms at once from her whole Countenance" in an affectionate smile which "our Heroe received full in his Eyes." Jones, already staggering, succumbs when his adversary "unmasked the Royal Battery, by carelessly letting her Handkerchief drop from her Neck."

In the film Joyce Redman and Albert Finney manage to convey, in images only, the sense of Fielding's metaphor of lust and appetite, Redman, especially, by rendering visually the epic sighs, ogles, and leers of Mrs. Waters. The scene is a triumph of the art of cinematic translation. Both the form of the adaptation and the comic effect could have been achieved in this way in no other medium: they are the result of the collaborative exploitation (by writer, director, photographer, commentator, actors, and editor) of peculiarly cinematographic techniques – here, specifically, the voice-over of the commentator introducing a series of "close-ups" arranged and controlled by expert "cutting." Entirely verbal effects in the novel are rendered in the film (except for the commentator's brief introduction) entirely in terms of visual images.

Consideration of the ways in which the film of *Tom Jones* is a successful adaptation of Fielding's novel can go no further than this scene of amorous gastronomics. Ultimately, of course, the film is meant to be judged as a work of art in its own right. The skill of Osborne and Richardson also appears in those elements and techniques only hinted at in the book. Most impressive of these is the use of visual contrasts in setting and situation for symbolic purposes. To establish at once the difference in nature between Jones and Blifil – the one free and wild and open-hearted, the other stiff and artful and cold – the filmmakers introduce the characters in diametrically opposing situations. We first see Jones as he prowls in the woods at night, breaking the game laws and tumbling in the bushes with Molly: Tom is at home with the fox and the beaver; he returns the wink of an owl; and Molly, disheveled, flips a fern as she lures him to another kind of illicit sport. Blifil, in contrast, is first seen in Allworthy's sun-drenched formal garden: he is dressed in formal frock coat and walks sedately, holding a book in fastidious hands and obsequiously following those twin custodians of virtue and religion, the philosopher Square and Thwackum the divine. The contrast between Tom's two sweethearts, the profane and the angelic, is equally deliberate. After we have been shown another night scene of Tom and Molly amidst the bushes, the camera shifts abruptly to a bright, idyllic setting: we see Sophia's image reflected in a pool; swans swim gracefully about, and Sophia is as fair and white as they. When Tom appears, bringing her a caged song bird (nature not wild, but tame and lovely), the lovers run from opposite sides of the water to meet at the center of a bridge. Sophia has been presented as the image of purity and light, the proper emblem of that chastity of spirit which (in Fielding's story at least) Tom must learn to seek and find.

The film is visually organized according to a scheme of such contrasts – Allworthy's formal estate with Western's sprawling, boisterous barnyard; Molly's disordered bedroom with Sophia's chaste boudoir. The color itself is varied in this way to signal the shift from the naturalness and simplicity of the country to the affectation and luxury, and man-made squalor, of London: scenes in the country are done predominantly in greens and browns, and in black, gray, and white; but London is revealed in a shock of violent colors. Tom and Partridge enter town amidst stark and vicious scenes recalling Hogarth's *Rake's Progress* and *Gin Lane*. And soon thereafter the screen is flushed with reds, purples, and oranges as Tom joins the masquerade at the Opera House, where he will meet Lady Bellaston.

Such contrasts are based on similar oppositions, thematic and structural, in the novel. For two of the film's most effective sequences, however, the filmmakers had little help from Fielding, yet the episodes serve to convey attitudes and themes more or less consonant with Fielding's intentions and essential, certainly, to the film Osborne and Richardson were making in the 1960s. The first of these sequences is the stag hunt,[15] for which there is no basis in the novel other than Fielding's characterization of Western as obsessed with hunting (of hares, however, not stags).

In filming the hunt the filmmakers abandoned, for once, their attempt to imitate in their own medium the distancing effects of Fielding's intrusive narrator and his irony; instead they aimed to depict vividly the brutal, predatory quality of eighteenth-century life in the provinces. "The hunt," as Osborne stipulates in the script, "is no pretty Christmas calendar affair but a thumping dangerous vicious business"; to achieve this effect he directs that "the camera will always be in motion to give the greatest feeling of speed and danger." This intent is skillfully executed: caught on screen are the fury of the chase and the sadistic elation of the hunters – the lashing of horses, the spurt of crimson as spur digs into flesh, the tumble of mounts and riders, the barnyard and the broken-necked goose trampled in the pursuit, the surge of the dogs as they tear the stag's throat out, and Western's triumphant display of the bloody prey (as Osborne directs, the actor "thrusts it almost into the lens"). The violence of this episode has no equivalent in Fielding's original; it calls to mind instead the novels of Smollett, whose comedy can be brutally physical. Even so, no one, surely, would wish the sequence out of the film.

In sharp contrast to the violence of this passage is the lyricism of the montage sequence portraying the courtship and deepening love of Tom and Sophia as Tom recovers from a broken arm on Western's estate.[16] Richardson achieves here a sense of Arcadia – an unfallen world of bright flowers and placid waters, of gaiety and innocence. The growing intimacy of the lovers is expressed in a playful montage in which their roles are interchanged: first Sophia poles Tom around the lake while he lolls and smokes a pipe, then their places are reversed; Sophia appears on horseback followed by Tom straddling an ass, then vice versa, then they appear together on the same horse; Sophia shaves Tom, and Tom then wades into mud chest-deep to fetch her a blossom. They sing, skip, and lark about together. When at length they silently declare their love with a deep exchange of glances and a kiss, the tone of the sequence modulates from the frivolous to the tender. In a few frames skillfully juxtaposed, Richardson and his editor convey how it feels to fall in love. From this moment there can be no doubt of the rightness and warmth of Tom and Sophia's affection – no doubt even when, afterwards, Tom succumbs to the temptations of Molly, Mrs. Waters, and Lady Bellaston.

Ultimately, of course, the film is not the novel, nor was it meant to be. The vision of the filmmakers is narrower than Fielding's: a consequence partly of the limitation of scope in the film, partly of commercial pressures precluding moral seriousness in a work meant to entertain millions, and partly of the Zeitgeist of the 1960s. We are not left with a sense of Fielding's balanced and ordered universe, nor are we made aware of the lesson he imparts in recounting the progress of his reckless hero toward self-knowledge. At the end of the novel, the marriage of Tom and the lovely woman whose name signifies Virtue does not, as one critic complains, lack "plausibility";[17] given the moral dimension Fielding's comedy implies, it is symbolically appropriate and necessary. In this respect the difference between Fielding's thematic intentions and those of the film is plain when Finney and Susannah York close their story with a kiss while the voice of the commentator speaks the *carpe diem* moral:

> Happy the man and happy he alone,
> He who can call today his own,
> He who secure within can say:
> Tomorrow do thy worst! For I have lived today.

Despite such thematic discrepancies, Osborne and Richardson's *Tom Jones* remains, in an impressive variety of ways, a model of the creative adaptation of a novel to film.

Thirteen years later Richardson, this time assisted by scriptwriters Allen Scott and Chris Bryant, attempted to repeat the success of *Tom Jones* by adapting another of Fielding's novels for the screen. *Joseph Andrews* (1976), however, is a travesty of the original.[18]

Viewed on its merits as an entertainment, the film is not without appeal. John Addison, who composed a delightful score for *Tom Jones*, provided another for this. The art director, Bill Brodie, conceived a hundred beautifully composed scenes, ranging from the May Day festival with which the film opens, to the traffic jams and gardens and elegant assemblies at Bath, to the rowdy country inn of the Tow-wouses and Parson Adams's country church bedecked with sheaves of grain and the fruits of the field as Fanny and Joseph wed at harvest time. Use is made of the works of artists who were Fielding's contemporaries: as Fielding in the Wilson episode borrowed from *A Rake's Progress*, so Richardson in adapting the episode brings Hogarth's plates to life on the screen; and when the heroine of Samuel Richardson's *Pamela* appears in the film, she is dressed as Joseph Highmore painted her. As a period piece the film is well done. The acting is always adequate and often superb. Much of the dialogue, moreover, is taken word for word from Fielding (Beryl Reid as Slipslop is hilarious with her malapropisms), and many of the scenes and images (the celebrated "Night Adventures" at Booby Hall, for example) are well adapted from the novel. Though a departure from the original, the decision to shift the town scenes from London to Bath, which remains an almost unspoiled eighteenth-century city, was sound.

For all its virtues, however, the film fails as an adaptation of the original. It alters utterly the essential character of Fielding's novel. In the film of *Tom Jones*, as we have seen, Richardson captured the spirit of

Fielding's comedy and he found in Fielding's narrative method inspiration for many of his best technical effects. In *Joseph Andrews* he abandoned this approach. Most offensive of the sequences that travesty the book is the treatment of the scene (III: vii) in which the "roasting" squire and his companions play practical jokes on Parson Adams at the dinner table while the servants ply Joseph and Fanny with drink in the kitchen in order to facilitate the squire's plans to deflower the girl. What in the novel is intended as a comic interlude, despite the threat to Fanny and the rude antics of the squire and his hangers-on, is in the film transmogrified into an episode out of "Monk" Lewis. "The gothic interests me greatly," says the squire, swilling wine out of a skull as he presides like some surrogate Sir Francis Dashwood over the Hell-Fire Club: "Its preoccupation with death I find absorbing." Enter then a file of chanting whores masquerading as nuns, bearing the body of Fanny and serving her up, drugged and naked, in a monstrous parody of the Eucharist, while Parson Adams looks on helplessly, his arms clamped to his chair, his outraged protests muffled by the hideous cast-iron scold's mask he has been forced to wear. After one of the company slurps wine from Fanny's navel, we expect the worst when her host announces: "After the blood, the body." But Joseph hastens to the rescue, having extricated himself from the greasy embraces of a buxom lady of the night in the scullery. From "Monk" Lewis, Richardson next turns to Dumas for inspiration and has Joseph treat us to an exhibition of swordplay worthy of D'Artagnan.

Some time after he decided to make this film Richardson lost his nerve. A comic story about a chaste young man and his innocent passion for a chaste young woman had to be spiced up. And so Joseph in the village festival that opens the film shimmies up a greased phallic pole in order to snatch a leek from the crotch of an earth-goddess effigy at the top; in crass allusion to the eating scene in the film of *Tom Jones*, Lady Booby in bed tilts back her head, opens her mouth, and suggestively swallows a plump asparagus; the rough lovemaking of Mr. Tow-wouse and his warm-hearted chambermaid takes place not in his bed but in the stable, where it is acted out in images such as Gulliver might have witnessed in Brobdingnag. Lady Booby (we are surprised to discover) was once a strolling actress with whom Wilson had an affair, and the bastard offspring of their passion (again put pantingly on display in flashback) proves to be none other than Joseph Andrews himself. But if all this was only good bawdy fun, the later scene, in which Joseph and Fanny consummate their love before they are married only to find they have committed incest (or so it appears), is a measure of how little concerned Richardson was to preserve the spirit of Fielding's comedy.

Not only in his graphic interpolation into Fielding's story of an explicit and perverse sensuality can we gauge the film's departure from the original. Richardson's political allegiance to Marxism results in a further violation of the character of Fielding's work. The ideology that informs such of Richardson's films as *The Loneliness of the Long Distance Runner* (1962) and *The Charge of the Light Brigade* (1968) ill accords with the tenor of Fielding's social satire. Fielding's Samaritans are often drawn from the lower orders of society: the postilion in the stage coach, Betty at the inn, the peddler, an impoverished country curate named Abraham. Fielding celebrates their humanity while he ridicules the selfishness and folly of their "betters." But in *Joseph Andrews* (II: xiii) the passage representing the relations of "high" people and "low" people in terms of a ladder of dependence makes clear that for Fielding there is nothing to choose, finally, between the pride of a lord and a footman.

Only once in the novel does Fielding sound like Dickens in a dark mood; and that is when he tells us – in a parenthesis – that the postilion who gave his only coat to clothe Joseph's nakedness "hath since been transported for robbing a Hen-roost" (I: xii). This interjection appears to have been for Richardson the key to unlock an esoteric political meaning in the novel. At the start, as the credits unroll, we hear a song of the peddler never sung in the book:

> To poverty and hardship this young man he was born,
> His kind and loving parents could scarcely feed their young.
> The times were hard and bitter, there was no work to do,
> Until at length in service this young lad was forced to go.

As if to apologize for having made the uninhibited Squire Western one of the harmless joys of the earlier film, Richardson introduced him into *Joseph Andrews*, this time in his character as a magistrate who metes out instantaneous justice to three lads who have mistakenly accused Adams and Fanny of being thieves: seizing a blunderbuss, Western blows away all three with a single shot. (Lest we miss the moral, the camera pans to the parson, who comforts Fanny and opines: "The justice of this world is very rough, child.") Later before Justice Frolick, Lawyer Scout accuses hero and heroine of stealing a twig: whereas Fielding had lightly held the threat of Bridewell over Joseph and Fanny's heads, Richardson injects a scene drawn from Hogarth's *Harlot's Progress*, taking us into the dreaded House of Correction where we are shown flayed backs and hear the rhythmic drumming of mallet on block as demoralized convicts beat hemp under the watchful gaze of sadistic turnkeys.

If Richardson had demonstrated surer control of his material, the film he produced might perhaps be defended as a "commentary" (to use Geoffrey Wagner's second category of adaptation) on Fielding's novel: the filmmaker has altered the original to suit a thematic purpose of his own.[19] Or it might perhaps, in the intellectually attractive terms proposed

10. Parson Adams (Michael Hordern) looks on as Squire Western (Hugh Griffith) dispenses "rough justice" in Richardson's *Joseph Andrews*

by Dudley Andrew, be justified as a work satisfying "the sociology of adaptation": "Let us use [adaptation]," Andrew advises, "not to fight battles over the essence of the media or the inviolability of individual art works. Let us use it as we use all cultural practices, to understand the world from which it comes and the one toward which it points."[20] For the world Fielding offers us in this, the first comic novel in English, the film of *Joseph Andrews* substitutes another, reconceived in the prurient imaginings and according to the political agenda of its director, our contemporary.

With its different constraints and advantages – chief among them a much smaller screen and a much greater temporal scope – the BBC television production of *Tom Jones*, in five parts, played in England in November 1997[21] and in the United States (on the Arts and Entertainment channel) in three parts in April 1998. Though it lacks the film's insights into the character of Fielding's novel, this production – written by Simon Burke and directed by Metin Hüseyin, and affectionately dedicated to Fielding – is not without compensating virtues. It is three hours longer than the film and, by including many more scenes from the book, conveys a better sense by far of the scope and intricacy of Fielding's plot. The scenes of life in the country and in London have been so carefully researched and represented that the viewer virtually experiences at first hand the whole sprawling panorama of mid-Georgian England. Burke and Hüseyin crowd into the production as much of the novel as possible; more often than not they render Fielding's scenes faithfully, at times using his own words.

In one important respect, this commendable impulse to preserve in images essential elements of Fielding's narrative proves an embarrassment. Recognizing that the life of the novel is the "character" of the omniscient narrator, whose voice is heard from the first sentence to the last addressing the reader like an entertaining companion on a journey, the authors of the production have made him, literally, a character in the film. Fielding himself (played by John Sessions) is physically present on the screen as the intrusive narrator who, unnoticed by the other characters, mixes with them as he speaks to us in words drawn verbatim from the novel. Unlike the subtler cinematographic strategies of the film version, this clumsy device necessarily reduces Fielding's wise and witty periods to mere sound bites. The narrator of *Tom Jones*, the providence who supervises what Fielding called his "great Creation" (x: i), here appears only as a sort of elfin interloper in tricorne, periwig and breeches.

No less discordant in this production is the authors' violation of the controlling modality of the novel: its deliberate and self-conscious artificiality. Fielding's scenes, whether comic or violent or "low," are presented in a style that, as the case may be, heightens our amusement or spares us discomfort. The aim of Burke and Hüseyin, however, was to present Fielding's story with (in the words of Max Beesley, who plays the lead) "a lot more realism than usual."[22] But "realism" in the conventional sense is precisely not Fielding's style. The authors' efforts at achieving this effect too often sink the production into vulgarity: we are shown Bridget Allworthy in the throes of giving birth to Blifil; Molly Seagrim's battle in the churchyard, done in the novel "in the *Homerican* Stile" (IV: viii), becomes on screen a female mud-wrestling match; in a fury after learning that Sophia has escaped marriage to Blifil, Western plunges his face in a pie and flings food about; in a pet at finding Jones with Sophia, Lady Bellaston rakes her fingernails down her footman's cheek. None of this is in the novel.

Nor, despite Fielding's (unfounded) reputation as a writer who revels in bawdy adventures, are the scenes we are shown of explicit sex: Tom with Molly Seagrim in the bushes, with Mrs. Waters at Upton, and, most flagrantly, with Lady Bellaston in London, who offers herself in the nude to Jones in his bath. Such scenes of erotic nudity are wholly inappropriate to the comedy of *Tom Jones*. Fielding's manner of treating his hero's sexual escapades is invariably oblique, provoking laughter rather than lust. He never depicts such matters graphically. Apropos of Jones's affair with Lady Bellaston, the narrator expressly repudiates pornography – here, for once, not at all regretting that he lacked his friend Hogarth's pencil:

> In the Evening *Jones* met his Lady again, and a long Conversation again ensued between them; but as it consisted only of the same ordinary Occurrences as before, we shall avoid mentioning Particulars, which we despair of rendring agreeable to the Reader; unless he is one whose Devotion to the Fair Sex, like that of the Papists to their Saints, wants to be raised by the Help of Pictures. But I am so far from desiring to exhibit such Pictures to the Public, that I would wish to draw a Curtain over those that have been lately set forth in certain *French* Novels. (XIII: ix)

The filmmaker who sets out to catch the essential character of Fielding's fiction on screen is faced with the difficulty that, more than most novelists, Fielding avoided exhibiting pictures. Description was an element of narrative better left to artists such as Hogarth, whose images, like those of the modern cinematographer, carry immediate and powerful emotive force. Yet the "sister arts," as practised by novelist and history-painter, were not quite incompatible. Their implements, words and images, differed; but their common intent was the faithful imitation of human character and action. In adapting *Tom Jones* for the screen, Richardson and Osborne succeeded by focusing on certain defining features of Fielding's novel: they sought to convey its distinctive comic spirit without vulgarizing it, and they saw that the *manner* of Fielding's narration was fundamental to the work. They mirrored these verbal effects in the novel by finding analogous effects in the visual medium of film: the eye of the camera substitutes for Fielding's omniscient narrator; the devices of the cinematographer mimic Fielding's word play; the exaggerated, yet controlled, performances of the actors recall Fielding's principle of revealing the "species," the type, in his characters. The film of *Joseph Andrews* and the television production of *Tom Jones* succeed in visually evoking the age of mid-Georgian England and in setting Fielding's characters in motion in that world. But neither work conveys a sense of the mode and tenor of Fielding's comic art. They serve chiefly as foils to the film of *Tom Jones*, illustrating how not to set about adapting novels to the screen.

NOTES

1 See "Osborne's 'Tom Jones': Adapting a Classic," *Virginia Quarterly Review* 42 (1966), 378–93. I use "analogy" in the normative sense of the word, which the *OED*, following Johnson, defines as "the resemblance of things with regard to some circumstances or effects." In this sense, for example, intrusive

camera tricks that call attention to the medium of the narrative, collapsing the distance between audience and filmmaker, are analogous to the rhetorical high jinks of Fielding's intrusive narrator. The present essay draws upon my article on the film of *Tom Jones* cited above, and upon my articles on the film of *Joseph Andrews* ("Fielding on Film," *Eighteenth-Century Life* 11 [1987], 110–13) and on the television production of *Tom Jones* ("*Tom Jones* on the Telly: Fielding, the BBC, and the Sister Arts," *Eighteenth-Century Fiction* 10 [1998], 501–5).

2 Brian MacFarlane, *Novel to Film: An Introduction to the Theory of Adaptation* (Oxford: Clarendon Press, 1996), p. 21.

3 References to *Joseph Andrews* are to the Wesleyan edition, ed. M. C. Battestin (Oxford: Clarendon Press, 1966; Middletown, CT: Wesleyan University Press, 1967).

4 Ronald Paulson, for example, "reads" these pictures in *Hogarth's Graphic Works*, rev. edn. (New Haven: Yale University Press, 1989).

5 Reproductions of LeBrun's picture, as well as others by Hogarth, Kneller, and Lely, to which Fielding refers in *Tom Jones* and which are cited later in the present essay, are gathered at the end of vol. II of the hardback Wesleyan edition, ed. M. C. Battestin and Fredson Bowers (Oxford: Clarendon Press, 1974; Middletown, CT: Wesleyan University Press, 1975). References to *Tom Jones* are otherwise to the revised paperback edition (Middletown, CT: Wesleyan University Press, 1975).

6 George Bluestone, *Novels into Film* (1957; reprinted Berkeley and Los Angeles: University of California Press, 1971), p. 1.

7 Pauline Kael, later principal critic for *The New Yorker*, refers to *Tom Jones* only incidentally in reviewing other films. What she chiefly admired about it was Gibbs's "innovative editing." (See "Trash, Art, and the Movies," in *Going Steady* [Boston and Toronto: Little, Brown, 1970], p. 120.) In *The New Yorker* (December 29, 1975), she used Richardson's film to express her contempt for Stanley Kubrick's *Barry Lyndon* ("Kubrick's Gilded Age," in *When the Lights Go Down* [New York: Holt, Rinehart and Winston, 1980], p. 103).

8 See Peter M. Nichols, ed., *The New York Times Guide to the Best 1,000 Movies Ever Made* (New York and Toronto: Random House, 1999), pp. 888–9.

9 "*Tom Jones*," in Kauffmann's *A World on Film: Criticism and Comment* (Harper and Row, 1966; reprinted Westport, CT: Greenwood Press, 1975), pp. 124–6.

10 References to the text of the film are to John Osborne, *Tom Jones: A Film Script* (London: Faber and Faber, 1964).

11 Wayne Booth, *The Rhetoric of Fiction* (Chicago: University of Chicago Press, 1961), p. 217.

12 For a detail of these cinematographic stunts in the film, see Annette Insdorf and Sharon Goodman, "A Whisper and a Wink," in *The English Novel and the Movies*, ed. Michael Klein and Gillian Parker (New York: Frederick Ungar, 1981), pp. 36–43.

13 See the novel, V: v; film script, Segment 150.

14 See the novel, IX: v; film script, Segments 280–4.

15 Film script, Segments 114–20.

16 Film script, Segments 138–42.

17 Laurence Behrens, "The Argument of *Tom Jones*," *Literature/Film Quarterly* 8 (1980), 22–34.

18 For a more favorable opinion, see Lawrence F. Laban, "Visualizing Fielding's Point of View," in *English Novel and the Movies*, ed. Klein and Parker, pp. 28–35.

19 *The Novel and the Cinema* (Rutherford, NJ: Fairleigh Dickinson University Press, 1975), p. 223.

20 J. Dudley Andrew, *Some Concepts in Film Theory* (Oxford: Oxford University Press, 1984), p. 106.

21 Reviewed by John Mullan, "Admirable Accidents," *The Times Literary Supplement*, December 5, 1997.

22 See Beesley's interview with Harriet Winslow, *Washington Post* ("TV Week," April 5–11, 1998).

Cynthia Wall

It seems to be a Johnsonian truth universally acknowledged that a reader in search of the "story" in Clarissa would hang herself. For all its million words, Richardson's novel (1747–8) covers an extraordinarily brief length of time (eleven months), with an even smaller parcel of actual *events* – "just enough plot," as one reviewer of the BBC adaptation put it, "to fill out a very acceptable short story."[1] Clarissa's confinement and flight, rape, and death; Lovelace's stratagems, duels, and death; a few mistimed repentances and more deaths – all are embedded in densely detailed correspondences that swell thought through slow time. Along with the vexed question of "fidelity," the usual problem with film adaptations is how to sift, compress, and interpret the plot and texture of the text, and in that sense *Clarissa* would seem ideal: nearly all the "action" can easily be accommodated, while epistolarity might be satisfied with a few shots of characters cutting quills, scratching lines, and rifling drawers. In other words, one typical problem with film adaptations is *time* – how compression affects interpretation. But *Clarissa* suggests another matter of interest to film, particularly in regard to eighteenth-century fiction: *space*. In the text, while time becomes strikingly attenuated and non-linear – almost immobile – space seems rather to disappear as well. The luxuriant details offered by the novel are not those of physical description – of parlor, house, grove, garden, brothel, or city – but of mind and heart, speculation and interpretation, moral principle and plotting stratagem. As with most late seventeenth- and early eighteenth-century narratives, space seems oddly, conspicuously *implied*; we have virtually no sense of color, line, shape, dimension, or decoration, but rather, an awareness of direction, relation, change, stasis – the boundaries of space, so to speak, without its details; the implication of image without image. Yet spatial matters do control a large part of the text, and for early readers those tagged spaces would have been more immediately explicit; and so one thing that a modern adaptation can do is to fill in its underdescribed spaces, to render them as visually full for the modern as for the contemporary reader. In other words, the usual possibilities of visual detail in film can be shaped to offer not just gorgeous costumes but also *interpretable* cultural imagery. And that, I will argue, is what the BBC *Clarissa* does exceptionally well. In its particular visual rendering of Richardsonian nuance, the depth of the text is replaced – or represented – by the depth of the image. Without remaining strictly faithful to some key issues of plot and character, un-derstandably irritating to Richardson critics, the adaptation manages to supply what the text always implies and only rarely describes: the physi-cal boundaries and loaded visual detail of Clarissa's fatal, claustrophobic, emblematic life.

A number of the reviewers of the BBC adaptation dwell with distinctly ambivalent admiration on the £2 million spent to produce a "classic cos-tume drama,"[2] noting the fusions of Hogarth, Gainsborough, Fragonard, and Highmore in the fifteen hundred costumes and elaborate sets. Lois Chaber frowns on what she sees as "the priority given to visual authentic-ity over textual," finding such priority "particularly ironic in the context of Richardson's novel; Lovelace's ability to exploit, and Clarissa's suscep-tibility to, visual and external detail (the pious library at Mrs Sinclair's, the impressive jewels of 'Lady Betty') help to bring about the downfall of the heroine. One is inclined to agree with Lovelace's cynical assertion that 'the whole world is governed by appearances.'"[3] She concedes that David Nokes's and Janet Barron's "concern for dramatization explains and, in varying degrees, justifies many of the liberties taken with the text," then concentrates mostly on the deviations from and misinterpretations of the novel's plot: Lovelace devouring a "much-glamorized" Arabella's neck; an inconsistent characterization of the heroine as too much attracted to Lovelace; the sadistically detailed visualization of the rape (Chaber, "Fatal Attraction," 259). This analysis is excellent along precisely such lines of plot, characterization, and cultural probability; what I want to argue here, however, is that when viewed from a primarily *spatial* perspective, the film on the one hand actualizes a different and very impressive kind of fidelity to the eighteenth-century perception of the text *as dramatic*, and on the other supplies for the twenty-first-century reader the sort of visual particularities that for Richardson's contemporaries would have been a cultural given – the architectural details, the interior structures, and their spatial/psychological implications.

The textual spaces of *Clarissa*

Richardson's *Clarissa* is a world of implied spaces, to a modern eye visually barren. We get few descriptions of rooms, but rather indices of *location*; the architectural details of windows, stairways, and doors emerge not so much in terms of setting but as sudden frames *for* action and narrative implication. Yet these visually vague spaces become quite specific axes of plot structure, sites of contestation and confrontation. As John Bullen argues, "The movement of the action from one location to another tends to formulate plot and geography into parallel patterns, made up, in both cases, of fixed points connected by imaginary lines."[4] I see at least three spatial axes that mark forms of psychological event: centers, as sites of power; margins, as sites of contestation; and "off-limits," or spaces beyond the known or apprehended, as sites of deduction and interpretation.

The novel in some ways begins and ends in Clarissa's parlor, which she describes as having "two doors . . . a wainscot partition only parting [it from the next parlor]. I remember them both in one: but they were separated in favour of us girls, for each to receive her visitors in, at her pleasure."[5] The "possession" of a parlor by daughters is a great mark of family honor, but it is in fact Clarissa's public ownership of space (both legal and social) – her parlor, her ivy summerhouse, her dairy house – that violates her brother James's patriarchal assumptions and so generates the family effort to dispossess and displace her. After all her submission, rebellion, and sacrifice, it is precisely this central occupation of internal domestic space – *her* parlor in her "father's" house – that Clarissa reclaims symbolically at the end, as her cousin Colonel Morden recounts:

> But when the corpse was carried into the lesser parlour, adjoining to the hall, which she used to call *her* parlour, and put on a table in the middle of the room, and the Father and Mother, the two Uncles, her Aunt Hervey, and her Sister came in (joining her Brother and me . . .) the scene was still more affecting. Their sorrow was heightened, no doubt, by the remembrance of their unforgiving severity: And now seeing before them the receptacle that contained the glory of their family, who so lately was driven thence by their indiscreet violence (never, never more to be restored to them!) no wonder that their grief was more than common grief. (VII:275 [1398])

Within her last and simultaneously most and least confining of enclosures, her coffin, Clarissa returns with terrible finality to mark by this occupation the emptiness at the center of her family.

But in addition to the spatial centers of the rooms of power (drawing rooms, parlors, dining rooms), many key events of the novel also "happen" in doorways or on staircases, as liminal sites for many kinds of passage or obstruction. "My brother took upon himself to fill up the doorway once when [Lovelace] came, as if to oppose his entrance," Clarissa observes (I:24 [51]). When her mother implores her to "go in again to Mr. Solmes, and behave discreetly to him; and let your papa find you together, upon *civil* terms at least," Clarissa writes: "My feet moved (of themselves, I think) farther from the parlour where [Solmes] was, and towards the stairs; and there I stopp'd and paused" (I:145 [115]). Until the

actual rape, much of the dramatic conflict between Lovelace and Clarissa
is centered on the control of "her" dining room, but the determination
of control depends on the manipulation of doorspace – on the power not
only to occupy but to *change the meaning of* spatial contours, as Lovelace
describes:

[S]he flew to the door. I threw myself in her way, shut it, and, in the humblest
manner, besought her to forgive me . . . but pushing me rudely from the door, as if
I had been nothing[,] . . . she gaining that force through passion, which I had lost
through fear; and out she shot to her own apartment [Thank my stars she could
fly no further!]; and as soon as she enter'd it, in a passion still, she double-locked
and double-bolted herself in. (IV:13[573])

Clarissa-at-the-door is as potent as Clarissa-in-the-room; she moves
through doorways as she moves through experiences of rejection, self-
protection, self-immurement. In the powerful post-rape penknife scene,
Lovelace describes Clarissa confronting her persecutors (himself and the
"ladies" of the house) in the dining room, asserting her position of unde-
filed honor first in the center of the room and then again in its doorway,
defining all the boundaries, commanding what will be closed, demon-
strating what remains open:

Now, Belford, see us all sitting in judgement, resolved to punish the fair
briberess . . . And hear her *unbolt, unlock, unbar*, the door . . . then *hear* her step
towards us, and instantly *see* her enter among us, confiding in her own innocence;
and with a majesty in her person and manner, that is *natural* to her; but which
then shone out in all its glory! . . . looking down my guilt into confusion . . . She
withdrew to the door, and set her back against it, holding the pointed knife to
her heaving bosom . . . [F]rom the moment she entered the dining-room with so
much intrepidity, it was absolutely impossible to think of prosecuting my villainous designs against her. (V:339–45 [948–52])

As Heidegger notes, "A boundary is not that at which something stops
but, as the Greeks recognized, the boundary is that from which something
begins its essential unfolding."[6] Clarissa's internal power increases paradoxically ("essentially unfolds") as she is pushed to the edges of filial, social,
and sexual vulnerability, and moves herself firmly into other rooms.

   But there is at least one more withdrawing of planes of space in this
text that equally illustrates moral, psychological, and structural position-
ings. Although key actions take place in the centers or on the boundaries
between rooms, a large portion of Clarissa's time is spent *deducing* the
patterns of space beyond her own field of vision – because she is vol-
untarily or involuntarily locked up someplace or another. "You are not
to be seen in any apartment of the house, you so lately govern'd as you
pleased, unless you are commanded down. In short, are strictly to confine

yourself to your chamber," orders her brother (1:154 [121]). Just before this edict, she had listened to and tried to interpret the new silences of space: "My father is come home, and my brother with him. Late as it is, they are all shut up together. Not a door opens; not a soul stirs. Hannah, as she moves up and down, is shunn'd as a person infected" (1:146 [115]). Clarissa frequently notes, as consequence and cause of various familial machinations, that "All is in a hurry below stairs." Both at Harlowe Place and in London Clarissa's perspective is that of imprisoned and therefore imperfect apprehension of spaces beyond her immediate boundaries, and thus she needs to interpret motives, events, and possibilities by deciphering the *sounds* that human beings make within architectural spaces.

In a sense *all* the characters operate within those blind parameters; the family below is speculating on Clarissa above; Lovelace, lurking at the garden gate of Harlowe Place to sweep Clarissa away, tells Belford: "The moment I heard the door unbolt, I was sure of her" (III:52 [399]). Later, when she has fled to Hampstead, he tries to recapture her by re-possessing her spaces: "I have been traversing her room, meditating, or taking up every-thing she but touched or used . . . From her room to my own; in the dining-room, and in and out of every place where I have seen the beloved of my heart, do I hurry; in none can I tarry; her lovely image in every-one" (IV:323 [740]). Like Clarissa reconstructing the actions and decisions of her family by listening for their steps or the sounds of their doors, Lovelace tries to *evoke* Clarissa from her rooms. In different ways every character in *Clarissa* moves within a space that *seems* clearly de-fined and understood – the father and brother issuing orders from Below Stairs, the lover plotting in the Next Room, the best friend reading help-lessly At Home, the aunt and mother shrinking into the Window – but the spaces are all oriented towards the location of Clarissa, their bound-aries converge on hers, and those boundaries are frequently implacable, misunderstood, unarticulated, unknown, or unavailable.

For the twenty-first-century reader, however, those spaces and bound-aries can seem underdescribed. We know where the characters are in space, and we know what that *means* in the context of the novel, but we do not necessarily know what that means *for us*. Those spaces are *implied* – yet for earlier readers, implied space was not necessarily *unvisualized* space. Description – and the absence of description – both rely to some extent upon the reader's quota of shared cultural referents. Philippa Tristram explains the lack of visual detail in eighteenth-century texts as a conse-quence of the "Rule of Taste" whereby, "just as a gentleman was de-fined by his likeness to other gentlemen, so a house should resemble other houses of a similar standing; it would therefore be redundant to describe what every courteous author must assume was already known

to his readers."[7] As Michel Beaujour argues of early generic poetic imagery, "the spheres of poetic culture and iconography" are united in a
reverse ekphrasis – an *ut poësis pictura* in which "the reader's store of cultural images come[s] from poems which all educated men have learned
by heart."[8] We tease out the implications of undescribed spaces that for
Richardson's early readers would have visually and culturally filled themselves. We *see* differently; as Virginia Woolf said of John Evelyn (and by
extension the early modern world): "*The visible world was always close to
him*. The visible world has receded so far from us that to hear all this talk
of buildings and gardens, statues and carvings, as if the look of things
assailed one out of doors as well as in . . . seems strange."[9] One basic justification for a "classic costume drama" is that it makes available to us a
world that, now lost, was once a given.

Clarissa as dramatic narrative

In their film adaptation of *Clarissa*, David Nokes and Janet Barron relied
on Mark Kinkead-Weekes's concept of "Samuel Richardson: Dramatic
Novelist" in an effort to make the production "pacey" (Chaber, "Fatal
Attraction," 259).[10] But the very idea of "paciness," Chaber argues, "con-
travenes the very essence of Richardsonian narration . . . eliminating thereby the subtle incremental repetition and gradual shifting of grounds so
crucial to Richardson's concept of human relations" (Chaber, "Fatal Attraction," 258). Chaber acknowledges that much of the cutting and prun-
ing was a necessary "fact of life for a television 'costume drama,'" but the
implication remains that the very demands of a television serial betray the
fundamental Richardsonian heart – the effect of the *method* – of *Clarissa*.
Before analyzing the spaces of *Clarissa* in film, I would like to offer four
contexts – two historical and two theoretical – for better appreciating the
adaptation's "concern for dramatization" and its privileging of the visual
over the textual. First, Richardson's earliest readers and critics describe
their experience of the novel in dramatically visual terms, authorizing the
stage, so to speak, for dramatic renderings; second, one such eighteenth-
century rendering puts Nokes and Barron to shame in its free-for-all of
cutting, splicing, inventing, and titillating, suggesting that the urge to
make a dramatic adaptation "pacey" is not simply an aesthetic embarrassment of the twentieth century; third, film theory itself has persuasively
countered the literary critic's passion for textual fidelity; and finally, I will
argue that the spatial representation in this production is particularly and
effectively Richardsonian in its structural emphases.

Long before Kinkead-Weekes, critics of Richardson emphasized the
dramatically visual qualities of his work. Richardson himself, in the

postscript to *Clarissa*, described the novel as a "History (or rather Dramatic Narrative)."[11] William Warburton's 1748 preface to the novel argues that Richardson's structural choice of epistolarity "afforded him the only natural opportunity that could be had, of representing with any grace those lively and delicate impressions which *Things present* are known to make upon the minds of those affected by them" (III:v). Sarah Fielding, in *Remarks on Clarissa* (1749), declares that one could point out "several Places in *Clarissa*, where we may see the very Look of the Eyes, and Turn of the Countenance of the Persons mentioned, and hear the Tone of the Voice of the Person speaking."[12] And Henry Fielding's response to the submerged rape scene and its surrounding narrative territory suggests an almost cinematic perception:

[W]hen I see her enter with a letter in her Hand, and after some natural Effects of Despair, clasping her Arms about the Knees of the Villain, call him dear Lovelace, desires, and yet unable to implore his Protection, or rather his Mercy, then melt into Compassion, and find what is called an effeminate Relief for my Terror. So I continue to the End of the Scene.
When I read the next Letter I am Thunderstruck; nor can many lines explain what I feel from Two.
What shall I say of holding up the License?[13]

Fade out, sharp cut, close-up? As Susan Stewart argues, "The printed text is cinematic before the invention of cinema. The adjustable speed of narration, the manipulability of the visual, turns the reader into a spectator enveloped by, yet clearly separated from, the time and space of the text."[14]

Thus Richardson's novel has seemed from the first to be visually compelling, dramatically *present* – early readers could *see* in ways that did not depend, as for post-Victorian readers, on detailed visual descriptions of faces and settings. That early critical emphasis on "seeing" is particularly suggestive in light of film adaptation theory. In 1897 Joseph Conrad claimed that his work as a writer "is by the power of the written word, to make you hear, to make you feel – it is before all, to make you see"; film theorists frequently pair this claim with D. W. Griffith's 1913 dictum: "The task I'm trying to achieve above all is to make you see."[15] Herbert Read's explanation recalls the Addisonian primacy of the visual imagination: the art of writing, he argues, is "to convey images by means of words" and that to convey images and "to make the mind see" is the definition of the ideal film – that we most fully and effectively inhabit the worlds of literature and film through *visual* imagination.[16] Richardson's novel made his early readers "see"; the BBC adaptation offers a more literal but equally interpretable field of vision.

Thus one historical defense of film adaptations of novels is that their rendering of visual detail supplies the modern viewer with some sort of experiential equivalence, an additional perspective in "seeing" the everydayness that would presumably have inflected eighteenth-century readings. The other historical context I want to offer is more on the side of bad precedents – not a defense of this (or any) adaptation, exactly, but a reminder that the desire to tamper with texts is hardly a recent or technologically based phenomenon.

Unlike the Fieldings, some of Richardson's early readers (as with later ones) felt the novel to be a trifle, well, *long*, and in need of some narrative "paciness." A particularly smug gentleman in Sarah Fielding's *Remarks on Clarissa* trots out a complete plot summary in a few paragraphs (to which Miss Gibson retorts: "that by his Rule of Writing, [an almanac] was the best History of *England*, and Almanack-makers were the best Historians").[17] In 1788, one Robert Porrett offered for the reading public his own stage adaptation, in which even the subtitle underscores the (melo)dramatic emphasis: *Clarissa: or, The Fatal Seduction. A Tragedy in Prose. Founded on Richardson's celebrated Novel of Clarissa Harlow.*[18] Porrett "sees" *Clarissa* in terms of the cheapest sensationalism, titillation, and vulgarity to which any bad Hollywood production could stoop. As Robert Giddings notes about film adapters, "there is a temptation . . . to follow the inclination towards the spectacular, to concentrate on what will look good in film. Consequently the memorable moments in moving films of the classics are not, as it were, the literary or poetic ones."[19] Unlike his contemporary literary critics, Porrett seems to have found *Clarissa* insufficiently dramatic for his representational medium; he therefore opens Act III "in a Cavern, with Banditti discovered at a table over their Wine" (51). In case the extra visual effects seem inadequate, the script underlines the drama. A scene in Act IV (in a thick, shady forest) has Colonel Morden watching the banditti's cave, reflecting: "The gloom that hangs o'er this retreat, suits well with the horror and distraction of my mind; and though revenge urges me on, I feel a strong propensity to pause here, and give vent to my feelings" (97). When Morden sees Young Harlowe and Arabella dragged thither, he asides: "Great God! What do I behold? my cousins! my hair stands stiff with horror" (98). Basically everyone dies gruesomely in this tragedy: Young Harlowe and Arabella are "justly" butchered by banditti; Lady Charlotte Harlowe collapses and dies when she sees their bodies brought back; James Harlowe Sr. collapses (presumably to die) when he sees his wife collapse; Anthony Harlowe collapses imminently upon hearing all this. All die promptly except for Clarissa herself, who, as the stage directions note in Act V: "[*seems in the agonies of death but recovers*]"; moments later: "[*seems again in the agonies of death, and again recovers – Morden all the time beholding her with unspeakable anguish*]"; then gasps, "'Oh!' [*This last interjection lengthened out, and with a sigh she expires*]" (131–2). And she's not dead yet. In the next scene her spirit appears to Lovelace in a roll of thunder, shouts at him, and disappears. This is a Clarissa who sighs profoundly (just in case we lost track of the Richardsonian moral import), "Alas! how difficult it is on such trying occasions to preserve that gentleness of temper which is so peculiarly becoming and graceful in our sex" (36).

Porrett's adaptation is a richly horrible example of the "inclination towards the spectacular" possibilities of literary texts. I include it here partly, I confess, because I think its sheer awfulness deserves a wider audience among *Clarissa* readers, but mostly to offer an historical illustration of the ways that Richardson's own contemporaries were prepared to "see" his texts under various dramatic lights. *Clarissa* seemed *already dramatic* in its visual as well as emotional immediacy. Because drama transforms narrative and psychological immediacy into physical and spatial representation, its very emphasis on plot, action, and dialogue – its "inclination towards the spectacular" – can bring a world of print alive for estranged eyes. Critics have accused the BBC production of exploiting the spectacular; my historical examples are meant to suggest readers have been doing this all along. I would argue that Porrett's adaptation is bad (very, very bad) because among other things it distorts beyond recognition, beyond sense, beyond meaning, and certainly beyond grace the theatrical possibilities of the novel; the BBC production, on the other hand, if not strictly "faithful" to the text, draws on the possibilities of the medium of film to reproduce something recognizably Richardsonian.

Given that outright aesthetic judgment, I would like briefly to address the issues of "fidelity" in screen adaptations of novels. Brian McFarlane argues that "the adducing of fidelity to the original novel as a major criterion" is pervasive in newspaper reviews and longer critical essays, and adds: "No critical line is in greater need of re-examination – and devaluation."[20] Fidelity criticism depends on the assumption that the text has a particular, *correct* reading (usually the critic's own visualization) that the filmmaker either grasps or betrays. But this assumption obscures the idea of adaptation as a convergence among arts and transforms reviews into accounts of what might be transferred as opposed to adapted.[21] As Jonathan Miller puts it:

The fact that someone is in a novel . . . does not mean that they are in the novel in the same way that someone else might be in Birmingham or in a cubicle. They cannot be taken out of the novel and put in a film of it . . . [They] are made out of the same materials as the novels in which they occur, and they cannot be liberated in order to make a personal appearance in another medium.[22]

Whereas, McFarlane notes, "the relentless linearity associated with the visual reading of a novel favours the gradual accretion of information about action, characters, atmosphere, ideas, and the mode of presentation,"[23] film transforms a linear wealth of narrative detail into a spatial sweep of visual detail. Marshall McLuhan points out that "in an instant [film] presents a scene of landscape with figures that would require several pages of prose to describe. In the next instant it repeats, and can go on repeating, this detailed information. The writer on the other hand has no means of holding a mass of detail before his reader in so large a bloc or *gestalt*."[24]

The point is to see where the limits of one medium permit the possibilities of another. Giddings suggests that the clash of limits for many critics lies in the fact that the image, unlike more ambiguous language, is "specifically representation[al]: not a room, but a specific room; not a bird, but a swallow."[25] I would like to approach the BBC *Clarissa* in the sense of Geoffrey Wagner's term for one kind of adaptation as "commentary" (a reemphasis or restructuring) or J. Dudley Andrew's "transforming" (reproducing something essential).[26] The BBC *Clarissa* reemphasizes and visually transforms the essential claustrophobia, the revealing angles, the implicative structures of Richardsonian spaces through the possibilities of light, close-up, framing, and cuts – through the historically reproductive "seeing" of the camera.

The filmic spaces of *Clarissa*

The BBC adaptation of *Clarissa* certainly emphasizes and frequently exaggerates the spectacular moments of the texts, as many critics have complained (the graphic rape scene, the suggestion of incest between James and Arabella, Lovelace's duel with Belford), but it also works with small gestures, subtle signs, and historically accurate sensibilities. Like the first two letters of Richardson's *Pamela* (1741), the first six minutes of the film can be "read" for all that follows. I will look at some of the more striking examples of filmic interplay between structures, angles, interiors, and shadows to suggest that this particular transformation of Richardson's text, unlike Porrett's absurd dramatization, exploits the specular (as well as the spectacular) to *recreate* something essential: the adaptation visually opens up the endless narrative sense of shutting down.

The film opens with a view of Harlowe Place, a shot that will be repeated over and over to introduce Harlovian scenes and underscore the Harlovian *gestalt*. The house is relentlessly Georgian, always seen from a slow swinging shot from the viewer's right, under some perpetually dark, hanging, framing tree. The repeated shots of the house of course efficiently introduce the Harlowe interior-to-come, but they also reinforce the set, symmetrical, utterly fixed and implacable sense of the family themselves. The view of the house does not change; the house does not change; the House of Harlowe does not change; and for Clarissa, more hopefully, her Father's House does not change.

The film consistently focuses on small things, on *parts*, suggesting fragmentariness, dismemberment, and epistemological as well as psychological isolation. The first shot of Clarissa moves from from house-shot into chamber-shot with an immediate close-up of her set face – she is *like* her house, *part of* her family, yet emphatically separated, isolated in her stillness, almost psychologically inviolate, as the servants dress her for the reading of her grandfather's will. She stares stonily into a mirror that reminds us of the multiple perspectives of the epistolary interchanges. Chaber sees the many mirror scenes as emphasizing superficiality and a false sense of Clarissa's personal vanity, but my own first viewing suggested the bleakness of sorrow or self-realization along with the sense of plural and contradictory points of view. Silence surrounds Clarissa; the opening shots offer no word from this novel-of-words until the reading of the grandfather's will. Then we see her hand sliding down the rail, visually dismembered – a lovely example of what Noël Burch calls the two different kinds of filmic space: "that included within the frame and that outside the frame."[27] The hand leads to its body: a shot from below of Clarissa coming resolutely down the stairs, alone on the wide bends of dark wood, to discover her fate.

The camera then moves into the parlor to introduce us to the family, assembled in a Highmore grouping, with telling close-ups of strikingly well-cast Highmorean faces. Each close-up reveals the facial display of *character* as the will is read: Anthony complacent, James suspicious, Arabella furious, Clarissa stunned, Charlotte concerned. Although, as George Bluestone points out, since film has "only arrangements of space to work with [and therefore] cannot render thought," the compensatory advantage, as Edward Branigan argues, is that "a narrative construction underlies every shot in a point of view structure."[28] That is, narrative detail is *interpretively* compressed into a visual moment: we see from Arabella's curl of the lip that she is jealous and spiteful before the dialogue from the text confirms it. The small, isolated, visual parts add up with an almost narrative effect.

The film also employs light and angle to construct its implicit narratives. The portrait of the family during the reading of the will is slashed by cuts showing the entrance of Lovelace into Harlowe Place. The camera watches him from above as he enters the front door, his back to the light from the door; as he stands alone on the black-and-white floor (we're given lots of ironic black-and-white in this film, as well as light-and-dark),

11. Clarissa (Saskia Wickham) escaping from Mrs. Sinclair's: the spatial implications of windows and stairs

his brilliant clothes contrast sharply with the black mourning of the Harlowes. Framed by the arch, shot from above, he is both splendid and minimalized – golden and dark, the fallen angel. More close-ups of the family punctuate the portrait of Lovelace, generating a temporal and spatial tension that prefigures plot. The various obsessions of the various Harlowes are deftly etched – and interrupted (thwarted?) by the economical repetition and comprehensiveness of the scene.

Like the novel, the film concentrates on interiors, and particularly on the *boundaries* of interiors. Staircases appear over and over again in the film as in the text: James Harlowe thrusting the black book of Lovelace's misdeeds at Clarissa's neck while forcibly grasping her hand; Lovelace looming over a writing Clarissa at St. Albans; the stairs of Mrs. Sinclair's looming over Clarissa as she attempts to escape; Lovelace on the stairs as Mrs. Sinclair and her ladies tell him Clarissa has escaped; Lovelace confronted by Belford's sword on the stairs of Clarissa's last refuge. Similarly, windows are (as in the text) relatively rare but structurally significant. Very early on we see from a darkly framed upper-storey window Lovelace and Arabella frisking about in the garden. The contained perspective suggests the limitations and restrictions that structure these social and personal worlds, but the windows in general, like the mirrors, also manage to convey both the plurality of perspectives and the limitations of vision. This

12. Lovelace (Sean Bean) looming over Clarissa (Saskia Wickham) in the lodgings at St. Albans

garden scene is one of the few staged outside; yet even as the camera angle moves from inside to outside, as Clarissa wanders out to interrupt their tête-à-tête, the scene manages to remain closed, contained, made up more of close shots and facial studies than of any real glimpses of a natural world. In Lovelace's outdoor scenes, particularly when he's instructing Belford on the rules of the rake, the camera remains stationary, focused locally, and unlike the wide-open hunting scenes of Tony Richardson's 1963 *Tom Jones*, never gives us anything panoramic beyond the fall of a shot bird – as if following Coleridge's pronouncement that, compared to Fielding, reading Richardson was like being in a sick room heated by stoves.[29] As in the novel, the interiors and their boundary-spaces supply scenes of transition, discovery, and the struggle for power; the film uses angles – shots from above or below, from Clarissa's or from Lovelace's point of view – in much the way the narrative marks the psychological angles of power or vulnerability. Power and point of view are visually expressed by points in space.

One of the most telling series of interior scenes articulates all sorts of dark boundaries as the camera drags the viewer steadily into the center of Solmes, the man the Harlowes insist that Clarissa marry. As Solmes arrives in his carriage and is brought into "Clarissa's" parlor, the camera itself seems reluctant, evasive, distant – avoiding his face. It is not until he has been cushioned next to Clarissa herself that the close-up confirms our growing dread: he is indeed a mincing, painted, terrible thing with abominable teeth. Then the adaptation adds a scene not in the novel itself: Solmes in his own home, in a close, dark room, hunched over a wooden cradle (invoking that other dark resting-place to come, Clarissa's coffin), rocking and snuffling and lisping some nasty fantasy. Part of the film's visual advantage lies in the way that (to paraphrase Branigan) it *reveals* the underlying narrative, *showing* us just what revolted Clarissa about the possibility of life with Solmes – the moral/sexual horror that utterly justifies her fear of committing to a man who has no interest in or respect for her own desires. Although this vivid rendering of Solmes may move us away from the rich ambiguity of the text (several characters suggest that Solmes isn't *quite* as morally or physically repugnant as Clarissa pretends), it illustrates the kinds of marital threats that have so completely disappeared from our cultural vision. Showing Solmes in the interior of his little nursery opens up both his own darkness and that of eighteenth-century marriage.

The film plays with darkness as intelligently as it explores spatial boundaries. The end of the first of the three parts shows us Harlowe Place in darkness for the first time – it is now empty of Clarissa. The next part begins with an outside shot of the lodging in St. Albans, also in darkness – the lodging contains Clarissa, trapped with a Lovelace who abandons his textual faux-respect and gloats visibly, astride the bedpost of the communicating room. Clarissa abruptly closes the communicating door, tries to drag a dresser in front of it, and sits, as he laughs on the other side. The dangerous threshold is emphasized; the barriers are obviously temporary, ineffectual, and soon to be violated.

The treatment of the rape in the film, to which so many critics object,[30] has some spatial and cultural justification for a 1990s audience beyond sadistic voyeurism. The *textual* power of the scene lies in its complete narrative omission. Henry Fielding recorded its power for the reader (quoted above); more recently, Dorothy Van Ghent wonderfully (albeit peculiarly) characterizes its cumulative novelistic rendering:

This slow and hovering form endows the physiological event – the rape – with profound attraction and significance by holding it up slantwise to view in a murk of shadows, turning it mysteriously, allowing it to emerge slightly, withdrawing it, allowing it to emerge again, and so on. It is as tantalizing and evasive as a trout. Only at long length are we permitted to get it into clear focus, while, in the meantime, we have been steadily bombarded, page after page, with an imagery deriving from various submerged but exceedingly powerful impulses and attitudes.[31]

The text permits the shock of the rape to occur, as Fielding experienced it, between lines, or rather, from the *clash* between lines, from her appeal for mercy to Lovelace's terrible words, "The affair is over. Clarissa lives" (v:222 [883]). Our own sense of shock, on the other hand, is produced by the combination of twentieth-century graphic violence – Lovelace shown thrusting, while the ladies of the house hold the writhing, drowning hands – and eighteenth-century details: the man seen from behind with his trousers open but on, the lady's skirts shoved up, her bodice ripped open. While perhaps not *exactly* as tantalizing and evasive as a trout, the filmic scene is, in its own medium, a literal presentation of murky shadows, the culmination of a steady bombardment, scene after scene, of imagery deriving from various submerged and powerful patterns: spatial constrictions, hunting scenes, hunting analogies, subversive voice-overs, and disconcerting transitional cuts from Clarissa happily secure in an opera box to Mrs. Sinclair's prostitute rifling and copying her stash of letters. The rape accomplished, Clarissa is left to a long still camera shot, a crucified form within the curtained boundaries of the bed – like the cradle before and the coffin to come, a darksome place of "rest."

Clarissa, her prison, and her coffin, dominate the spatial energy of the last part. In her prison-room, the camera shows Clarissa from the far end of her coffin, which takes up all the visual space and precedes her at the same moment that she commands it. Then the camera travels slowly up the surface of the coffin in the darkness, dogs barking outside; the shot moves from coffin to Belford to a startlingly gaunt and shadowed Clarissa with eerily bright eyes. The death scene in the film is as proportionately *consuming* as the death scene in the novel. The space surrounding Clarissa tightens steadily until her face consumes the screen; after her death, the camera watches from some remote elevation the progress of the coffin home as it carries the presence of the dead center vividly and darkly back into the heart of her father's house. The faint suggestion of residual light from Clarissa's deathbed scene should evoke even for modern audiences her Father's House.

Despite its deviations from the text, but precisely because of the way it invokes and employs contemporary spatial details and structures, I find the BBC adaptation of *Clarissa* to be a powerful "commentary" or "transformation" of Richardson's novel – emphasizing the spatial elements of boundaries and shadows that invoke the novel's powerful energy of constraint, confinement, and claustrophobia. The spatial representation emerges intelligently in the reiteration of stairways, the impotence of windows, the progressive loss of light, the several qualities of confinement, and the cuts from moments of apparent peace to realities of subverted securities. What this adaptation offers is not exactly *fidelity* to a text but a visual *interpretation* that supplies both the iconography of place and its specific possible details. We are given here a visual realm of detail and an interpretation of that visual detail that through several avenues offers our twenty-first-century sensibilities access to some eighteenth-century "givens" of space and boundary. We are *shown* some of the lights and shadows, the possibilities within confinement and the impossibilities of escape, that the text of words so much wants us to *see*.

NOTES

1 Sean Day-Lewis, "Out of the Doll's House," *The Sunday Telegraph*, November 24, 1991.

2 *The Radio Times* of November 23–29, 1991 so billed the adaptation on its front cover.

3 Lois A. Chaber, "A 'Fatal Attraction'? The BBC and Clarissa," *Eighteenth-Century Fiction* 4:3 (April 1992), 258.

4 John Samuel Bullen, *Time and Space in the Novels of Samuel Richardson* (Logan, UT: Utah State University Press, 1965), p. 27.

5 Samuel Richardson, *Clarissa. Or, The History of a Young Lady: Comprehending the Most Important Concerns of Private Life*, ed. William Warburton, 7 vols. (London: Printed for S. Richardson, 1748), II:180 (303). All quotations will be from this first edition; after the volume and page number, however, I will also add parenthetically the equivalent page number in Angus Ross's more widely available paperback edition (Harmondsworth, England: Penguin, 1985).

6 Martin Heidegger, "Building Dwelling Thinking" (1951), *Basic Writings*, ed. David Farrell Krell (New York: Harper and Row, 1977), p. 332.

7 Philippa Tristram, *Living Space in Fact and Fiction* (London: Routledge, 1989), p. 5.

8 Michel Beaujour, "Some Paradoxes of Description," *Yale French Studies* 61 (1981), 29.

9 Virginia Woolf, "Rambling Round Evelyn," *The Common Reader* (New York: Harcourt Brace, 1925, 1953), p. 84 (my emphasis).

10 See also David Shannon, "The Innocent and the Rake," *Radio Times* November 23–29, 1991, 22, 20; Sean Day-Lewis, "Out of the Doll's House."

11 Samuel Richardson, *Clarissa: Preface, Hints of Prefaces and Postscript*, intro. R. S. Brissenden (Los Angeles: William Andrews Clark Memorial Library and UCLA, 1964), p. iv.

12 Sarah Fielding, *Remarks on Clarissa Addressed to the Author. Occasioned by some Critical Conversations on the Characters and Conduct of that Work* (London: Printed for J. Robinson, 1749), pp. 8–9.

13 Henry Fielding to Samuel Richardson, October 15, 1748, quoted in William C. Slattery, ed., *The Richardson–Stinstra Correspondence and Stinstra's Prefaces to Clarissa* (Carbondale and Edwardsville: Southern Illinois University Press, 1969), p. 118.

14 Susan Stewart, *On Longing: Narratives of the Miniature, the Gigantic, the Souvenir, the Collection* (Baltimore: Johns Hopkins University Press, 1984; reissued, Durham, NC: Duke University Press, 1993, 1998), p. 9. Both Eisenstein

and Griffith acknowledged getting filmic hints from Dickens (see Robert Giddings, Keith Selby, Chris Wensley, *Screening the Novel: The Theory and Practice of Literary Dramatization* [London: Macmillan, 1990], p. 7).

15 Quoted in Giddings, *Screening the Novel*, p. 1.

16 Quoted in Giddings, *Screening the Novel*, p. 1.

17 Sarah Fielding, *Remarks on Clarissa*, p. 5.

18 Robert Porrett, *Clarissa: or, The Fatal Seduction. A Tragedy in Prose. Founded on Richardson's celebrated Novel of Clarissa Harlowe* (1788). Further references will be cited in the text.

19 Giddings, *Screening the Novel*, p. xv.

20 Brian McFarlane, *Novel to Film: An Introduction to the Theory of Adaptation* (Oxford: Clarendon Press, 1996), p. 8.

21 McFarlane, *Novel to Film*, p. 10.

22 Jonathan Miller, *Subsequent Performances* (London: Faber and Faber, 1986), p. 229.

23 McFarlane, *Novel to Film*, p. 27.

24 Marshall McLuhan, *Understanding Media* (London: Routledge and Kegan Paul, 1969), p. 307.

25 Giddings, *Screening the Novel*, p. 6.

26 Geoffrey Wagner, *The Novel and the Cinema* (Rutherford, NJ: Farleigh Dickinson University Press, 1975); J. Dudley Andrew, *Some Concepts in Film Theory* (Oxford: Oxford University Press, 1984).

27 Noël Burch, *Theory of Film Practice*, trans. Helen R. Lane (Paris: Gallimard, 1969), p. 17.

28 George Bluestone, *Novels into Film* (1957; reprinted Berkeley and Los Angeles: University of California Press, 1971), p. 48; Edward Branigan, *Point of View in the Cinema: A Theory of Narration and Subjectivity in Classical Film* (Amsterdam: Mouton Publishers, 1984), p. 103.

29 Samuel Taylor Coleridge, *Specimens of the Table Talk of the late Samuel Taylor Coleridge*, ed. Henry Nelson Coleridge, 2 vols. (London: John Murray, 1835), II: 339 (July 5, 1834).

30 Chaber notes that "Nigel Forde's polite queries, on the radio programme 'Bookshelf,' about the (im)morality of this lurid scene elicited justificatory comments by Nokes, Barron, and Loader that bore a discomfiting resemblance to the reflexive rationalizations of Richardson's own letter-writers" (Chaber, "Fatal Attraction," 261).

31 Dorothy Van Ghent, *The English Novel: Form and Function* (New York: Harper and Row, 1953), p. 47.

7   *Jacques le fataliste* on film: from metafiction to metacinema

Alan J. Singerman

There is a long tradition of adaptation of eighteenth-century French novels into film. These works include a remarkable dozen versions of the Abbé Prévost's *Manon Lescaut* between 1908 and 1968,[1] René Jolivet's *Les Aventures de Gil Blas de Santillane* (1955), five versions of Laclos's *Liaisons dangereuses*,[2] an evocation of Sade's Justine by Roger Vadim,[3] Jacques Rivette's adaptation of Diderot's *La Religieuse* (1966), and two films based on Diderot's *Jacques le fataliste et son maître*: Robert Bresson's *Les Dames du Bois de Boulogne* (1945), which modernizes one episode of the novel, and Claude Santelli's 1984 téléfilm, *Jacques le fataliste et son maître*, which is the main subject of interest in this study.[4] Bringing Diderot to the screen has not been an easy matter. The first two film adaptations of Diderot's novels were subjected to severe criticism. Bresson's *Dames* met with an icy reception from the public, bringing financial ruin to its producer, and was soundly reproached by critics, not the least of whom was Georges Sadoul, for attempting to place in a contemporary context a social problem, marriage beneath one's own class, which appeared as an irrelevant anachronism in the twentieth century.[5] Rivette's *La Religieuse* was banned by the conservative Gaullist government even before being shown in public, on the pretext that it was a "film blasphématoire qui déshonore les religieuses" ["a blasphemous film which dishonors nuns"].[6] Like Vadim's *Liaisons dangereuses 1960*, also initially banned, Rivette's film benefited commercially from the incident when the interdiction was lifted. Nevertheless, *La Religieuse*, which was based on a stage adaptation of Diderot's novel co-written by Rivette and Jean Gruault in 1963, was criticized by some as too long and too "classical" and never really enjoyed the favor of the public, despite later critical praise (Bonnet, "Revoir La Religieuse," 65). As regards the specific character of the adaptations of Diderot's narratives, Bresson chooses to adapt a single, albeit major, episode of *Jacques*, the story of Mme de la Pommeraye's revenge on the marquis des Arcis for his inconstancy (comprising about one sixth of the work), narrated in Diderot's novel by the hostess of the Grand Cerf Inn. Bresson conventionalizes the narrative by eliminating the presence of the narrator and, consequently, the continual interruptions of her account which, drawing the reader's attention again and again back to her role as narrator, serve to foreground the narrative as a theme in the novel. While it may be argued that Bresson attempts to create filmic equivalents to Diderot's narrative technique through the use of various rhetorical figures (Roger, "Diderot, Cocteau, Bresson," 49–54), he shows no interest in transposing either the levels of narration or the persistent intrusions by author and reader, the metafictional side of Diderot's work. Rivette, for his part, abandons from the outset the first-person narrative of Suzanne, the protagonist of Diderot's *La Religieuse,* opting for a more objective approach which eschews overt psychological analysis by avoiding close-ups and adopting a generally "theatrical" distance, while at the same time emphasizing the "tableau" aesthetic of which Diderot was fond. Claude Santelli, contrary to his two predecessors, embraces Diderot's narrative project wholeheartedly, attempting to adapt to the medium of film the whole scope of the novel with its multiple narrative levels and its metafictional richness and complexity. Moreover, Santelli transposes the very phenomenon of metafiction by foregrounding, as we shall attempt to illustrate, the narrative specificity of the seventh art itself. In the process, the adaptation of Diderot's metafictional techniques comes to mirror, to a certain extent, the metacinematic character of Santelli's work itself. The main focus of this study will thus be the narratological techniques in Santelli's film which, on the one hand, adapt the metafictional features of Diderot's novel and, on the other, create a level of metacinema in the film. I would mention here, given the multiple uses of the concept of "metafiction," that when I speak of metafiction in this essay, I am using the term primarily as defined by Patricia Waugh: "Metafictional novels tend to be constructed on the principle of a fundamental and sustained opposition: the construction of a fictional illusion (as in traditional realism) and the laying bare of that illusion. In other words, the lowest common denominator of metafiction is simultaneously to create a fiction and to make a statement about the creation of that fiction."[7] Before moving on to a discussion of the metadiscourse(s) specific to Santelli's film, let me recall the main lines of Diderot's novel.

Jacques le fataliste, Diderot's 1771 metafictional masterpiece, tells the story of a journey undertaken by Jacques and his master, on horseback, somewhere in France roughly between 1765 and 1770. The main thread of the action is the story of Jacques' love life, which he relates to his master as they amble through the countryside. Jacques' narrative is constantly interrupted, however, either by incidents which befall the two travellers, or by more or less philosophical discussions with his master, or by embedded narratives of various lengths told by the two main characters or by other delegated narrators. In addition to the interruptions within the story itself, the extra-diegetical author-narrator himself intervenes constantly, either to dialogue with a fictional reader about his own narrative choices, to add various and sundry anecdotes which have little or nothing to do with the story of Jacques' loves, or even to intrude into the diegesis itself on occasion.

It is no secret that *Jacques le fataliste* is a sharply critical, if humorous, parody of the conventional French novel of the period, defined by a French classical theorist as "des fictions d'aventures amoureuses, écrites en Prose avec art pour le plaisir et l'instruction des Lecteurs" ["imaginary amorous adventures written in artful prose for the pleasure and the edification of the readers"].[8] When Diderot insists in his novel that "ceci n'est point un roman" ["this is not a novel"] or "je n'aime pas les romans" ["I don't like novels"], the statements are only paradoxical in appearance;[9] he is referring to the stereotypical insipidly sentimental novel, whose falseness he finds intolerable.[10] In his metafictional project, however, Diderot goes much further, demystifying the novel genre itself, whose pre-modernist defining characteristic was traditionally the creation of the illusion of reality. Like Sterne, his model, Diderot purposefully sabotages the illusion of reality in his novel through the constant intrusions of his author-narrator, interrupting the tale of the journey to tell the tale of his own narration, drawing the reader's attention precisely to the freedom of the author in determining the chain of events in the novel. At the same time, Diderot demonstrates how the author's freedom is limited by forces such as historical truth and intertextual influences,[11] as well as by readerly expectations – expectations which he intentionally frustrates by refusing both to maintain an air of reality and to get on with the story of Jacques' amorous encounters. Like the author, however, the reader in Diderot's work is endowed with his own character and does not hesitate to stand up to the latter, demanding that he satisfy the reader's expectations and chiding the author when he oversteps the ontological limits of his role (577, 592).[12] In essence, Diderot makes explicit the normally implicit relationship between author and reader underlying all works of fiction. Moreover, in a thoroughly modern ("pragmatic") move, Diderot's author involves the reader in the act of fictional creation itself by inviting him or her to assume responsibility for narrative choices, including the choice of a denouement (515, 777).

It would be reasonable to wonder if anyone could make a film of this metafictional labyrinth. A few years before the 1984 airing on French television of Claude Santelli's adaptation, Milan Kundera, who had just published a very personal adaptation ("variation–homage") of *Jacques le fataliste* for the stage, declared in his introduction that the work is unadaptable as such for either stage or screen: "In all literature there are two novels that are absolutely irreducible, totally unrewritable: *Tristram Shandy* and *Jacques le Fataliste*. How can one simplify such brilliant disorder and be left with anything?"[13] Kundera's proclamation must be taken with a substantial grain of salt, of course, in light not only of his own adaptation of *Jacques*, but also of an earlier stage adaptation in Paris by Francis Huster,[14] but it is likely that Santelli was familiar with Kundera's text, published in Paris in 1981, and took up the "challenge" contained in that piece on the occasion of the bicentennial of Diderot's decease. Moreover, Kundera's "variation" may have served as a catalyst for Santelli in another way as well, because the novelist-playwright's rewriting of *Jacques* is a case study in the violation of convention. Not only does Kundera exhibit the same sort of temporal playfulness, the intermingling of present and past, that Santelli highlights in his film, but he transgresses further by alternating bits of dialogue from different stories, much like the cinema's "alternating montage," and by bringing into contact in his play characters from various stories in Diderot's novel (such as Jacques and Saint-Ouen) who have never met before. Thus, Kundera demonstrates how the spirit of transgression found in Diderot can be adapted to another medium, despite his argument that Jacques is "unrewritable."[15] Santelli follows suit in a brilliant narratological and cinematographic exercise which seems to accomplish exactly what Kundera, however seriously, denied could be done.

From a strictly anecdotal and thematic viewpoint, Santelli transposes to film a judicious selection of the primary plot elements and motifs which structure Diderot's novel. In approximately fifty carefully crafted sequences, his characters recreate the principal stages of Jacques' journey with his master, with digressions to evoke the story of his wounded knee, his sojourns in the peasant's and the doctor's houses, his "gagged" upbringing, his charitable act, the attack upon him by thieves, and his eventual meeting with Denise, the object of his affections, at Desglands' castle. His master narrates and plays out his own duping by the chevalier de Saint-Ouen and Agathe, while the author-narrator (Diderot) in the film adds the stories of the poet of Pondichéry and of Gousse. As in the novel, the two travelers debate a broad range of metaphysical and philosophical subjects, including fatalism and determinism, morality, human liberty, cosmic justice, and social reproduction. The author-narrator adds reflections on the author's liberty and prerogatives, his relationship to the reader, his insistence on verisimilitude and his distaste for conventional novels, as well as on the relationship between fiction and reality. The film is necessarily reductive, picking and choosing from the wealth of material in Diderot's novel. Despite a long sequence at the Grand Cerf Inn,

Santelli makes no reference to the hostess's narrative concerning Mme de la Pommeraye (understandably, in light of Bresson's film), nor to the marquis des Arcis's relation of the Father Hudson affair, nor to the story of Jacques' captain's incessant dueling with his best friend, nor to those of M. Pelletier and M. de Guerchy, to mention the principal episodes left out. These omissions notwithstanding, Santelli's work effectively represents the novel's central action and thematics.

From a narratological standpoint, *Jacques le fataliste*, the novel, offers a dazzling interweaving of the two narrative registers of mimesis and diegesis, that is, of showing and telling, or story and discourse, depending on whose terminology you wish to use.[16] For this very reason, despite Kundera's categorical pronouncement, Diderot's novel lends itself particularly well to screen adaptation. While "showing" is used metaphorically in Percy Lubbock's celebrated opposition – narrative discourse cannot literally "show" anything – showing is, of course, the fundamental nature of film. Cinema can both show and tell, combining word and image – in addition to music and sound effects – to tell a story. Santelli plays masterfully on this natural quality of the film medium to transpose and focus on the opposition of story and discourse in Diderot's novel. The filmmaker also takes advantage of cinema's oft-noted inherent relationship to the present tense – the image on the screen is always in the present for the spectator – to transpose Diderot's practice of using the present to render action more immediate and thus more "mimetic," the mediation of the narrator "disappearing" in certain episodes.[17] In a novel nothing is closer to pure mimesis, "showing," than dialogue, and the journey of Jacques and his master is dominated by dialogue between the two protagonists as Jacques narrates his past, responds to his master's queries, and debates human behavior and philosophical questions. Santelli has merely to transpose elements of the dialogue to the screen to adapt this aspect of Diderot's novel. The real challenge to the filmmaker is posed by the telling of the story, or, more precisely, the representation of the act of discourse itself in relation to the story, which is foregrounded by Diderot in his novel. In the following pages we shall examine a sampling of the specific techniques employed by Santelli to highlight the interplay of story and discourse in both novel and film.

At the beginning of his film, Santelli, like Diderot, quickly establishes the two main narrative registers – first that of the author-narrator, presented briefly in voice-over, and then that of Jacques himself as he relates how he received a knee injury in the battle of Fontenoy, an episode which is then shown in the film (as opposed to being simply narrated by Jacques).[18] Santelli then proceeds to give the author a veritable persona in his film, granting him the same independent existence he has in Diderot's novel. In a long down shot showing Jacques and his master riding slowly along the road at the bottom of a high hill, the camera slowly tracks backwards and pans to the right to reveal the author, following his characters' progress through a telescope as he continues his narration. By framing the author and his characters simultaneously, the filmmaker is able to assert more forcefully the relationship between the extra-diegetical author and his fictional creations established in Diderot's novel. At the same time, Santelli insists on the ontological distance between the author-narrator's space and that of his characters by using both the telescope (an overt signifier of distance) and deep-focus photography. The sequence also introduces the temporal interplay which characterizes the entire work as we move from the present of Jacques the narrator, which is the past of the author, to the past of Jacques (Fontenoy), then back to the present of Jacques and from there to the present of the author, juxtaposed in the same shot to the narrative past (Jacques' present). At the end of the sequence, the author turns, in a close shot, to speak directly to the camera, establishing the relationship between the author and his interlocutor, the reader qua spectator, which Diderot stresses throughout his work in the numerous interruptions of the story by the author-narrator.

Shortly thereafter, Santelli begins to develop more fully the metafictional dimension of Diderot's work while at the same time introducing a clearly self-reflexive cinematic theme. From a shot of Jacques philosophizing with his master about fatalism, Santelli returns again to the author watching his characters through the telescope lens – much as the filmmaker watches his characters through the camera lens and is separated from them by a similar ontological distance. We hear the end of Jacques' sentence in voice-over, finished by the author's ironic "etc., etc." as the latter strides directly up to the camera to address the spectator again. Conflating several authorial intrusions (in the novel) in this shot, Santelli's Diderot tells the spectator that he should be grateful for all the omitted details, reminding him of the various fanciful turns he could give his narrative, insisting that he doesn't like "novels," and complaining of the reader–spectator's infatuation with love stories (499, 495, 731, 671–2, in order of appearance in the novel). Then, as the camera pans to follow him, the author walks over to a segment of wall in the middle of a meadow and, tossing his cane and telescope out of the frame, steps up to a writing desk which has slid into the frame from the right. The camera tracks to a tight close-up, followed by a cut to an identical close-up of the author shot on a studio set and a rapid zoom backwards as the main wall slides down behind him to create the author's salon before our very eyes.

In the first part of this sequence, shot in the space of Jacques' voyage, Santelli, by placing the author in a space which encompasses both mimesis and diegesis, suggests the ontological intermingling of the intra- and extra-diegetical spaces, the weaving together of story and discourse practiced by Diderot in his novel. The remainder of the shot, however, in which the author moves to his desk, makes the leap from metafiction to metacinema by "focusing" on the cinematic construction of illusion, the self-conscious utilisation of artificial elements to create the illusion of reality. When Santelli cuts to the close-up of the author, featuring segments of the salon in the clearing, followed by the close-up in the studio revealing the placement of the main wall panel behind the author, the creation of cinematic illusion of reality is clearly demystified; we are confronted with the fundamental facticity, as well as the art, of cinematic representation, stripped of its mimetic pretensions. The transition itself, from shot to shot, is charged with transsemiotic inferences. The author begins a sentence in the first close-up in the diegetical space in the meadow – "Si je faisais . . . " – which is completed in the second close-up in the author's narrative space in the studio: ". . . /z/un roman." The emphasis on the exaggeratedly theatrical phonetic liaison /z/ between "faisais" and "un" is a playful reference to the startling continuity, or "liaison," between the two ontologically disparate shots. As the full wall panel now slides down behind the author, the camera zooms rapidly backward, revealing at his side a female servant holding the cane and telescope he had tossed off-camera in the previous shot, and thus strengthening the link between the two incongruous spaces. The author's remarks will be addressed, throughout the remainder of the film, alternately to his servant and to the spectator. Santelli's female house-servant, who sometimes looks over the author's shoulder to peek at his text, serves as an incarnation of the author's reader-interlocutor (in the novel) to whom he directs some of his remarks, while the filmmaker, at the same time, again brings more clearly into play, through the author's address to the camera, his own specific public, the spectator. The author-narrator ties the two addressees together in this scene by accusing them both of only being interested in love stories, but makes the reader–spectator conflation much more explicit later in the film. In response to a question by his servant about Jacques' master, he answers, addressing the camera: "Comme vous, il était homme, homme passionné . . . comme vous, lecteur; homme curieux comme vous, lecteur"; then, swooping toward his servant, "homme importun, comme vous . . . homme questionneur," after which he returns to address the camera again, adding "homme importun, comme vous, spectateur" (see *Jacques*, 538). As in Diderot's novel, the relationship between Jacques and his master in the film appears, on the level of narrative, as a *mise en abyme* ["mirroring'] of the relations between the author and his reader . . . and, by extension, between the filmmaker and his or her public.

The sequence which follows demonstrates more clearly how Santelli successfully transposes to the screen the interplay of story and discourse in Diderot's novel. We find Jacques in bed at night in a peasant's home, suffering from his knee wound while the peasant and his reluctant wife make love in the background. In a series of asides to the spectator, Jacques and his master discuss why people who live in misery tend to make more children (cf. *Jacques*, 511). At the beginning of this scene, the foreground and background of the shot are in the same fictional time and space, that of Jacques' narrative past. When Jacques turns to address the camera, however, and then is joined by his master in the same shot, the story register is momentarily coalesced with the plane of discourse; that is, we literally do not lose sight of the subject of Jacques' narration (the *énoncé*) when the focus is drawn to the act of narration itself (the *énonciation*). While Diderot, in his novel, does not expect the reader to lose sight of the love-making scene either, the story must, of necessity, yield to the discourse as Jacques and his master discuss his narrative – they cannot be represented simultaneously. However, in the film both can be observed at the same time, and the filmmaker seems, therefore, to realize Diderot's metafictional project more fully than Diderot himself, to the extent that the film expresses more clearly the inextricable relationship between the utterance and the uttering in discourse. The background of the shot remains wholly in the story space, while the foreground, through the "metaleptic" move (the intrusion of the extra-diegetical narrator and narratee into the fictional universe),[19] combines story and discourse (Jacques' past and present) before returning completely to the story when Jacques cries out in pain from his wounded knee.

At the end of this sequence, it becomes clear that the transparently artificial and mobile scenery has an ontological function in Santelli's film. After a fade-out, there is a rapid fade-in as the wall panel behind Jacques' bed (in the inn where he is telling the story) slides down into place, evoking the barrier between the character's story and discourse spaces. Santelli's camera then tracks slowly backward as Jacques and his master finish speaking, their space becoming a smaller and smaller spot of light as the camera moves into the author's darkened bedroom and pans to catch him emerging from his bed. The lights come up and a second panel of wall slides down to separate the author's story (the voyage of Jacques and his master) from his own narrative register. Throughout the film, in fact, various wall panels serve as ontological signifiers as they slide up and down to open or close the story space, allowing the narrator (author or character) to pass from one space to the other at will. The best example of this aspect of Santelli's film is certainly the staging of the story of Gousse, the eccentric, and Prémontval's affair with his pupil,

Mlle Pigeon. As Gousse leaves the author's house, where he has been chatting with members of the household, he departs through an opening created as a wall panel slides up, leading to another story space. As the author follows him into the new space, the lights come up revealing the school of mathematics and drawing where the liaison between the teacher and his pupil begins. As the author narrates, we see the love story unfold behind him. When Prémontval and Mlle Pigeon elope, the lights go out, ushering in yet another story space as a spot light singles out Gousse, snow falling around him, as he returns on foot from the Alps after giving all his money to the young couple. In addition to the clever play between story and discourse highlighted in this sequence, it should be noted that the mobile scenery and lighting effects, creating separate story spaces with their own temporality, is blatantly theatrical rather than cinematic. The school scene, with students, teachers, and a nude model, is a striking tableau, reflecting the predilection for such scenes in Diderot's novel (e.g. 622, 682–4) and adding another vein to Santelli's adaptation.

In a later episode Santelli again mixes story and discourse registers, while adding a new twist by doubling the hero's own persona. In this case, we see Jacques attacked by three thieves who, thinking him wealthy because he gives some money to a poor woman, beat him and attempt to rob him (cf. *Jacques*, 572). As Jacques hoists himself onto his crutches and moves up a long set of stone steps out of our sight, his master, to whom he has been narrating the story, erupts into the same shot, overcome with indignation, sword in hand, threatening to attack the thieves and avenge his servant. Jacques the narrator, in voice-over, tries to calm his master, then rejoins him in the foreground of the shot – literally "foregrounding" the narrative act – as Jacques the character moves slowly away up the stairs in the background. The presence of two Jacques compounds the narrative trangression initiated by the master's entry into the mimetic space and the time of Jacques' past. Here again, showing and telling are distinguished by the opposition of foreground and background, but the intimate connection between the two, the act of narration and the story itself, is expressed through their appearance in the same frame.

As the sequence draws to a close, when Jacques recalls his anguish at the thought that he now had no money to pay the doctor, his master panics and cries out: "Mon pauvre Jacques, que vas-tu devenir?" ["My poor Jacques, what will become of you?"]. To which Jacques responds, bemused: "Mon maître, rassurez-vous. Me voilà" ["Don't worry, Master. I'm right here"]. In addition to the preceding metafictional play, the master's agitated state, in both novel and film, mocks the illusion of reality both discourses are purported to create. In this respect, the transposition of this episode to film is particularly successful, since the illusion of reality, while remaining an illusion, is more directly (if not more effectively) realized in the images of cinema, by the analogical nature of the medium, than in the language of prose fiction.

In a subsequent episode, where the author intervenes to demonstrate his freedom to invent the vicissitudes of his story and to reject falsity in fiction, Santelli brings the means of cinema increasingly into play to express both the metafictional reflections of Diderot's novel and the metacinematic character of his own film. In Diderot's novel, this particular authorial intrusion occurs in the middle of the master's story of his relationship with the chevalier de Saint-Ouin and Agathe, when the author–narrator confides to the reader that he is tempted to shut the master up by pointing in the distance to an old soldier arriving on a horse, or a young peasant girl in a straw hat riding along on her donkey: "Et pourquoi le vieux militaire ne serait-il pas ou le capitaine de Jacques ou le camarade de son capitaine? [...] Pourquoi la jeune paysanne ne serait-elle pas ou la dame Suzon, ou la dame Marguerite, ou l'hôtesse du Grand-Cerf, ou la mère Jeanne, ou même Denise, sa fille? Un faiseur de roman n'y manquerait pas; mais je n'aime pas les romans, à moins que ce ne soient ceux de Richardson [...] Mon projet est d'être vrai, je l'ai rempli" ["And why couldn't the old soldier be Jacques' captain or his captain's comrade? Why couldn't the young peasant girl be Suzon or Marguerite, or the hostess of the Grand-Cerf, or Jeanne, or even her daughter Denise? A scribbler of novels wouldn't hesitate; but I don't like novels, other than Richardson's. My plan is to be true, and I've kept to it"] (731). The author then adds that he is free to stop a carriage approaching them and let out its occupants, which would lead to the narration of a long series of stories postponing indefinitely the story of both Jacques' and his master's loves – a choice which he renounces. Santelli masterfully transposes this scene by developing the motif of the carriage introduced at the very end of the author's intervention, absorbing into the carriage scene the essential elements of the whole preceding passage. We find Jacques and his master in a village square, with Jacques nursing a severely sore throat. As the camera pans around a large tree, we discover the author, again intruding into the fictional space of his characters as he muses to the spectator, over a background of fanciful, playful music, about the turn of events he could impose. To demonstrate his freedom of narrative choice, a stagecoach suddenly arrives in town and discharges one by one a series of characters which he could, if he so desired, bring into the story at this point: "Il ne tiendrait qu'à moi d'arrêter le carrosse et d'en faire sortir, que sais-je, une paysanne en chapeau de paille? un vieillard porteur d'un message tragique? le frère Jean revenu de Lisbonne grâce à un miracle? le capitaine [de Jacques] échappé à la mort?" ["If I wanted to, I could stop the coach and let out, let me see now – a peasant girl with a straw hat? an old man bringing a tragic message? Friar John miraculously returning alive from Lisbon? Jacques' captain escaped from death?"]. But the author then states, emphatically, as an accelerated reverse projection packs the four characters back into the stagecoach, "Non, non, et non, je ne fais pas de roman; la vérité et rien que la vérité" ["No, no, this is not a novel; the truth and nothing but the truth"], upon which we see the stage arrive in town again to discharge Agathe, the female lead in the master's story soon to follow. In this sequence the filmmaker creates a more graphic but completely "faithful" version of Diderot's incessant musing over his narrative choices, while foregrounding, through the reverse projection, the narrative technique of cinema itself.

In the sequence that follows the scene in the town square, as the master begins the story of Saint-Ouen and Agathe – with frequent interruptions from Jacques – the author appears for a moment in the background framed in a small space between the two characters. The brief shot recalls not only the metalepsis motif in the novel, but, more importantly here, the "presence" of the author in the dialogue of his characters. This point is also made earlier when the author begins a sentence of dialogue in his salon, which is then repeated by Jacques, on horseback, after we cut to the next shot. Diderot's remarks on the theater in *Jacques* apply fully to the dialogue in his novel: "Je vous défie de lire une scène de comédie ou de tragédie, un seul dialogue, quelque bien qu'il soit fait, sans surprendre le mot de l'auteur dans la bouche de son personnage" ["I defy you to read any scene from a comedy or a tragedy, a single dialogue, however well it may be written, without perceiving the author's words in his character's mouth"] (763). In short, the glimpse of the author behind his characters in the scene in Santelli's film suggests that it is impossible not to detect the author's voice behind his characters' words; completely transparent, unmediated, literary representation (pure mimesis) simply does not exist.

As a final example of Santelli's metadiscursive adaptation, let us examine a short segment of the master's narration of his relationship with Agathe, as he and Jacques rest by the roadside. In this part of the episode, the master begins to relate, in voice-over, his night with Agathe. As he speaks, we see him climb up a ladder to her window, enter her bedroom, and begin to undress while the unclad girl waits smiling in her bed. Suddenly, he turns back toward the open door of the bedroom and calls out: "Tu m'écoutes? Tu dors? Jacques!" ["Are you listening to me? Are you asleep? Jacques!"]. In the next shot, Santelli cuts back to the roadside where we see the master step out of the door to Agathe's bedroom, a segment of scenery now removed from the studio and set down in the open field. The master walks over to the apparently bored Jacques, who has dozed off, and upbraids him for his lack of attention. In Diderot's novel (747), the interruption of the master's story brings us back to the "present," that is, the space of the master's discourse – which is a present once removed, because it is also the space of the author–narrator's framing story, the journey, and thus situated in the past with respect to the authorial figure. The spatio-temporal narrative play in the novel is again rendered cleverly in the film by the montage, cutting from Agathe's bedroom to the clearing where Jacques and his master have stopped to rest. The master's role as both character (in the author's story of the journey) and narrator of his own story (in which he is again a character) is metaphorically and metonymically represented by the presence of the entrance to Agathe's bedroom in the field, that is, in the narrator's space – the improbably placed prop functioning, like the improbable montage itself, on the metanarrative level. The spectator, like Diderot's reader, is denied the illusion of reality (i.e. prevented from immersing himself or herself in the master's titillating story) and forced to remain conscious of the narrative register – the doorway, an ironic mocking of cinematic "realism," serving also as a materialization of the novel's references to the master's interrupted and unfinished story. This point is driven home when, after recovering the master's stolen horse, the two men ride past the bedroom door, still standing out in the field, prompting Jacques to cry out: "Vous oubliez la porte, la porte d'Agathe, la porte!" ["You're forgetting the door, Agathe's door, the door!"] – which is the signal for the master's story to continue with a cut to a shot of the door as it bursts open and the whole household rushes into the bedroom to trap the duped master in bed with Agathe. Here again, Santelli finds an ingenious way to adapt Diderot's playful commingling of story and discourse, at the same time calling attention to cinema's specific means of expressing metadiscursive thematics.

It should be mentioned, finally, that Santelli exploits a wide range of cinematic techniques which produce an indisputable self-referential effect, particularly as regards the *raccords*, or transitions between shots, both within and between sequences. In addition to the standard cut, fade-out and fade-in, blurring and unblurring of the focus, and stop-action-type transitions, some combined with zooms backwards (like the cut from the close-up of the author in the meadow to the author in his salon), Santelli resorts to a number of particularly creative devices which draw attention to the specificity of the medium. To effect a transition from the peasant's home back to the author's salon, for instance, he combines a move from voice-over to "voice-in" (dialogue) by the author with an overlapping action: the peasant's wife drops a plate and the filmmaker cuts to a shot of a plate dropped by the author's servant that crashes to the floor in the

author's home. On other occasions, characters slide into or out of the
frame with no visible means of locomotion, as in the passage near the
end of the film when Jacques completes his story about Denise. Seated at
the roadside with his master, Jacques slides out of the frame, still seated,
accompanied by a long lateral tracking shot to the right, picking up speed
until the film cuts to a shot in the castle room into which he slides from
the left, holding onto his hat. At the very end of the film, Santelli links
the final reflections of both the author and Jacques (on cuckoldry and
destiny) through a combination of pans and swish pans which imply both
the continuity and the discontinuity between the author's and his character's spaces. In all of the preceding examples, the transitions are effected
by means overtly specific to the medium of film and which unequivo-
cally call attention to themselves as such, with the result that Santelli
persistently thematizes cinematic devices at the same time that he adapts
Diderot's novel.

A final example of transition technique in Santelli's film is worthy of
note because it constitutes a clever transposition to cinema of the theory
of fiction that Diderot elaborates in his novel. On two separate occasions,
the author uses a free-standing pivoting mirror in his salon to introduce
a new sequence. In the first instance, we see in the mirror, beside which
the master is standing, a reflection of Jacques and his master preparing
for bed in the first inn where they stop. The author spins the mirror, creating an effect similar to a swish pan and leading to a cut to the author's
room. In the second case, the author looks in the two-sided mirror, turns
it around, and sees only his own reflection in each side, followed by a cut
to Jacques' master asleep on the roadside. The two shots are highly suggestive, not only of cinema, which has had a long love affair with mirrors,
but also of the concept of art as imitation (reflection) of life: we remember Stendhal's celebrated description of the novel as "un miroir que l'on
promène le long d'un chemin" ["a mirror one carries down a road"].
Diderot's concept of good fiction differs little from Stendhal's. Throughout his novel he promotes the criterion of "truth," that is, verisimilitude, in
works of fiction and demonstrates in his anecdotes the affinities between
historical reality and fictional representation, as in the parallel stories
of M. de Guerchy and the friend of Jacques' captain (609–10) and in
Gousse's involvement in the elopement of Prémontval and Mlle Pigeon
(554–5).[20] In both novel and film, Diderot states clearly to his interlocutor: "Je m'amuse à écrire sous des noms empruntés les sottises que vous
faites" ["I enjoy attributing to fictional characters the follies you commit"] (714). As a novelist, Diderot portrays the reality around him, and
the reader must beware of assuming his text is merely fictional: "Celui qui
prendrait ce que j'écris pour la vérité, serait peut-être moins dans l'erreur

que celui qui le prendrait pour une fable" ["Someone who considers what I write to be the truth would perhaps be closer to the truth than someone who considers it a fiction"] (505). The author's liberty to invent, which Diderot also invokes, is circumscribed not only by the reader's expectations and various literary influences (Molière, Rabelais, Montaigne ...), but, most importantly, by reality itself, the criterion of "truth."[21] As an eighteenth-century theorist, Diderot, contrary to modern trends, does not conceive of fiction as independent of reality.

While Santelli uses the mirror motif, as well as the author-figure's discourse, to reflect Diderot's belief in the mimetic mission of fiction, he no less clearly transposes Diderot's insistence on the author's liberty to invent into a demonstration of the filmmaker's freedom to create a fictional universe rather than just to record reality. Diderot's fictional creed might thus be formulated, in opposition to Robbe-Grillet's famous "Je ne transcris pas, je construis" ["I don't copy, I create"],[22] as "Je transcris et je construis." The fundamental difference between Diderot's metafiction and that of the modern metafictionists, from Borges and Nabokov to John Fowles and William H. Gass, might indeed be summed up by the difference between Santelli's adaptation of *Jacques le fataliste* and Alain Robbe-Grillet's *Trans-Europ-Express* (1966), which has also been treated as an "adaptation" of Jacques.[23] While both films, like the novel, focus on the ambiguous relationship beween fiction and reality, Robbe-Grillet emphasizes that what appears as reality might only be fiction, whereas Diderot, as we have seen, promotes the opposite position that what appears as pure fiction might indeed be a representation of reality. Diderot's mimetic theory of fiction is firmly rooted, like his deterministic universe, in the French eighteenth century, where techniques of illusion reigned supreme. Santelli faithfully transposes this theory to the screen, while also clearly representing Diderot's more modern intuition of the fictional world as, simultaneously, a creation of the author.

NOTES

1 The most well-known versions are H.-G. Clouzot's *Manon 49* (1949) and Jacques Aurel's *Manon 70* (1968).
2 Roger Vadim, *Liaisons dangereuses 1960* (1959), Charles Brabant, *Liaisons dangereuses* (1979), Stephen Frears, *Dangerous Liaisons* (1988), Milos Forman, *Valmont* (1989), and Roger Kumble, *Cruel Intentions* (1999). For a discussion of the films by Vadim and Frears, see Richard Frohock's essay in this volume.
3 *Le Vice et la vertu* (1963) is, in fact, a loose conflation of motifs from Sade's two novels, *Justine, ou les Malheurs de la vertu* (1791) and *Histoire de Juliette, ou les Prospérités du vice* (1797).

4 Santelli's 135-minute téléfilm is available through the French catalog of the "Films for the Humanities & Sciences" collection (PO Box 2053, Princeton, NJ 08543-2053; web site: www.films.com).

5 Georges Sadoul, *Histoire du cinéma mondial* (Paris: Flammarion, 1949), p. 289. For a fuller account of the reception of Bresson's film and additional commentary, see Philippe Roger, "Diderot, Cocteau, Bresson, ou 'L'Histoire d'un mariage saugrenu'" in Elisabeth de Fontenay and Jacques Proust, eds. *Interpréter Diderot aujourd'hui* (Paris: Sycomore, 1984), pp. 31–57; and Daniel Millar, *The Films of Robert Bresson* (New York: Praeger, 1969), pp. 33–41.

6 Jean-Claude Bonnet, "Revoir La Religieuse" in *Interpréter Diderot aujourd'hui*, ed. Fontenay and Proust, p. 60. See Kevin Jackson's essay in this volume for a discussion of the banning of Rivette's film.

7 Patricia Waugh, *Metafiction. The Theory and Practice of Self-Conscious Fiction* (London and New York: Routledge, 1984), p. 6. The definition of metafiction offered by Larry McCaffery is, of course, no less relevant to Diderot's novel: "that type of fiction which either directly examines its own construction as it proceeds or which comments or speculates about the forms and language of previous fictions" (*The Metafictional Muse* [Pittsburg: University of Pittsburg Press, 1982], p. 16).

8 Daniel Huet, *Lettre à M. de Segrais sur l'origine des romans* (1678) in Henri Coulet, *Le Roman jusqu'à la Révolution*, II (Paris: Armand Colin, 1968), p. 66.

9 *Jacques le fataliste et son maître* in *Œuvres romanesques* (Paris: Garnier, 1966), pp. 528, 278. All subsequent references to *Jacques le fataliste* are to this edition and will be given in parenthesis in the body of the essay.

10 For example, he refers to the contemporary novel, at the beginning of his *Eloge de Richardson*, as "un tissu d'événements chimériques et frivoles" ["a jumble of fanciful and frivolous events"], in *Œuvres esthétiques* (Paris: Garnier, 1965), p. 29. All translations from the French in this essay and in the notes are mine; all quotes from French critical sources in the following notes are translated into English.

11 Cf. Stephen Werner, as regards Diderot's representation of the origin of fictional discourse: "Fiction is to be viewed as sandwiched between free invention and the determinants of reality, imagination and nature [...] Now the subjective, now the objective" ("Diderot's Great Scroll: Narrative Art in *Jacques le Fataliste*" in *Studies on Voltaire and the Eighteenth Century* 78 [1975], 97–8).

12 For a good discussion of the role of the reader in *Jacques*, see Kathryn Simpson Vidal, "Diderot and Reader Response Criticism: The Case of *Jacques le fataliste*," *Studies in Eighteenth-Century Culture* 15 (1986), 33–45.

13 Milan Kundera, *Jacques and His Master. An Homage to Diderot in Three Acts*, trans. Michael H. Heim (New York: Harper and Row, 1985), p. 9. The original text was *Jacques et son maître* (Paris: Gallimard, 1981). Kundera's play consists of an intertwining of three relationships in Diderot's novel, each of which is shown to be a variation on the others: the master and Agathe, Jacques and Justine, and the marquis des Arcis and Mme de la Pommeraye.

14 *Les Amours de Jacques le fataliste* (performed at the Théâtre de l'Atelier in 1970). The play was revived in 1986 (Théâtre du Rond-Point), a couple of years after the appearance of Santelli's film.

138 Alan J. Singerman

15 For an in-depth study of the originality of Kundera's work, see Eva Le Grand, "Milan Kundera, auteur de *Jacques le fataliste*" (*Stanford French Review* 7: 2–3 [Fall 1984], 349–62); see also Christine Kiebuzinska's interesting comparison of Diderot's and Kundera's versions, "Jacques and his Master: Kundera's Dialogue with Diderot" (*Comparative Literature Studies* 29: 1 [1992], 54–76).

16 The "telling–showing" opposition was introduced by Percy Lubbock in *The Craft of Fiction* (New York: The Viking Press, 1957), p. 62; for the "story–discourse" terminology, see Seymour Chatman, *Story and Discourse: Narrative Structure in Fiction and Film* (Ithaca, NY: Cornell University Press, 1978); the "mimesis–diegesis" formulation was popularized by Gérard Genette in *Figures III* (Paris: Seuil, 1972), pp. 184–5.

17 One of the best examples is the story of Gousse; see William F. Edmiston, "L'Histoire de Gousse n'est pas un conte: Présence et absence du narrateur dans un épisode de *Jacques le fataliste*" (*Kentucky Romance Quarterly* [renamed *Romance Quarterly*] 30: 3 [1983], 323–9). As regards the constant "present" of cinematographic representation, there is a general consensus among theoreticians, expressed succintly by François Jost: "The cinematographic image has a single temporal register: the present" ("De Diderot à Robbe-Grillet: *Jacques le fataliste* dans *Trans-Europ-Express*" in *Interpréter Diderot aujourd'hui*, ed. Fontenay and Proust, p. 90).

18 Since Diderot makes no distinction between author and narrator in his novel and is clearly reflecting on the author's production of his/her text, we shall often refer to the "author" in the following remarks, despite the modern distinctions between author, narrator, and implied narrator.

19 See Gérard Genette's discussion of the "narrative metalepsis" in *Figures III*, p. 244.

20 For example, as we saw above: "Mon projet est d'être vrai" ["My plan is to be true"] (p. 731); cf. pp. 505, 576, 551, 553, 777. While Thomas Kavanaugh may be justified in his admonitions about "approaching this novel as mimesis" ("The Vacant Mirror. A Study of Mimesis Through Diderot's *Jacques le fataliste*" in *Studies on Voltaire and the Eighteenth Century* 104 [1973], 44), it should be kept in mind that "le vrai" remains Diderot's ideal in fictional creation; if he constantly breaks the illusion, it is largely to plead for a more "truthful" illusion.

21 See François Jost's remarks ("De Diderot à Robbe-Grillet," in *Interpréter Diderot aujourd'hui*, ed. Fontenay and Proust, pp. 84–7) on the tension between liberty and constraint in Jacques. See also, on this subject, Wim De Vos, "La Narration est-elle un acte libre? La Métalepse dans *Jacques le fataliste*" (*Les Lettres romanes* 44: 1–2 [Feb.–May 1990], 3–13).

22 Alain Robbe-Grillet, *Pour un nouveau roman* (Paris: Gallimard, 1963), p. 177.

23 François Jost points out in Robbe-Grillet's film the same "entanglement of narrative levels" as in Diderot's novel, the same intrusions of the narratee (the script-girl and the producer here), the same constraints imposed by "reality," the same "interpenetration of the fictional and authorial worlds"; "De Diderot à Robbe-Grillet," pp. 88, 91, 92.

Kevin Jackson

Improbable as it may now seem, Jacques Rivette's *La Religieuse* [*The Nun*] – an all but forgotten work[1] by a director who has neither sought nor attained any great measure of international celebrity – was once the most notorious film in France. Banned by the French Ministry of Information on April Fool's Day, 1966 (an unusual display of self-deprecating wit?), Rivette's version of Diderot's novel gave rise to a blizzard of impassioned articles in the national press. *Le Monde* actually ran a special daily feature, *L'Affaire de la Religieuse*, to which readers would regularly turn for the latest developments. Filmmakers, writers, religious leaders, and politicians clubbed together for protests and counter-protests; there were petitions, declarations, denunciations, public meetings, and angry open letters on all sides, though no broadcasts – the director of French television and radio had strictly forbidden any mention of the *affaire* on his airwaves. The arguments dragged on for months, until finally, on May 30, 1967, the ban was lifted and the adult public was allowed to see Rivette's film, distributed under the title *Suzanne Simonin, la religieuse de Diderot*. Naturally, the box office was healthy.

Like D. H. Lawrence after the triumph of Penguin Books in the *Chatterley* trial in England a few years earlier, Denis Diderot had suddenly and unexpectedly become a best-selling author. New editions of *La Religieuse*, some of them so hastily printed that they had barely been proofread, were selling out almost as quickly as the bookshops could display them. The gloomy prediction of the Benedictine Superior Marie-Yvonne had come true: "How many people will now read Diderot's book, which is even more noxious than the film!"[2] But prurient cinemagoers, tempted by the prospect of frenzied naked nuns and lesbian romps,[3] were doomed to disappointment. (Ken Russell's lurid vision of erotic frenzies within convent walls, *The Devils*, was still four years away.) *La Religieuse* proved to be – as a contemporary British reviewer justly put it – "a quiet, classically austere work . . . rigorously self-effacing."[4] The scandal soon faded from popular memory, and Rivette returned to comparative, if productive, anonymity. His next film, *L'Amour fou* [*Mad Love*] (1968) was not much shown outside France, and the number of people who have sat through the full twelve and a half hours of its successor *Out One: Noli Me Tangere* (1971) can probably still be measured in the dozens. Nor is it solely among the ranks of the unconverted that *Suzanne Simonin, la religieuse de Diderot* has fallen into oblivion: even Rivette's coteries of admirers have by and large tended to consider the film as something of an aberration – the most conventional and, in the pejorative sense, "literary" work of an *auteur* who has otherwise been committed to restless experimentation with the narrative possibilities of cinema. Today, the most obvious trace left by the whole *affaire* is the cover of the GF–Flammarion paperback edition of Diderot's novel, which continues to feature a black-and-white shot of Anna Karina in the role of Suzanne.

There are a number of good reasons for regretting this state of collective amnesia. Despite the limited circulation of his films outside France, Rivette has been seriously proposed, by those critics who have addressed his work with sympathy, as one of the cinema's greatest living talents,[5] and though he has expressed his own dissatisfactions with *La Religieuse*, Rivette evidently does not subscribe to the orthodoxy that the feature has little connection with his other work:

La Religieuse may appear to be an uncharacteristic work, but it isn't one for me ... *Toutes proportions gardées* ["all things in due proportion"; that is, in a spirit of appropriate humility], it was my idea to make a film in the spirit of Mizoguchi ... There was an attempt to make a film with extended takes or even one-shot sequences, with a flexible camera and rather stylised performances.[6]

Another sound reason for reconsidering *La Religieuse* is that it is a work of such manifest seriousness, not to say earnestness, as well as "simply the most telling portrayal of eighteenth-century society ever to appear in French cinema," in the words of a contemporary journalist.[7] Finally, and not least, there is the consideration implicit in the bitter open letter addressed by Jean-Luc Godard to André Malraux, Minister of Culture, in the pages of *Le Nouvel Observateur*: "If it were not prodigiously sinister, it would be prodigiously beautiful and moving to see a UNR minister of 1966 fear the spirit of an encyclopaedist of 1789."[8] This is well-aimed and suitably high-flown rhetoric, but it is more than simply rhetoric. For many of the pious objectors to *La Religieuse*, Rivette's offense was not so much in launching his personal "noxious" attack on the honor of French nunhood as in restoring currency to a still more noxious text; he was not charged with distorting a classic French author (who, by piquant coincidence, was the subject for that year's *concours général* [general certificate of education] examination in the nation's *lycées*), but with perpetuating that author's outrage to decent Christian feeling in a peculiarly dangerous manner.

It was a remarkable achievement: in the middle of the 1960s, Rivette provoked his fellow countrymen to reenact an ideological battle worthy of the Enlightenment.

Plainly, for all that there have been several thoughtful and searching accounts of the film,[9] *La Religieuse* deserves more detailed critical attention than it has so far received. Rather than take on that worthwhile task myself, however, I'd like instead to examine here a few of the pertinent facts in the case of *La Religieuse*, the book and the film, suspecting that there are aspects of its tangled history which are of greater moment than might be immediately apparent.

In the three or four decades following its publication, Diderot's novel became so well known in France that by 1844, when Baudelaire composed his early verses "Epître à Sainte-Beuve" ["Epistle to Sainte-Beuve"], the poet could take it for granted that "everyone" would be aware of what would now be called its "adult" content:

> L'œil plus noir et plus bleu que la Religieuse
> Dont chacun sait l'histoire obscène et douloureuse ...
>
> [An eye more dark and more blue than the Nun
> Whose melancholy, obscene tale is known to everyone ...][10]

Yet the novel's reputation for salacious detail was in many ways ill deserved. Rather than being one of those gleeful exercises in pornography with which eminent French men of letters, from Beroalde de Verville to Georges Bataille, have titillated or shocked their readers, *La Religieuse* was mischief of a more innocent order. The fiction which culminated in a cinematic scandal had began two centuries earlier with an entirely good-natured hoax.[11] Towards the end of the 1750s, the Marquis de Croismaire – a devout Christian who nonetheless maintained cordial relations with the sceptical Diderot and his fellow Encyclopaedists – became keenly interested in a case of clerical injustice. A few years earlier, in 1752, a nun named Marguerite Delamarre had begun proceedings to have her vows anulled, but was eventually turned down by the ecclesiastical court of Paris. She protested, and went to the higher authority of the appeals court of the Parlement de Paris. Despite the Marquis de Croismare's attempts at influencing the outcome, in 1758 her second plea was also refused. She was forced to remain a nun for another three decades, until convents were dissolved during the Revolution. Following the failure of his efforts, the marquis retired to his estate near Caen. He was sadly missed by Diderot and company, who therefore dreamed up a plot to bring him back. Early in 1760, they set about composing a series of pleading letters which purported to come from a young nun who had fled her convent and was now living in hiding in Versailles, at the home of a friend of the pranksters, Madame Moureau-Madin.

The hoax worked. The compassionate marquis declared himself deeply moved by the plight of "Suzanne Simonin," as the letters were signed, and offered her a position in his household. This was not precisely the outcome the hoaxers had looked for, and Diderot had to stall by inventing all sorts of reasons why Suzanne was incapable of travelling to Caen. These worked for a while, but the joke was clearly getting out of hand, so Diderot hardened his heart, "killed" Suzanne, and on May 10 sent a letter, ostensibly from Mme Madin, detailing the agonies of the young refugee's passage from this world to the next. It was not until 1768, when Croismare came back to Paris and tried to discuss the whole sad business with a baffled Mme Madin, that the deception came to light.

This collaborative spoof had unforeseen consequences for the history of literature, for the "dead" Suzanne refused to lie down quietly. Diderot, intrigued by the implications of the tragic yarn he had spun and then cut short, spent the months after May 1760 working on a longer account of Suzanne's life. He kept the manuscript more or less private until 1770, when his co-conspirator Friedrich Grimm published a memoir of what they had done in the pages of the *Correspondance littéraire*, together with the texts of the letters and a hint that further "revelations" about Suzanne might be forthcoming. It took another ten years before those details were made public: a subsequent editor of the *Correspondance* persuaded Diderot to let him have the text of his novel, which he duly published in 1780. This was the only version of *La Religieuse* circulated in Diderot's lifetime – a discreet publication, since the *Correspondance* was read by only a small circle of subscribers. Sixteen further years passed before the first proper edition was available to a wider public. The same revolutionary Directory which finally released the unfortunate Marguerite Delamarre from her pious incarceration also granted liberty of the press to Suzanne Simonin. But by that time, Diderot had been dead for a dozen years.

The novel bore many marks of its improvised origins. Its very first sentence – "The Marquis de Croismare's reply, if he does reply, will serve as the opening lines of this tale" (21) – must always be mildly puzzling to readers unaware of the Encyclopaedist's game with the soft-hearted aristocrat. And though Diderot played freely with his historical sources, the bones of the real-life case of Marguerite Delamarre are frequently to be discerned beneath the fictional flesh he put upon them. Since Baudelaire's assumption that "everyone" knows the Nun's story now seems somewhat old-fashioned, a brief summary is in order here.

Written almost entirely in the first person singular, *La Religieuse* tells the story of Suzanne Simonin, one of three daughters of an advocate who married late in life. Though, by her own modest admission, both more beautiful and more gifted than her conceited siblings, she was always treated coolly by her parents. As the three girls reach nubile age, the parents grow alarmed that potential suitors always gravitate towards the charms of Suzanne, so they pack her off to a convent until her sisters are safely wed. Suzanne is reasonably contented with her lot, expecting an early release, but is shocked to find that her parents, having spent a fortune in dowries, now expect her to take orders and remain a nun for life. She resists, but is eventually browbeaten into joining the novitiate. From this point on, *La Religieuse* is essentially the tale of Suzanne's rebellions, persecutions, and despairs.

Suzanne completes her novitiate, but as a result of her rebelliousness is transferred to the convent at Longchamp. At first, life here is not so bad: she is tutored by the relatively humane Madame de Moni. But her protector soon dies, and is succeeded by the fanatical Sister Sainte-Christine, who, seeking to crush Suzanne's spirit, enforces a brutal regime of abuse. Though strongly tempted by suicide, Suzanne continues to fight for her freedom and eventually wins a transfer to the liberal convent of Saint-Eutrope. The place seems like a well-lit paradise of sisterly affection, and Suzanne is doted on by the Mother Superior, Madame ***. For alert readers, those coy asterisks tell their own tale. Madame ***'s motives are not altogether holy; nor are her kisses and hugs altogether maternal, though Suzanne (for all her meekly vaunted intelligence) is far slower than the reader to grasp what is going on.

The hand she had rested on my knee wandered all over my clothing from my feet to my girdle, pressing here and there, and she gasped as she urged me in a strange, low voice to redouble my caresses, which I did. Eventually a moment came, whether of pleasure or of pain I cannot say, when she went as pale as death, closed her eyes, and her whole body tautened violently, her lips were first pressed together and moistened with a sort of foam, then they parted and she seemed to expire with a deep sigh. I jumped up, thinking she had fainted, and was about to go and call for help. (137–8)

Sexual exploitation is no joke, but a sexually naive narrator can be.[12] Though Diderot is in the main compassionate towards his sorrowing creature, he is far from uncritical, and it is not only her inability to recognize a female orgasm when she sees one that makes Suzanne seem just a shade dim-witted. (Rivette's film, recounting this event in the conventional third-person form of film narrative, shreds it of nearly all of its comic tone.) Suzanne is compliant when her confessor, Father Lemoine, urges her to shun Madame *** completely. The Mother Superior grows sad, then morbid, then frenzied. The other nuns, blaming Suzanne for the demise of their beloved leader, organise a fresh campaign of persecution.

A new confessor, Dom Morel, comes to investigate the case, and thanks to his investigations, our less than perspicacious heroine finally realises her Superior's true motives.

The ten or so remaining pages of Suzanne's confessions grow increasingly fragmentary: a previously invisible "editor" comes forward to comment on the scrappy state of the available documents. Suzanne flees the convent one night with the help of a young Benedictine, who promptly tries to rape her. She is taken to a brothel and held there for two weeks before making a second escape, suffers various additional humiliations and then manages to secure a menial job in a laundry. The novel ends with a final appeal to the marquis, hinting at the possibility of suicide if she is forced back into the convent.

Such is the principal content of Diderot's novel, and, since the director remained uncommonly faithful to his source, such is the plot of Rivette's film. Rivette makes just one substantial change. His film concludes with Suzanne in a brothel, powdered and primped and clearly more desperate than ever. Where the action of Diderot's novel is left hanging, Rivette has Suzanne fall – she jumps from an upper-storey window and is last seen lying dead, spread out on paving stones in an attitude which echoes that of a penitent before the altar.[13] Some scholars have objected strongly to Rivette's act of licence here, but it cannot be said to have added greatly to the potential offensiveness of the film as far as the pious were concerned, as a review of the scandal will show.[14]

It was as early as 1962 that Rivette first took Jean Gruault's scenario to the board responsible for issuing production visas. He was rejected. Despite being rewritten and trimmed of its offending material, the script was turned down three times in all, and eventually passed in a bowdlerized version on the understanding that it would also be retitled as *Suzanne Simonin, la religieuse de Diderot* and furnished, by the producer Georges de Beauregard, with a disclaimer pointing out that it was a work of fiction and not a comment on modern-day convent life. These laborious negotiations took the better part of three years, and it was not until September 1965 that Rivette was at last able to begin shooting.

In the meantime, religious groups had been alerted. The president of the *Union des Supérieures Majeures* wrote to the Minister of Information, one M. Peyrefitte, demanding his intervention "in the name of the 120,000 nuns of France." Peyrefitte replied that he would do everything in his power to prevent the film's release, but appears to have made no move before being succeeded in his ministerial post by Yvon Bourges: our villain, as it were. Before long, Bourges's office was being flooded with angry petitions – so many that he phoned the local archbishop to request that a team of nuns be despatched to help him sort the mail. What had happened was that children in Catholic schools were being required to write down dictated letters of complaint, take them home to be signed by their parents, and post them to the Ministry. One of these petitions, drawn up by the APEL (Association des parents des écoles libres ["Parents' association of free schools"]), declared:

This film, which defames and travesties the life of religious orders, injures
—the dignity of woman;
—the honour of nuns;
—wounds the moral sense;
—draws a distorted picture of nuns, former educators of our mothers and our wives; most often at present still the educators of our children.

On all these grounds, we firmly protest against this project – however advanced that it may be in its realization – and we urgently appeal for the total banning of its projection.[15]

Surprisingly, perhaps, the twenty-three members of the Censorship Board, having viewed Rivette's completed film, declared on March 22, 1966 that it was quite suitable for public exhibition. Bourges was not happy. A week later, on March 29, he "invited" the members of the board to view the film again, and reconsider their verdict. This time, one of the Censors brought along a Mother Superior, who – it is pleasant to record – thought that the film was perfectly realistic and nothing to be upset about: "All that's happened hundreds of times in convents," was her phlegmatic response. Unfortunately, Bourges had also sent along his own expert – Maurice Grimaud, the director of the Sûreté Nationale, who warned the board of the riots which would surely break out if *La Religieuse* were to be distributed.

Votes were cast and, once again, the Censors passed *La Religieuse* by a large majority. They did, however, restrict the film to viewers over the age of eighteen, and recommended that it should not be exported to any part of Africa or to Cambodia, Laos, Vietnam, Lebanon, Syria or Madagascar – that is, to countries in which there were French missions, where the locals might not fully appreciate that the film was set in the bad old pre-Revolutionary days, and where they might form a false impression of modern nuns, "whose cultural activities participate in the world-wide radiance of France." Unappeased, Bourges decided to overrule his own Censors, and announced a total ban on Rivette's film. *Le Monde* reported the wording of the Minister's objections:

This decision is motivated by the fact that this film, because of the behaviour of some characters, as of certain situations, and similarly because of the audience and the range of a commercially distributed film, is of a nature to affront gravely the feelings and the consciences of a large part of the population.[16]

To arms, Citizens! Intellectuals, filmmakers, writers and even sympathetic priests hastened to the defense. The 200,000 members of the federation of ciné-clubs volunteered for any form of protest Rivette's group saw fit; Rivette and his fellow film director Claude Chabrol went on a "Free the Nun" tour of French campuses ("Censors belong in convents," Chabrol told their supporters); Beauregard began a legal action against Bourges, accusing him of "misappropriation of power," and began a petition of his own, aiming for the symbolic total of 1,789 signatures; *Paris Presse* leaked a rumour that the members of the Censorship Board were planning to resign as a body, believing that Bourges had made them look like "clowns"; and the editorial columns fired salvo after salvo. The Abbé Lenfantin wrote to *Cahiers du Cinéma* with "tears in my eyes," and rose to a pitch of truly splendid disgust:

Oh, how I should like to have M. Bourges in the secrecy of the confessional! I will tell him, that ignoble servant of a totalitarian State, some home truths. That such men, such fools that one is flabbergasted, exist still and govern us! I say out loud to M. Bourges and to his masters that they will remain in the memory of history on the same grounds as the judges of Flaubert and of Baudelaire – as those powerless curs who cling with all their teeth to the skirts of Beauty![17]

Jean-Luc Godard composed and published two blazing open letters: one in *Le Monde*, in which he sarcastically offered his thanks to Yvon Bourges who, by banning "one of the most celebrated classics of freedom," had shown him the true face of contemporary Fascism; and a still more intemperate one in *Le Nouvel Observateur* to his one-time supporter André Malraux, Minister of Culture, who had not long since rescued his own film *Une Femme mariée* [*A Married Woman*] from "the axe of Peyrefitte."

Being a *cinéaste* [filmmaker] as others are Jews or blacks, I was beginning to be bored with going every time to see you and with asking for you to intercede with your friends Roger Frey and Georges Pompidou to obtain mercy for a film condemned to death by censorship, that gestapo of the spirit. But God in heaven, I did not really think I should have to do so for your brother, Diderot, a journalist and a writer like you, and his *Religieuse*, my sister, that is to say, a French citizen who prays simply to our Father to protect his independence.

Blind man that I was! I should have remembered that letter for which Denis had been put in the Bastille.[18]

For their part, the opponents of *La Religieuse* were equally intemperate. In *Le Figaro Littéraire*, François Mauriac complained that "It would never occur to those who chose to film Diderot's poisoned book to make a film against the Jews – whereas against the Catholics, anything goes!" while the conservative weekly *Carrefour* thundered that "if, in the name of freedom, we let this film be shown, we might as well open the doors of France to all the dirty hairy beatniks of the earth." The plot thickened when the ever-shrewd Malraux gave permission for *La Religieuse* to be screened at Cannes, thereby sparing the French government the embarrassment of seeing the nation's most famous film festival boycotted by each and every one of the French directors whose films had already been submitted for exhibition.

Eventually, Bourges was himself succeeded as Minister of Information by a M. Gorse, and the ban was lifted some thirteen months after its first imposition. In practical terms, it had done Rivette's career no harm at all. Beauregard had been quick to trade on the film's notoriety and sold it to distributors from eight countries, so that *"La Religieuse* became [Rivette's] only solid financial success."[19] On balance, critics around the world treated the film intelligently and with respect, but it is fair to suspect that the majority of audiences were "rather bored" by its uncompromising severity and its remarkable lack of features that any save the most prickly could find offensive.[20] It swiftly became obvious to all who saw the film that outraging the sensibilities of the devout had never been among Rivette's ambitions for the film. So what, then, had the director been hoping to achieve by bringing *La Religieuse* to the screen?

Rivette's involvement with *La Religieuse* began with work on a stage adaptation. While he was still editing his first full-length film, *Paris nous appartient* [*Paris Belongs to Us*] (1960), the director was approached by that film's co-screenwriter, his actor friend Jean Gruault, who had composed the draft of a stage play of Diderot's novel in hotel rooms while on a theatrical tour in Brussels and Switzerland. Since Rivette's various accounts of his own motives in tackling Diderot tend towards the gnomic, not to say cryptic,[21] it is Gruault's recent book of memoirs, *Ce que dit l'autre* [*What the Other One Says*], which offers the clearest and most substantial statement of what the filmmakers found appealing in *La Religieuse*. A man who had spent the better part of three years of his youth in a seminary himself, Gruault introduces the possibility that he was working out some autobiographical themes in his screenplay, only to dismiss it. No, Gruault says, what really appealed to him was the chance to write dialogue rather more elegant and sparkling than the ponderous ruminations and sibylline apophthegms which had filled *Paris nous appartient*. Besides which, he continues, he found himself moved by the plight of a hunted, persecuted young woman who, rather than submitting passively to her fate, fights back with an energy which reminded him of Lillian Gish in *Orphans of the Storm*.[22]

Gruault's completed play had its initial staging in 1960 by the Théâtre Quotidien in Marseille, with Betty Schneider in the title role, and was a

13. Suzanne Simonin (Anna Karina) in her cell in Jacques Rivette's
La Religieuse

great success. In 1963, Rivette directed a new production at the Théâtre
du Studio des Champs-Elysées, with Anna Karina as Suzanne; finance
was provided by Karina's husband, Jean-Luc Godard, and the producer
was Antoine Boursellier. In later years, Rivette was diffident about this
staging: "*La Religieuse* was an opportunity that presented itself, and it
wasn't very successful. Luckily, there was Anna Karina, who wanted to
play the main part. She gave an interest to the play, which was otherwise
quite unsuccessful."[23] The show ran for less than a month, from February
6 to March 5. Critical response to the production appears to have been
at best lukewarm, though *Cahiers du Cinéma* was appropriately loyal: its
reviewer, Jean-Louis Comolli, enthused that it "restored to the theatre a
simplicity, an efficacy and a freedom which it has long been lacking."[24]
Unabashed by the comparative failure of his first venture onto the stage,
Rivette pressed on with plans for a feature film version. When he was
interviewed in 1968 about the place of this film between its predecessor
Paris nous appartient and its successor, *L'Amour fou*, Rivette was modest
and frank: He saw *La Religieuse*, he said:

as a seductive error. At first, I felt like doing it only as an adaptation, in order to get
people to know the book; then there was directing the play, and I felt like filming
the play and sometimes wanted to see passages of it become a film while still

remaining within a theatrical performance ... for me it remains a very theatrical film. I wanted to play on the fact that there were some very theatrical passages, which were intentionally played for a theatrical effect, and that sometimes it became more just physical actions and therefore became cinematic.[25]

Rivette's interest in bringing some of the qualities of the theatre to his film work was not, it should be stressed, an accidental byproduct of his brief career digression onto the stage. The theatre – and, particularly, the process of staging – was the ruling obsession of Rivette's early work. "All films are about the theatre, there is no other subject," ran his memorable declaration to a group of interviewers from *Cahiers du Cinéma*.[26] Thus, *Paris nous appartient* is the story of a young woman (Betty Schneider) who becomes involved in rehearsals for a production of Shakespeare's *Pericles* which never reaches the stage. For *L'Amour fou*, Rivette asked the theatrical producer Jean-Pierre Kalfon to form a company to rehearse Racine's *Andromaque*: part of the film follows their rehearsals to the brink of the first night, while the other part concerns a TV crew who are themselves making a documentary about the performers. Rivette's gargantuan, all but unseen film *Out One: Noli Me Tangere* and its slightly more available shortened (four hours and twenty minutes) version *Out One: Spectre* also depict, among various other matters, the efforts of two rival theatrical troupes as they prepare, but never stage, productions of Aeschylus's *Prometheus* and *Seven Against Thebes*.

In the light of this fascination, *La Religieuse* appears not so much a contradiction of Rivette's usual procedures as a logical complement to them. Where *Paris nous appartient*, *L'Amour fou*, and the *Out One* films show the process of bringing (or failing to bring) a play to the stage, *La Religieuse* displays the end product. In fact, Rivette goes out of his way to signal the theatricality of the enterprise: before the opening credits roll, the soundtrack is filled with the noise of an audience shuffling and murmuring, to be silenced by the traditional *trois coups* [three knocks] which announce that a play is about to begin. The film's first shot also drops a strong hint about the nature of what is to come. Rivette pans to the right over a seated gathering of spectators – our on-screen surrogates – before coming to rest on the image of Suzanne, dressed as a Bride of Christ, being led to her vows behind the grille which separates the sacred world from the profane. Screaming "I have no vocation," she rebels, is dragged away howling, and the tragedy begins to unfold. The religious ceremony, in other words, is regarded as a species of staged performance. Rivette later revealed that he had wanted to sustain the analogy between ritual and performance throughout the film, but had been hampered by the production budget; above all, he regretted that "I couldn't show the ceremonies, the paraphernalia of the offices."[27]

14. Simonin, isolated and oppressed in the convent, in *La Religieuse*

Well and good, and no doubt an accurate account of his aims and errors. But what is odd, almost bizarre about Rivette's repeated emphasis on the essential theatricality of the film is that it so blithely disregards all the qualities which made *La Religieuse* scandalous. He never seems to have abandoned this puzzling reticence. When asked about his reasons for making the film, Rivette gave any number of different accounts, but the property common to all his responses is that they refer exclusively to formal ambitions: questions of tempo, rhythm, cinematic allusion (Mizoguchi), decor and space, even linguistic conceits. At one point, he suggested that "The original idea of *La Religieuse* was a play on words:

making a 'cellular' film, because it was about cells full of nuns." Seconds earlier, however, he had told the very same interviewers that "The origin of *La Religieuse* was mainly music, the ideas of [the avant-garde composer and conductor, Pierre] Boulez – though very badly assimilated. The idea was that each shot had its own duration, its tempo, its 'colour' (that is, its tone), its intensity and its level of play."[28]

Now, contradictory statements, to paraphrase Johnson's Imlac in *Rasselas*, cannot both be true, but they may both be honest, and when Rivette insists that he started *La Religieuse* with an idea about music, or with a pun, or with a desire to investigate theatricality, or with the ambition to imitate Mizoguchi or what have you, what he is presumably saying is that his mind was teeming with all sorts of ideas about his film, some of which found their way into the finished product, some of which became compromised en route, and some of which were simply forgotten or dropped. But not once does he let slip any indiscretion about wanting to attack nuns. In fact, Rivette's words are so thoroughly sober in tone, so guilelessly unruffled by *La Religieuse*'s (still very recent) standing as the greatest popular scandal of French cultural life, that it is almost tempting to see him here as a hapless victim of other people's malign intentions – as a sort of holy innocent, albeit a highly thoughtful innocent, who had simply stepped into a trap built for him by the Church and its fellow travelers. *Suzanne Simonin, c'est lui?* ["For Suzanne Simonin, read Jacques Rivette?"] Well, not quite.

In other words, perhaps the most baffling aspect of the affair of *La Religieuse* is the yawning gap between the way in which the film was conceived by its creators and that in which it was perceived by the pious. On the one side, we have Rivette and Gruault, the director wholly preoccupied with austere questions of cinematic form, the writer full of imaginative sympathy for Diderot's Lillian Gish-like heroine and her fight for freedom; on the other, the irate protestors and their belief that France was threatened by indecency, blasphemy, and sedition. One need not be particularly soft on censorship matters to feel that the splenetic reaction was excessive, especially since it is by no means self-evident that either the novel or the film need be construed as even remotely irreligious. To make this point is not (or not necessarily) to play the rhetorical card which is often brought out when liberal secularists rush to defend works which have outraged the faithful, from Scorsese's *Last Temptation of Christ* to Rushdie's *Satanic Verses* – that is, to argue, however implausibly, for the deep if paradoxical underlying piety of the offending piece. This somewhat embarrassing ploy tends to satisfy neither the faithful (who remain unconvinced) nor the secularists (who do not much care for questions of dogma).

Still, the records imply – more than imply – that both Diderot and Rivette had quite other things on their minds than besmirching the good name of the Catholic Church. It is an enlightening fact that the Church, though it certainly put many of Diderot's works on the Index of prohibited books side by side with the entire oeuvre of Voltaire, chose to let *La Religieuse* go free; that decision indicated greater powers of discrimination than the Index's tarnished reputation would suggest. By and large, modern critics seem to agree with the verdict of the novel's English translator, Leonard Tancock: "It is not an attack upon Christianity, or even the Catholic Church ... The tone throughout is respectful of sincere religion. The attack is against misconceived Christianity, applied by ignorant, warped and unnatural people in a social system where the civil law protects the persecutor and penalises the victim."[29] In similar vein, Peter France observes that "unlike Voltaire in his campaign against the *infâme* [that is, the 'infamous' Church] ... Diderot does not seem to have pursued the religion of his fathers with great venom," and proposes that Diderot's "attitude to nuns is like his attitude to the blind: they can tell him something new about humanity. Thinking about monasteries and convents, he asks: What happens to normal human beings in such (to him) unnatural surroundings? The novel is like the account of a scientific experiment."[30] While Diderot, then, was happy enough to associate himself with such fervent atheists as Holbach, his unbelief was of the serene rather than the militant order. In so far as *La Religieuse* may legitimately be regarded as a satire – and it remains debatable how much real crusading intent can be ascribed to a work deliberately kept private for so many years – it is a satire on the ways in which human beings are driven to cruelty, fanaticism, and despair by their own institutions.

Rivette's private views on Christianity may come as a still greater surprise. Far from sharing the derisive or dismissive atheism of so many young intellectuals of his generation, he seems to have been a startlingly ardent believer, and his youthful critical writings bear witness to his wish to bear Christian witness. Take his extraordinary essay on Rosselini's film *Voyage to Italy*, a magnificent and anguished portrait of a marriage in crisis which ends, or appears to end, with the couple being reconciled by the action of Divine Grace.[31] Rivette declares in his review that "Rossellini's genius is possible only within Christianity"; that Rossellini's burden (of which Rivette manifestly approves in the strongest terms) is "that only a life in God, in his love and his sacraments, only the communion of saints can enable us to meet, to know, to possess another being than ourselves alone; and that one can only know and possess oneself in God"; and – a disconcerting maxim – that Rossellini "is not merely Christian, but Catholic; in other words, carnal to the point of scandal." Out of that

Catholic carnality, the young Rivette believed, a new form of cinema was about to emerge – "our cinema, those of us who are in our turn preparing to make films."[32] He continues:

A fig for the sceptics, the rational, the judicious; irony and sarcasm have had their day; now it is time to love the cinema so much that one has little taste left for what presently passes by that name, and wants to impose a more exacting image of it.[33]

There is not a single sequence in *La Religieuse* which suggests that Rivette had, a decade later, come to rue his fervent expressions of Catholic belief, or his hopes for the cinema he thought adumbrated in Rosselini's great film. As in the novel, the genuinely pious characters of Rivette's work are treated with due respect, and Suzanne's own yearnings towards the comforts of faith – her prayers and claspings of the cross – are never made to seem hypocritical, hysterical, or grotesque. To an agnostic viewer, the film will appear either to be dispassionately neutral towards Christian faith or, possibly, to be exercised with distinctions between sincere religion and the corrupt exploitation of religious institutions by their senior members. It will also – recall the words of Gruault's memoir and Godard's protest to Malraux – appear to be a film greatly preoccupied with the question of freedom, and not only the freedom of the cloistered.[34] For all that, it would be wrong to conclude that Rivette's detractors were simply making a fuss about nothing.

"The cinema," Rivette once maintained, "is necessarily fascination and rape": a strong contender for his most arresting policy statement ever, though it has many worthy competitors elsewhere in his writings and interviews.[35] The enemies of *La Religieuse* might not have put their case in quite those pungent terms, and certainly not in a spirit of approval, and yet their very outrage at Rivette's work hints a curious kind of intuitive acquiescence in its essential accuracy. With the hindsight of three decades, it becomes clearer than ever that those who opposed *La Religieuse* were frequently objecting not so much to any particular repugnant aspect of the film – loyal as it demonstrably was to Diderot's readily available novel – as to its having been made as a film at all. The wording of Bourges's original complaint repays attention: what he has in mind as a censor, what alarms him most, is "the audience and the range of a commercially distributed film." Bourges's assumption here is surely that film is a massively more potent and dangerous medium than print – a view that may or may not stand up to serious scrutiny, but which has often been at the heart of debates on cinema censorship.[36] Film, so the Bourges-oisie of the world has long assumed, can inflame the passions of the young, the irresponsible and the illiterate – both at home and in our colonial possessions – as the chillier and more elite medium of the printed word can never do; it bypasses the critical faculties even of the supposedly educated mind; it shouts to the mob in darkened rooms, where literature murmurs to the discerning, solitary individual. All highly dubious assumptions, all ripe for vigorous rebuttal; and yet the young Rivette who said that the cinema is "necessarily fascination and rape" was conceding that the powers of his adopted medium are indeed peculiarly overwhelming. To take this article of faith as seriously as Rivette did may involve the surrender of at least one patch of the moral high ground to those driven by the urge to keep cinema safely under wraps. In short, at a deeper, quieter level than the rowdy to-and-fro of public debate, Rivette and his censors were in a surprising degree of accord.

To be sure, the affair of *La Religieuse* was, like the *Chatterley* trial and other highly publicized censorship cases, something of a media circus and a five minutes' wonder, but – again, like other such cases – it also touched on issues of policy and aesthetics which have yet to be settled at all satisfactorily. The fight to free *La Religieuse* can easily be presented as nothing more than an all-too-familiar conflict between faith and secularism, conservatives and progressives, censors and libertarians. In another light, though, while it was indeed a battle over issues of faith, the contesting beliefs were not only those of Christianity and Enlightenment humanism. They included the convictions held by those puritans who instinctively dread the power of moving images to stir unruly emotions, and those held by all the filmmakers and viewers who are – at least at times – willing to invoke and relish that potentially hazardous power.

NOTES

1 Of the first half dozen histories of French cinema I consulted by way of putting this assumption to the test, only one so much as mentioned the film in passing.
2 Elliot Stein, "*Suzanne Simonin, Diderot's Nun*," *Sight and Sound* (Summer 1966), 133.
3 For a sympathetic general treatment of this topic, see Sara Gwenllian Jones, "Sexing the Soul: Nuns and Lesbianism in Mainstream Film," *Perversions* 1 (1994–95), 41–59. I owe this reference to Peter Swaab.
4 Tom Milne, untitled review of *La Religieuse*, *Sight and Sound* (Winter 1967/8), 38–9.
5 David Thomson, *A Biographical Dictionary of Film* (London: Andre Deutsch, 1994), p. 636.
6 Jonathan Rosenbaum, Lauren Sedofsky, and Gilbert Adair, "Interview with Jacques Rivette," *Film Comment* (September 1974), 24.
7 Stein, "*Suzanne Simonin*," 131.
8 Jacques Bontemps, "Jottings from Other Publications," *Cahiers du Cinéma in English*, 7 (January 1967), 6–7, 64.

9 A short list of criticism in English should include Milne (see note 4); Peter Lloyd, "Jacques Rivette and *L'Amour Fou*," in *Mongram* 2 (Summer 1971), 12; and James Monaco, *The New Wave* (Oxford and New York: Oxford University Press, 1976), pp. 315–18.

10 Charles Baudelaire, *Baudelaire*, introduced and edited by Francis Scarfe (Harmondsworth: Penguin, 1961), p. 33.

11 I owe the details of this account mainly to the relevant sections of Denis Diderot, *The Nun*, intro. and trans., Leonard Tancock (Harmondsworth: Penguin, 1974); Peter France, *Diderot* (Oxford: Oxford University Press, 1983); Vivienne Mylne, *Diderot: La Religieuse* (London: Grant and Cutler, 1981); and Christine Clark-Evans, *Diderot's La Religieuse: A Philosophical Novel* (Montreal: CERES, 1995). Reference to Diderot's novel will be to the 1974 Penguin edition and will be given parenthetically in the text.

12 The question of Suzanne's precise degree of sexual ignorance is considered at great length in Eve Kosofsky Sedgwick, "Privilege of Unknowing," in *Tendencies* (London: Routledge, 1994), pp. 23–51. Sedgwick considers the narrator "unmistakably a pain in the neck" (28).

13 In an interesting essay "Génie de la Mélancholie" ["Genius of Melancholy"], in which she proposes that Rivette's body of work as a whole may be regarded as belonging to an allegorical tradition of Melancholy (that discussed by certain art historians, notably Panofsky and Saxl), Suzanne Liandrat-Guiges suggests that this terminal shot is crucial to Rivette's melancholic intentions. Suzanne Liandrat-Guiges, *Jacques Rivette, critique et cinéaste* (*Etudes cinématographiques* Vol. 63) (Paris–Caen: Minard, 1998), 38.

14 Tancock, introduction to *The Nun*, pp. 7–8.

15 Bontemps, "Jottings," 6.

16 Bontemps, "Jottings," 7.

17 Bontemps, "Jottings," 7.

18 Bontemps, "Jottings," 7.

19 Monaco, *New Wave*, p. 306.

20 Thomson, *Biographical Dictionary*, p. 636.

21 And since, I am obliged to confess, he made no reply to my requests for an interview.

22 Jean Gruault, *Ce que dit l'autre* (Paris: Julliard, 1992), p. 190.

23 Rosenbaum et al., "Interview with Rivette," 23. It seems only fair to add that Anna Karina's memories of the run are quite different. When I interviewed her in July 2001, she recalled a considerable hit – houses packed with profusely weeping spectators of the most fashionable and glamorous kind. Brigitte Bardot, she stressed, had been spotted in the audience.

24 Jean-Louis Comolli, "Théâtre" [Review of the stage production of *La Religieuse*], *Cahiers du Cinéma* 142 (April 1963), 38.

25 Jonathan Rosenbaum, *Jacques Rivette: Texts and Interviews* (London: British Film Institute, 1977), p. 29.

26 Rosenbaum, *Rivette*, pp. 36–7. This remark seems even stranger when taken out of context. A partial explanation of what Rivette meant by the assertion that films have "no other subject" but the theatre follows a few lines later: "Because that is the subject of truth and lies, and there is no other in the cinema:

it is necessarily a questioning about truth, with means that are necessarily untruthful. Performance as the subject." Rosenbaum, *Rivette*, p. 27.

27 Monaco, *New Wave*, p. 316.

28 Rosenbaum, *Rivette*, p. 30.

29 Tancock, introduction to *The Nun*, p. 11.

30 France, *Diderot*, pp. 37, 38.

31 Rosenbaum, *Rivette*, pp. 54–64; the Rossellini essay was first published in *Cahiers du Cinema* 46 (April 1955).

32 Rosenbaum, *Rivette*, pp. 58, 62, 63, 64.

33 Rosenbaum, *Rivette*, pp. 64.

34 Rivette's film has notable formal similarities to many prison movies, and above all – though in interviews, the director was anxious to play down any suggestion of direct influence by Robert Bresson – of *Un condamné à mort s'est échappé*.

35 Rosenbaum, *Rivette*, p. 37.

36 Compare, for example, the highly publicized debates and wrangles between producers and censors over the film versions of *A Clockwork Orange*, *The Last Temptation of Christ*, J. G. Ballard's *Crash*, or even – in some parts of the world – *The Canterbury Tales*.

9

Adaptation and cultural criticism:
Les Liaisons dangereuses 1960 and
Dangerous Liaisons

Richard Frohock

Choderlos de Laclos's epistolary novel *Les Liaisons dangereuses* (1782) has
proven to be of continual interest to European and American filmmakers.
Five major adaptations of the novel have been made for cinema and television in the span of four decades.[1] These adaptations have received much
attention from film and literature scholars, but the question of the novel's
appeal persists: what makes this eighteenth-century novel attractive for
repeated retellings on screen? Although some of the filmmakers retain
an eighteenth-century setting, the continual adaptations do not result
from an abiding interest in dramatizing the decadent aristocratic culture of pre-Revolutionary France; rather, filmmakers are drawn to this
eighteenth-century narrative because of its usefulness as a basis for examining and critiquing contemporary culture. Written at the end of over a
century of sustained European consideration of the libertine in literature,
Laclos's *Les Liaisons dangereuses* presents the complex relations among
sex, sadism, gender, and power in notoriously ambiguous terms. Its fascinating and repulsive characters, driven by sometimes ambivalent motives,
provide filmmakers with wide-ranging possibilities for assessing, from
various viewpoints, the manifestations of libertine philosophy within their
own cultural experience.

A comparison of the male and female libertine protagonists in Roger
Vadim's *Les Liaisons dangereuses 1960* and Stephen Frears's *Dangerous
Liaisons* (1988) – both to Laclos's original and to one another – illustrates
the range of interpretive opportunities that Laclos's characters present.
Vadim transfers Laclos's plot and characters to 1960, and Frears painstak-
ingly recreates an eighteenth-century world through Academy Award-
winning costumes, sets, and script.[2] Both, however, exploit the potential
Laclos's novel offers filmmakers for illuminating the libertinism of their
own cultures. One key to understanding the interpretive intentions of
each adapter is the implicit and/or explicit account of the motives behind
characters' sexual predations in the films themselves. A second key is
the filmmakers' perceptions of the cultural ethoi they inhabit and their
conviction that their art – or even their lives – can function as cultural

critique. In autobiography or in interview, both filmmakers have broadly summarized their views of the dominant cultural climate in which they made their films and have assessed their art as serving political, social, even moral purposes. The striking differences between the adaptations and the sometimes antithetical realizations of the principal libertines by these two filmmakers are less attributable to their interest in fidelity to Laclos than to the intent to critique a dominant cultural ethos variously configured by each filmmaker.[3]

Valmont, Laclos's male libertine protagonist, embodies principles and evinces motives articulated in libertine literature of the period. In its seventeenth- and eighteenth-century context, libertinism was viewed as a part of the Enlightenment impulse to free the individual from the constraints of traditional social authority. As John Wilmot, Earl of Rochester argues in *A Satyr against Reason and Mankind* (1679), reasonable people should allow desire, rather than convention, to govern behavior:

> Your reason hinders, mine helps to enjoy,
> Renewing appetites yours would destroy.
> My reason is my friend, yours is a cheat;
> Hunger calls out, my reason bids me eat;
> Perversely, yours your appetite does mock:
> This asks for food, that answers, "What's o'clock?"[4]

The motives for and meanings of Valmont's sexual promiscuity include and exceed Rochester's simple injunction to disregard social mores in fulfilling natural appetites. As scholars have observed, the sexual pursuits of many Enlightenment libertines have more to do with the accumulation of power than with the gratification of the senses.[5] Like Dorimant, the rakish protagonist in Sir George Etherege's *The Man of Mode* (1676), who "has subordinated sensuality to aggression, discovering in sexual pursuit the triumph of the will and celebration of the ego," Laclos's Valmont places much of the value of his sexual pursuits in the social prestige they afford him.[6] The full gratification of sexual conquest is not complete for Valmont until it has been publicized, often through Merteuil, who plans ultimately to write his memoirs for him.[7] In a world of inverted values, seduction becomes a heroic act, as Valmont's frequent military metaphors indicate: as he writes to Merteuil, "we are fated to be conquerors and we must follow our destiny" (14). A chief ambition of conquerors is fame derived from public celebration of their feats.

In addition to physical pleasure and social esteem, Laclos's Valmont aims to assert, through sexual conquests, his capacity to transcend mortality. Valmont aspires not only to secure his reputation as the greatest male seducer of his time but also to become the absolute maker of his own fate and to create others in his own image. In addition to military language, Valmont uses religious metaphors to describe his pursuits, such as when he writes of Tourvel "I shall truly be the God whom she loves best" (20). Not only does he, in the course of the seduction, become the object of adoration and worship. Valmont is nothing if not methodical in his endeavors, and a successful seduction confirms for him his power to transcend accident, happenstance, and providence and control destiny. Letter 71, in which Valmont describes his seduction of the Vicomtesse de M—, encapsulates key components of Valmont's philosophic libertinism. The appeal of the seduction is cerebral more than corporeal: Valmont is attracted by the challenge of the situation – the Vicomtesse occupies a room situated between her husband's and her lover's – and he stresses to Merteuil that he wants to do precisely that which is considered to be "impossible" by the Vicomtesse. When the Vicomtesse accidentally locks herself out of her room, Valmont thinks of a ruse to save her reputation, priding himself on his refusal "to be at the mercy of events like any ordinary mortal," and triumphantly proclaiming, "how could I allow a woman to be ruined through me but not by me?" (136). For Valmont, sexual conquests are confirmations of the quasi-divine powers of man, and he fittingly describes himself as a *"deus ex machina"* (145). Valmont concludes his anecdote by casually stating that Merteuil need not keep it to herself; the escapade promises to provide further pleasure to Valmont through its dissemination.

In his film *Liaisons dangereuses 1960* (1959), Vadim presents a Valmont who differs considerably from the original in motivation and intent. For Vadim's Valmont, sexual pleasure is a primary goal rather than a means to an end. In his confession to Marianne Tourvel, Valmont explains: "In love we [Valmont and Juliette] sought only pleasure, all the pleasures; even to the point where pleasure itself becomes pain. You think that everything is finished; but it's not. You can still go further, and further."[8] Vadim's Valmont, in contrast to the original, does not insist that sex serve as a means of increasing social prestige or power: when Juliette proposes to him that he seduce Cecile, he does not hesitate on the grounds that the seduction is beneath his abilities and therefore a detraction from his reputation. This Valmont is not concerned with positive or negative publicity. Vadim emphasizes instead the pleasure Valmont takes in defying sexual taboos, heightening the audacity of the seduction by making Cecile Valmont's cousin.

If Vadim's Valmont has an agenda, it is to live according to inclination – Rochester's "right reason" – rather than convention. Vadim avoids making his Valmont too deliberate in his actions or too explicit about his purposes, and in this regard, too, Vadim's Valmont differs significantly from Laclos's original. Whereas Laclos's Valmont calculatingly seeks out Tourvel, choosing her as a target because of the degree of difficulty involved in seducing a woman known for her high moral standards and the notoriety her seduction will garner for him, Vadim's Valmont accidentally encounters her on the ski slope after he has taken a fall. Only later does he begin to describe Tourvel as an "enemy worthy of my powers" (87) and speak of his desire to demonstrate that there are no "impregnable fortresses" (102). In addition, Vadim's Valmont plays no part in the exposure of Juliette – he never communicates her secrets to Danceny. Even the manner of death of this Valmont is freakishly accidental: when Danceny strikes him, Valmont falls, cracks his head on andirons, and dies. In contrast to Laclos's original, Vadim's Valmont works neither to aggrandize the self nor to probe his capacity to rise above all circumstances and direct his fate and the fates of others.

Vadim's transformation of Valmont's motives reflects his interest in exploring libertinism in contemporary rather than Enlightenment terms. Whereas it is difficult to know how Laclos viewed his protagonist, Vadim's description of his own way of life in his autobiography *Memoirs of the Devil* (1975) suggests that he remade Laclos's character approvingly in his own image.[9] Vadim complains that throughout his career critics in the press have labeled him in a variety of ways, yet Vadim repudiates all such classifications. He denies that he is an existentialist, insisting that there was no distinct philosophy behind his way of life in his early years (61); he disallows that he was ever a Machiavellist, arguing that he was merely "a victim of circumstance" (96); and he disputes the label of hedonist, claiming, "I have always met my political responsibilities" (100). Tales of his profligacy in the years prior to the making of *Les Liaisons dangereuses 1960* were greatly exaggerated, he insists: "The papers were full of stories of extravagant spending, scandal and debauchery, with us [Vadim, Brigitte Bardot, and Françoise Sagan] cast in the leading roles. Cha-cha sessions on the Esquinade and our pitched battles with sodawater syphons took on epic proportions. And yet it was only the carefree playfulness of children who refused to grow up despite being successful and almost thirty" (110). Vadim, in opposing "carefree playfulness" to all attempts to characterize his life in terms of an distinct philosophy with identifiable principles, sharply distinguishes himself from his friend Roger Vailland, co-author of the *Les Liaisons dangereuses 1960* screenplay, whom he describes as something closer to the eighteenth-century model of the libertine: "Like the saints, he was extremely strict in the application of philosophical and intellectual ideas to his private life . . . He has frequently been depicted as an intellectual and a libertine. Perhaps he was" (113–14). Vadim's Valmont, who reacts to situations more than he creates them and who is not explicit about his philosophy, is better characterized by Vadim's non-dogmatic disregard for social constraint rather than Vailland's systematic enactment of intellectual principles. Vadim identified filmmaker with character in an interview in which he declared "Valmont? C'est moi!"[10]

In adapting Valmont to the screen, Vadim exploits the potential of this libertine character in order to critique a conservative culture burdened with needless inhibitions. Thus, in *Memoirs of the Devil*, Vadim situates his filmmaking career in a time of cultural change when new notions of sexuality – famously conveyed, for example, by Bardot in Vadim's first film *And God Created Woman* (1956) – challenged conservative values, represented by the Censor's Committee and "family men." "Smashing the strictures of the old morality, [Bardot] was giving the world its first taste of the new morality, upsetting the Ten Commandments by showing that sex was no longer a sin" (3). For Vadim, this revision of attitudes toward sexuality had wider cultural implications; adjusting the relationship of sex and sin involved a destabilization of traditional notions of marriage and the family. In Vadim's adaptation, Valmont and Juliette freely break the rules of marriage in order to avoid sexual boredom. In addition, the film's libertinism is strongly associated with jazz, which relies on improvisation and generates power and novelty by defying traditional conventions of modality, harmony, and rhythm. Thus, for Vadim, libertinism in 1960 is part of a widespread challenge to traditional constraints in various cultural arenas, from sexuality and domesticity to music and filmmaking itself.

In his *Memoirs*, Vadim argues that he is not the devil solely responsible for cultural revolution, though he finds the accusation flattering. Vadim relishes the idea that he was on the vanguard of a large shift in ethos that had impetus beyond that supplied by his films and that was unstoppable for the censors and other cultural conservatives. As Vadim delights in noting, his film, so scandalous upon its release in 1959, and barred from export for three years, could be broadcast on television fourteen years later "to a family audience, on a Sunday" without any complaints (117). The new morality had lost its capacity to shock after it had succeeded in displacing the "moral order" that was "the order of the day" in 1959 (116). Vadim's transformation of Valmont's motives indicates his participation in, and approval of, the emergence of a new morality at a culturally conservative time. The libertinism of his Valmont constitutes an implicit, rather than explicit, revolutionary critique: instead of demanding, or even theorizing, a new morality, Vadim's Valmont simply manifests its arrival by refusing to be limited by existing moral codes.

By contrast, Frears creates a Valmont in *Dangerous Liaisons* (1989) who acts in accordance with a clearly defined set of libertine principles.

Frears's Valmont docs not simply seek liberation in breaking taboos, and sexual pleasure is, for him, of secondary importance.[11] Like Laclos's original character, Frears's Valmont is more immediately concerned with the social esteem and the "celebration of the ego" that seductions bring him. In Frears's film Valmont is guided in his choices by a larger libertine framework in which he sees himself as heroic conqueror, ever in pursuit of more prestige and fame. He declines Merteuil's suggestion that he seduce Cecile on the grounds that it would be too simple and therefore might damage his "reputation,"[12] and explains the necessity for disappointing Merteuil by declaring "I have to follow my destiny. I have to be true to my profession" (9). Frears's Valmont agrees to seduce Cecile only when he has his own revenge to enact against her mother, Madame Volanges, for warning Tourvel about his character and reputation.[13] Frears parallels Valmont to Tourvel, his primary victim, by depicting him as committed to libertinism with the same fervor as she is to Christian ethics.

Frears is more faithful to Laclos in rendering Valmont on screen, but like Vadim his characterization of Valmont is also guided by an interest in critiquing contemporary culture. Although Frears does not modernize the story in the explicit way that Vadim does, he nonetheless creates a film that is a comment on the 1980s as well as, if not more than, pre-Revolutionary France. Scholars have noted the topicality and political engagement of much British cinema in the 1980s, particularly the frequent attacks on Margaret Thatcher's economic and social policies.[14] At the center of the ideology of Thatcherism was, as Leonard Quart describes it, the creation of an "individualist ethos and an entrepreneurial culture where the acquisition of wealth and the consumption of goods became the prime values, while the ethic of social responsibility and mutual aid began to unravel. It was now more stylish 'to consume rather than to care.'"[15] Scholars have furthermore situated Frears's films of the 1980s – *My Beautiful Laundrette* (1986), *Prick up Your Ears* (1987), and *Sammy and Rosie Get Laid* (1988) – within this anti-Thatcher cinematic movement,[16] and Frears himself has described *Sammy and Rosie Get Laid* as "an attempt to bring Margaret Thatcher down."[17] The topicality of *Dangerous Liaisons* is less overt, but in an interview Frears, at first somewhat resistant to the idea, gradually works his way toward an acknowledgement of his interest in illuminating cultural similarities between the 1780s and the 1980s:

Dangerous Liaisons, for example, isn't clearly about the conditions in Britain, although people try to suggest it is. It may well be, however, that my interest in the material, in the novel, is due to these deeper interests. When the play [Christopher Hampton's *Les Liaisons Dangereuses* (1985)] came out it was a huge success. Somehow it captured the spirit of the times: when very rich people

15. The libertine Valmont (John Malkovich) in Stephen Frears's *Dangerous Liaisons*

behaved very selfishly. Some people think that's the way we are now, which may be some of the reason behind its success... Seeing the same ways we all behave, that was what we were really after. It was actually quite the opposite of trying to construct a portrait of the [eighteenth-century] society. At the time, you start to notice certain things going on underneath the basic information, attitudes between people that are very similar, things you're more interested in than to merely reconstruct.[18]

Frears's interest in matters beyond reconstruction – his interest in critiquing 1980s British culture – manifests itself in his creation of a libertine who embodies cultural traits that Frears perceives to be common to both cultural environments: conspicuous consumption, class arrogance, and a diminished sense of social responsibility. For instance, Frears unveils Valmont (and Merteuil) slowly to viewers in a dressing sequence that shows servants preparing them for the day. They are surrounded by ostentatious wealth evident in the rows of shoes, wigs, and perfumes from which they make their selections, and they command an excessive number of servants to tend to all of their needs (one even trims Valmont's nostril hair). The elaborate dressing rituals not only indicate that these heroes are preparing for battle but also provide the first indication of the inordinate consumption that is part of their moral failing. Vadim, by contrast, uses clothing for symbolic black and white contrasts, and indicates the bestial nature of Juliette by dressing her in furs.

In keeping with his critical emphases, Frears dramatizes the exploitation of the lower class by the wealthy, showing, for instance, Valmont's coercion of Tourvel's maid and her naked powerlessness to resist. Frears also chooses to dramatize Valmont's attempt to convince Tourvel that he is reforming into a compassionate humanitarian by staging an act of charity for Tourvel's footman to observe. Frears's Valmont and Azolan, his servant, comment ironically on the experience of relieving an impoverished family:

VALMONT And all that humble gratitude. It was most affecting.
AZOLAN Certainly brought a tear to my eye. (15)

Frears's decision to film this scene and Hampton's anti-sentimental dialogue underscore the theme of the callousness of the rich to the poor. The episode works as a neat inversion by making an act of charity exploitative and self-serving: saving a family from destitution matters only as it may advance the ends of the competitive individualist, whose entrepreneurial spirit and pursuit of consumable goods (in this instance Tourvel herself) override all other concerns. Because the exploitation of one class by another is not an important theme for Vadim, he includes no parallel scenes in his film.

Laclos's malleable male libertine serves each filmmaker as a means of leveling broad cultural critique, though from opposing points of view. For Vadim, Valmont illuminates cultural problems by challenging dominant mores and representing an alternative to them; for Frears, Valmont exemplifies a dominant culture that stands in need of social and moral reform. Frears's Valmont, in a sense, follows societal rules rather than breaks them – he can be understood as exceptionally adept in a world that institutionalizes selfish ambition. In Frears's film, characters beyond Valmont and Merteuil are similarly self-serving and unscrupulous (they are like in kind, if not degree). After all, an embarrassed Madame Volanges has difficulty explaining to Cecile why she, along with everyone else, receives Valmont in spite of his scandalous reputation (4). And, when Valmont tells tales about Madame Volanges's former profligacy to Cecile, those tales are never exposed as the stratagems they are in the novel. Little or no space remains for a moral critique from within the film: Frears levels his attack at a culture that produces people with Valmont's values, not at a single profligate who has invented his own immoral code of living.

A comparison of the Merteuils, the female libertine protagonist as she appears in the novel and is transformed in the two films, also reveals each filmmaker's perception of contemporary culture and interests in critique. Laclos's presentation of Merteuil's motives indicates that, in his view, libertine theory and practice are gendered. Whereas Laclos's Merteuil shares Valmont's penchant for military metaphors – such as when she claims that she must "conquer or die in the attempt" (169) – she does not share in all the motives for his libertinism. Valmont enjoys augmenting his notoriety, but Merteuil must take all possible precautions to avoid being implicated in any sexual intrigue. She cannot seek the pleasures of publicity and rakish reputation as he can (her fame as libertine can be established only posthumously). Given that she must constantly play roles in order to continue safely in her chosen way of life, Merteuil makes use of metaphors of the theater as much as she does metaphors of battle. Moreover, Merteuil seems to have little interest in experiencing quasi-divinity in the manner in which Valmont seeks it. While Valmont wishes to become Tourvel's god and transcend the limits of humanity, Merteuil, as has often been noted, is interested primarily in transgressing the social limits placed upon women. Although she occasionally uses transcendent language similar to Valmont's in order to describe herself – such as when she tells him, "if you don't spend the rest of your life offering up thanks to me, you're an ungrateful beast" (177) – Merteuil is more focused on defining her freedom in relation to men, and exercising vengeance on them, for their confinement of the female sex.

Merteuil articulates her feminist motives most explicitly in Letter 81, in which she declares bluntly to Valmont that she has been "born to avenge my sex and subjugate yours" (162). Rather than following societal rules fashioned for her sex, she creates and lives by her own principles and can describe herself as a truly "self-made woman" (163). In Enlightenment fashion, she rejects sentiment in favor of rationality and relies on her own observation, rather than traditional authority, for instruction and guidance. She seeks to gain knowledge rather than pleasure from experience, explaining: "I didn't want the delights of love, I wanted to know about it" (164). Her self-education is systematic: writing of her first sexual experience, she declares, "I took accurate note of the pain and the pleasure and saw my various sensations merely as a means of gathering information for later evaluation" (165). She also reads novels, philosophers, and moralists to educate herself in "what you could do, what you ought to think, and the appearances you must keep up" (166).

As she learns to circumvent the limitations placed on women – inadequate education, restricted ability to control (sexual) behavior and to determine identity – Merteuil also seeks to punish men for their presumptions and willingness to exploit society's double standards regarding sexual promiscuity. Her motive in corrupting Cecile is to make Belleroche, who has slighted her, publicly ridiculous. This desire to punish is most clearly illustrated in her account of her affair with Prévan, a rake who plots to seduce and expose her. She outmaneuvers him, however, by consenting to having sex with him and then falsely accusing him of attempted rape, which results in his imprisonment. For the female libertine, power is exercised to make the point that women need to be avenged for the oppressions they suffer and the social disadvantages with which men burden them. Merteuil appropriately describes herself as a "modern Dalila," capable of bringing the powerful male to a catastrophic fall (168).

Vadim's Juliette – his version of Merteuil – articulates different motives for her libertine behavior. As several critics have lamented, Vadim's Juliette loses the feminist agenda of Laclos's Merteuil.[19] Juliette's only explicit analysis of her sexual promiscuity comes early in the film when she is having a conversation with her would-be suitor, Prévan. In the exchange, she indicates that her open marriage with Valmont is a way of avoiding the ennui that plagues other couples: "Look around you. What do you see? The women are as bored with their lovers as they are with their husbands. With Valmont I am never bored" (27). Her libertinism, like Valmont's, seems embedded in an interest in abandoning social mores for a more fulfilling, less inhibited life.[20] Vadim reduces Prévan's role to that of rebuffed lover in order to make this comparatively insipid point. The possibilities for dramatizing sexual double standards, woman's social confinement, or the vengeance of a suppressed gender remain untapped.

Although Juliette's interest in transgressing sexual protocols mirrors Valmont's, she and her husband are not, finally, the same type of libertine. Although Claude Brulé, one of the screenwriters for Vadim's film, describes Valmont and Juliette both as "monsters," it becomes clear in the course of the film that Juliette is the more monstrous of the two.[21] Danceny calls Juliette "even worse" than Valmont (239), and several moments in the film encourage viewers to accept his judgment. For instance, Vadim films a portrait of Juliette that hangs in their apartment and depicts her "entirely nude, a black, spiny plant twisted about her body" (28). A note in the screenplay makes the symbolism of this painting explicit:

16. Juliette (Jeanne Moreau), the female libertine as *femme fatale*, in Roger Vadim's *Les Liaisons dangereuses 1960*

"Painted in the surrealist style, her naked body, twined in thorny tendrils, seems poisonous and evil" (222). In keeping with this vilification of Juliette, the screenplay indicates that she "seems harder now, inhuman" when she confronts Valmont with loving Marianne (159); by contrast, Valmont is never dehumanized in this manner.[22]

Juliette's wickedness is consistent with traits of female protagonists as depicted in *film noir*.[23] In prominent examples of the genre from the 1940s and 1950s, male and female protagonists cooperate in immoral practices, yet, frequently, the woman is the more devilish of the two, often instigating and drawing the man into crime, and for her greater culpability she often receives the greater punishment.[24] This pattern is evident in Vadim's adaptation: Juliette is the attractive, yet deadly and essentially evil, seductress, whereas her male counterpart is, by contrast, more innocently pleasure-seeking. When Juliette burns herself at the end of the film, the scar on her face "disfigures her without, however, making her horrible" (254). As in the novel, Madame Volanges provides the interpretation of her disfigurement: "Her face is the image of her soul" (255). Vadim's Valmont, although treacherous, is never presented as being corrupted to the core in an analogous way.

Laclos created his Merteuil at a time when women were socially, economically, and politically disenfranchised with little reason to hope for improvement. Merteuil offers this gender discrimination as a primary motive for her behavior, and Laclos is widely held to have sympathized with Merteuil's complaints if not her solutions to social injustice. His unpublished (and unfinished) essays on the education of women indicate that he was something of an early feminist himself.[25] Because of the legitimacy of her grievances, some readers interpret Laclos's triple punishment of Merteuil through ostracism, financial ruin, and disfigurement by smallpox as belying the author's true sentiments although it was necessary to appease the censors who demanded retribution for crime. In contrast, Vadim wrote at a time when new opportunities for women were emergent, and the attributes he gives to his female libertine are characteristic of a larger cultural vilification of the woman of power. Scholars have interpreted the prevalence of the *femme fatale* of *film noir* as a misogynist response to women's advancements during and after World War II. Less confined to domestic spheres, women were enjoying new prominence in powerful arenas, and this social shift was widely perceived as threatening.[26] Vadim's Juliette wields significant economic and political power: as one of her party guests comments, "She has enough ambition for two" (21), and her ambition is realized in that, during the course of the film, she manages to get her husband a commission for the United Nations. Powerful herself and directing her husband's fate, she is emblematic of threatening social transformations. Responding to a cultural moment in which women's rights were expanding, Vadim exchanges Merteuil's feminist motives for Juliette's unaccountable evil and uses Laclos's character to make a case for women having less rather than more power; there is no temptation to interpret her fall in the denouement as belying the author's judgment of her. Vadim not only strips Juliette of Merteuil's feminist agenda but also fashions her into an embodiment of anti-feminist sentiments.[27]

Frears's Merteuil is very unlike Vadim's Juliette. Frears's Merteuil articulates, in condensed form, the rationale and purpose of her libertine behavior in terms that echo Merteuil's self-description in Letter 81, and she thereby reintroduces the feminist motives of Laclos's protagonist. Explaining her libertinism in terms of sexual politics, she complains of the passive, dominated role she is "condemned to" as woman (25). Like Laclos's character, Frears's Merteuil believes her destiny is to revenge her sex – "I was born to dominate your sex and avenge my own" – and she describes her self-education and preparation for that task in equally systematic terms:

I learned how to look cheerful, while under the table I stuck a fork into the back of my hand. I became a virtuoso of deceit. It wasn't pleasure I was after, it was knowledge. I consulted the strictest moralists to learn how to appear, philosophers to find out what to think and novelists to see what I could get away with. And, in the end, I distilled everything down to one wonderfully simple principle: win or die. (26)

Although Frears's Merteuil is in this sense more faithful to Laclos's original and verbalizes a larger agenda that Juliette lacks, scholars have noted that the feminism of Frears's character is not, finally, as pronounced as in the novel.[28] This point is valid, especially when one considers that the Prévan narrative, the primary example of Merteuil's philosophy in practice, is dropped completely from Frears's version. In having Prévan arrested under the false accusation of rape, the original Merteuil takes vengeance on a man who intended to exploit sexual double standards by seducing her, publicizing her indiscretion, and consequently ruining her reputation. Merteuil outwits and punishes him for his attempt, thereby giving Valmont and readers an excellent example of her manner of avenging her sex and dominating males. Thus, in spite of Frears's inclusion of a feminist rationale for his Merteuil, the triumph of his character over the limitations and double standards placed on her sex is less prominent than it is in Laclos's novel.

Instead, the primary conflict for Frears's Merteuil is internalized. In his portrayal of libertinism, Frears indicates that the culturally sanctioned desire to aggrandize the self involves the willful suppression of sentiment, which may return involuntarily and disruptively for the libertine. This holds true for male and female libertines, and therefore Frears, finally, makes less distinction and creates more symmetry between his male and female protagonists than any other adapter of *Les Liaisons dangereuses*. Frears relishes the duplicity of his libertines: Merteuil is frequently associated with mirrors that split her image and suggest not only her calculated deception and her love of theater but also her fractured sense of self.[29] She is not a source of evil, doubled in a surrealist painting like Juliette, but is, like Frears's Valmont, the product of a materialist culture that encourages suppressing, even mocking, sentiment in the interest of validating the egotistic will. The culture that sanctions this orientation toward the world – rather than a culture that oppresses women, or the powerful woman as evil incarnate – is the primary target at which Frears aims through his characterization of Merteuil.

A comparison of final scenes in the two films underscores the different conceptions of the moral failings represented in Vadim's Juliette and Frears's Merteuil. The former, disfigured by fire (just as the original Merteuil, who is scarred by smallpox) has her evil soul publicly exposed. Frears, by contrast, does not punish Merteuil corporally for her crimes, and he also eschews the political rendering of the final scene of Hampton's stage play, *Les Liaisons dangereuses* (1985), which indexes the imminent collapse of the French aristocracy by depicting Merteuil playing cards while the silhouette of a guillotine shows on the wall.[30] Frears opts instead for a more subtle shot of an exposed and socially ruined Merteuil sitting alone at her dressing table and removing her makeup as tears roll down her cheeks. The cause of her tears is ambiguous – the stripping of her facade, her public humiliation, the death of Valmont and her remorse for her role in it, may all pain her – but it is evident that emotion rather than evil surfaces as her public and private faces are integrated. Hampton notes in his screenplay that as Merteuil removes her makeup, "a new MERTEUIL seems for the first time to be revealed, weary, fragile, vulnerable almost" (75). Juliette, by contrast, is never moved by her exposure and according to the screenplay looks "proud, defiant, scornful, and cold" as the crowd gazes on her half-burned face (255). Merteuil's final moments in Frears's film parallel Valmont's in that he, too, experiences the surfacing of sentiment in the denouement. During his duel with Danceny, the action is interrupted by Valmont's tender thoughts of Tourvel, and he is so moved by his reflections that he condemns himself and thrusts his body onto Danceny's sword. Because the female libertine, like her male counterpart, is more, rather than less, human than she appears to be, her libertinism results in a destructive, fractured, psychological condition, and is ultimately unsustainable.[31]

Unfortunately, we do not know how Laclos viewed his own libertine protagonists. Laclos wrote only one novel and the sparse comments he made about it in letters tantalize more than they elucidate his intentions. The novel itself offers only ambivalent evidence: Valmont and Merteuil are appealing for their assertions of freedom and their desire to move beyond cultural prudishness and constrictiveness, yet they are repulsive in their callous and systematic exploitations of often defenseless victims. Laclos's punishment of each character at the end of the novel might seem to clarify his evaluation of them, but questions persist about the fall of each. Are we to understand Valmont as having committed suicide on Danceny's sword? Is the punishment heaped upon Merteuil the result of Laclos's idea of justice, or acquiescence to censors' demands? Laclos's readers remain divided over whether Laclos intended his novel to be a libertine manifesto, a moralistic condemnation of a decadent aristocracy, or something in between.[32]

The appeal of this novel for filmmakers comes out of this ambiguity. As they discover, Laclos's ductile characters offer a range of possibilities for refashioning their motives to suit contemporary purposes. Filmmakers tend to diminish the original ambivalence of the novel by amplifying some character motives while muting others, but what Laclos's characters lose in roundness they gain in pointedness useful for cultural critique. Although I have focused on Frears and Vadim, other adapters of *Les Liaisons dangereuses* can be approached in the same manner.[33] What makes Laclos's novel so eminently adaptable, so suitable for diverse purposes, is the undecidability of his libertine characters. Alluring yet abhorrent, subversive yet conservative, they serve filmmakers equally well as harbingers of liberating cultural shifts or as exemplars of a dominant ethos in need of reform.

NOTES

1 Roger Vadim, the first adapter, modernized Laclos's story in his controversial *Les Liaisons dangereuses 1960* (1959); Charles Brabant's television adaptation *Les Liaisons dangereuses* (1979) followed twenty years later. In the late 1980s, two major film productions were released: Stephen Frears's *Dangerous Liaisons* (1988) and Milos Forman's *Valmont* (1989), both of which retain the novel's eighteenth-century setting. The latest adaptation, Roger Kumble's *Cruel Intentions* (1999), uses contemporary Manhattan teenagers as the principal characters, perhaps with an eye to repeating the adaptive strategy of the successful *Clueless* (1995), a modernized version of Jane Austen's *Emma*. Kumble's direct-to-video prequel, *Cruel Intentions 2*, was released in 2000.

2 Frears's film won Academy Awards for best art direction/set direction, best costume design, and best screenplay adapted from another medium. It was nominated for Academy Awards for best actress, best supporting actress, and best music, original score.

3 Brian McFarlane, *Novel to Film: An Introduction to the Theory of Adaptation* (Oxford: Clarendon Press, 1996) argues for the merits of a structuralist approach to filmic adaptations. He does, however, acknowledge the value of

historical "intertextual" readings, at least in some instances. See pp. 10–11, 21–2, and his "Special Focus" section on Scorsese's *Cape Fear* (1991), pp. 187–93.

4 John Wilmot, Earl of Rochester, *The Complete Poems*, ed. David M. Vieth (New Haven: Yale University Press, 1968), p. 98, lines 104–9.

5 For discussion of links between Hobbesian philosophy and Restoration libertinism, see Warren Chernaik, *Sexual Freedom in Restoration Literature* (Cambridge: Cambridge University Press, 1995), pp. 22-51.

6 Harold Weber, *The Restoration Rake–Hero: Transformations in Sexual Understanding in Seventeenth-Century England* (Madison: University of Wisconsin Press, 1986), p. 81.

7 Choderlos de Laclos, *Les Liaisons dangereuses*, trans. and ed. Douglas Parmée (Oxford University Press, 1995), p. 11. Subsequent references will be given parenthetically in the text.

8 Roger Vailland, Roger Vadim, and Claude Brulé, *Roger Vadim's Les Liaisons Dangereuses*, trans. Bernard Shir-Cliff (New York: Ballantine, 1962), p. 99. Subsequent references will be given parenthetically in the text.

9 Roger Vadim, *Memoirs of the Devil*, trans. Peter Beglan (New York: Harcourt Brace Jovanovich, 1975), p. 3. Subsequent references will be given parenthetically in the text.

10 Quoted in Joseph Brami, "Mme de Merteuil, Juliette, and the Men: Notes for a Reading of Vadim's *Liaisons dangereuses 1960*," *Eighteenth-Century Life* 14 (1990), 63.

11 For a contrasting view, see Majda K. Anderson, "The Reigns of Power: Foucault, Feminism, and *Dangerous Liaisons*," in *Literature and Film in the Historical Dimension*, ed. John D. Simons (Gainesville: University Press of Florida, 1994), pp. 75–88, who argues that Frears's Valmont is "motivated entirely by pleasure, not an unyielding desire for power" (p. 82).

12 Christopher Hampton, *Dangerous Liaisons: the Film* (London: Faber and Faber, 1989), p. 7. Subsequent references will be given parenthetically in the text.

13 For an alternative reading, see Marina Warner, "Valmont – or, the Marquise Unmasked" in *Don Giovanni: Myths of Seduction and Betrayal*, ed. Jonathan Miller (Baltimore: Johns Hopkins University Press, 1990), pp. 93–107, who argues that Valmont in Frears's film acquiesces to the will of the masculine, controlling woman.

14 As Lester Friedman puts it in the Preface to *Fires Were Started: British Cinema and Thatcherism*, ed. Lester Friedman (Minneapolis: University of Minnesota Press, 1993), British filmmakers of the 1980s were connected in "their revulsion, to one degree or another, for the ideology of Thatcherism" (p. xix). Similarly Leonard Quart, "The Politics of Irony: The Frears–Kureishi Films," in *Re-Viewing British Cinema, 1900–1992: Essays and Interviews*, ed. Wheeler Winston Dixon (State University of New York Press, 1994), argues that in many British films of the decade "the meanness, greed, and absurdity of much of contemporary English life during the Thatcher era was corrosively skewered" (p. 242).

15 Leonard Quart, "The Religion of the Market: Thatcherite Politics and the British Film of the 1980s," *Fires Were Started*, ed. Friedman, p. 20. Quart

quotes Hugo Young, *The Iron Lady* (New York: Farrar Strauss Giroux, 1989), p. 537.

16 See Susan Torrey Barber, "Insurmountable Difficulties and Moments of Ecstasy: Crossing Class, Ethnic, and Sexual Barriers in the Films of Stephen Frears," in *Fires Were Started*, ed. Friedman, pp. 221–36.

17 Stephen Frears, "Keeping His Own Voice: An Interview With Stephen Frears," interview by Lester Friedman and Scott Stewart, *Re-Viewing British Cinema*, ed. Dixon, p. 233.

18 Frears, "Keeping his Own Voice," pp. 223–4. Similarly, Christopher Hampton, interview by Robert Maccubbin, *Eighteenth-Century Life* 14 (1990), indicated that contemporary politics and culture informed his portrayal of libertinism in *Les Liaisons Dangereuses* (1985), at least obliquely: "I think that what was in my mind was that throughout the '80s in this country there's been a sort of sanctification of institutionalized selfishness. And I think that was at the back of my mind" (82). Paradoxically, Hampton asserts that the decision to retain an eighteenth-century setting reinforces the film's applicability to contemporary times: "I decided that it would be *more* modern if it were in costume than it would if it were in modern dress. I just thought that the modernity of it would stand out in a way that wouldn't if you modernized it" (83). For a contrasting viewpoint, see Stephanie Barbé Hammer, "Romanticism and Reaction: Hampton's Transformation of *Les Liaisons Dangereuses*," in *Christopher Hampton: A Casebook*, ed. Robert Gross (New York: Garland Publishing, 1990), pp. 109–31, who reads Frears's play as in collusion with some aspects of the Thatcherite ethos (p. 127).

19 Brami, "Notes"; John L. Fell, "The Correspondents' Curse: Vadim's *Les Liaisons dangereuses 1960* (1959)," in *Modern European Filmmakers and the Art of Adaptation*, ed. Andrew Horton and Joan Magretta (New York: Frederick Ungar Publishing, 1981), pp. 51–62; Karen Hollinger, "Losing the Feminist Drift: Adaptations of *Les Liaisons dangereuses*," *Literature/Film Quarterly* 24 (1996), 293–300; Geoffrey Wagner, *The Novel and the Cinema* (Rutherford, NJ: Fairleigh Dickinson University Press, 1975), pp. 83–90.

20 As Brami, "Notes," has pointed out, Vadim in his "Brief Word" describes Juliette in terms of her "emancipation from all moral constraints" (56).

21 Vadim et al., *Les Liaisons dangereuses*, p. 7.

22 Elise F. Knapp and Robert Glen, "'The Energy of Evil Has Diminished': Less Dangerous Liaisons," *Eighteenth-Century Life* 14 (1990), 41–8, argue that "evil as a concept disappears" in filmic versions of Laclos's novel (p. 41); I suggest that Vadim's Juliette constitutes an exception to this general diminution of evil. See also Fell, "Correspondents' Curse," who considers Juliette to be "even more villainous than the marquise" (p. 56).

23 Brami, "Notes," 59–60, observes that Jeanne Moreau, who plays Juliette, specialized in *femme fatale* roles.

24 See the chapter on "*Noir* Women" in Jon Tuska, *Dark Cinema: American Film Noir in Cultural Perspective* (Westport, CT: Greenwood Press, 1984), pp. 199–214.

25 Choderlos de Laclos, "On the Education of Women," trans. Lydia Davis, *The Libertine Reader: Eroticism and Enlightenment in Eighteenth-Century France*, ed. Michel Feher (New York: Zone Books, 1997).

26 See Tuska, *Dark Cinema*, p. 204, and Stephen Farber, "Violence and the Bitch Goddess," *Film Comment* (November 1974), 8–11.

27 For an alternative approach to this problem, see Brami, "Notes," 63–5, who interprets the disempowerment of Juliette in terms of Vadim's and Vailland's personal misogyny.

28 See Hollinger, "Losing the Feminist Drift," 295–6, and Warner, "Valmont – or the Marquise Unmasked," p. 97.

29 Production designer Stuart Craig, interviewed by Robert Maccubbin, *Eighteenth-Century Life* 14 (1990), 94, notes the "shameless" use of abundant mirrors in screenplay and film. For a psychoanalytical reading of Frears's Merteuil, see Alan J. Singerman, "Merteuil and Mirrors: Stephen Frears's Freudian Reading of *Les Liaisons dangereuses*," *Eighteenth-Century Fiction* 5 (1993), 269–81.

30 Christopher Hampton, *Les Liaisons dangereuses* (London: Faber and Faber, 1985). Frears considered a dramatic version of this ending and filmed Glenn Close losing her head at the guillotine.

31 Alan J. Singerman, "Variations on a Denouement: *Les Liaisons dangereuses* on Film," *Eighteenth-Century Life* 14 (1990), 49–55, argues that in the end of Frears's film, Merteuil is made "psychologically fragile, less satanic, more human" (53). For an alternative reading, see Hollinger, "Losing the Feminist Drift," who argues that only Valmont is "redeemed by romantic love" while Merteuil is transformed into a "diabolical villainess" (295).

32 See David Coward, introduction to *Les Liaisons dangereuses*, ed. Douglas Parmeé, pp. vii–xxxiv, for an overview of criticism on Laclos's novel.

33 It would be intriguing, for instance, to study how Milos Forman's concern to avoid a Marxist reading of the novel manifests itself in his *Valmont* (1989). See Milos Forman, interviewed by Elise Knapp and Robert Glen, *Eighteenth-Century Life* 14 (1990), 98–107.

10

Mapping Goethe's *Wilhelm Meister*
       onto Wenders' *Wrong Move*

Margaret McCarthy

Two hundred years of *Bildungsroman* literature and criticism sit implacably before any scholar concerned with the historical trajectory between Johann Wolfgang Goethe's novel *Wilhelm Meister's Apprentice Years* (1794–6) and Wim Wenders' filmic adaptation *Wrong Move* (1974). Geographical tropes seem highly appropriate for a terrain both far-flung and richly stratified. After all, the *Bildungsroman* put German literature quite literally on the map, earning it recognition beyond Germany's borders as the form spread to, and established literary landmarks in, other cultural contexts. Despite the genre's subsequent wanderlust, layer upon layer of a distinct, collective German self emerged in a mountain of literary works produced on German soil. Before Germany even existed as a unified, geographical entity, intrepid scholars began scaling the mountain, and for two hundred years have charted every dent and fissure in hopes of defining the *Bildungsroman*. In most general terms, critics agree: the *Bildungsroman* depicts a young man progressing from adolescence to young adulthood, who abandons provincial roots to travel to an urban environment. His goal, as expressed by *Wilhelm Meister*, is to realize the intellectual, emotional, moral, and spiritual capacities inherent in his character. Whether nurturing or inimical, the protagonist's new environment very often facilitates the growth of his inner qualities, and sometimes leads him to the ultimate attainment of wisdom and maturity. *Bildung* is both the cultivation of inner talents – a process of self-formation – and a self-integration within the larger social field. Given the complicated ways in which individuals and their surroundings interact, however, the concept of *Bildung* remains highly mobile, despite that immovable mountain of literary and scholarly works.

Attempts at defining the *Bildungsroman* have nonetheless often reflected an impasse in both genre and subject theory. Establishing paradigmatic boundaries, no matter how tentative, has often hindered attempts to trace the various historical ways *Bildung* has been narrated and to what ends. Similarly, scholarship concerned with the subject within *Bildung* has bogged down around questions of "agency" versus "structure," or the extent to which individuals are free agents within cultural and social constraints.[1] To bypass the culs-de-sac reached in both genre and subject theory, one must first recognize that the human subject, as Steve Pile and Nigel Thrift argue, lacks precise boundaries and is always on the move, both culturally and in fact.[2] What is needed, then, is not a map that designates specific coordinates along a structure/agency continuum, but rather the dynamism of a compass which tracks an individual's movement and encounters in time and space. By putting *Wilhelm Meister* on wheels in his road-movie version of *Bildung*, Wenders plays up the peripatetic nature of selfhood, meaning that we are always "on the move," whether literally within shifting topographies or more generally as subjects in process.

If efforts to track mobile selves have been hindered by the inherent stasis in *Bildungsroman* scholarship, many scholars have at least recognized that the genre itself was never on firm ground. Despite the status of Goethe's novel as prototypical *Bildungsroman*, *Wilhelm Meister* is only tenuously integrated into the larger field by the novel's end, and only when the Tower Society and his impromptu marriage thud their way into the plot. It is tempting, of course, to view the Tower Society, that secret group that charts Wilhelm's progess and guides his integration into society, as exemplary of Enlightenment selfhood based on autonomy, consciousness, and reason. By helping him to cultivate those stable, inherent qualities within, they guide Wilhelm away from artificial foundations of self in the theater world he inhabits for the better part of the novel. From this model of selfhood one then traces a negative trajectory to the damaged selves who figured so prominently in Germany's period of "New Subjectivity" during the 1970s. Countless New Subjectivity texts and films attempted to convey an autobiographical or subjective immediacy that both countered the objective, political dogmatism of the late 1960s and belied the inadequacies and mediated nature of language itself.[3] In many ways, though, Goethe's *Wilhelm Meister* is, in fact, the prototype for Wenders' displaced heroes, but not because one finds in novel and film optimistic beliefs in either Enlightenment models of selfhood or the healing powers of language. Rather, attention to spatial metaphors uncovers the shaky foundations not only of Wilhelm's *Bildung* and thus of the genre, but also, more fundamentally, of subjectivity itself. Even within relatively static environments, the grounds of subject formation continually shift if one observes how subjects variously inhabit larger, structural determinants in time and space. Registering such shifts offers a way past static paradigms of selfhood and creates new maps for reading both novel and film.

The visual field set up by Wenders' title – *Wrong Move* – points us back to the physical coordinates sustaining Goethe's novel and the flimsy, attenuated selves one initially finds there. Many characters are described in the novel as being *bewegt* or moved. In visual terms, such movement figures as dangling in space, either literally or metaphorically, and manifests itself in Wilhelm's fascination with puppets, acrobats, and tightrope walkers. Traditional concepts of *Bildung*, where characters resign themselves to social structures, presume a fairly stable individual not so markedly different from the Enlightenment model of selfhood. Yet Wilhelm's *schweben* or "hovering" in the theater world and final insertion into the firm structures of both matrimony and the Tower Society create visual effects similar to those in Wenders' film, where characters skid uncertainly across a shifting landscape, before Wenders' Wilhelm himself finally deadends at the Zugspitze, Germany's highest mountain. Novel and film are each full of wrong moves, since selfhood again quite literally lacks firm grounding and instead exists at every turn as an effect of the ways subjects map themselves and are mapped within their surroundings. Tracking both puppets and cars paints a much more variegated landscape of *Bildung* than one in which selfhood and its surround seem relatively stable from start to finish. More important, both novel and film offer spatially informed metaphors for the complicated interface between self and environment not only as it exists, but also as it could ideally be, although the film is much more oblique in suggesting utopian possibilities.

How one imagines the notion of interiority so central to selfhood and *Bildung* has everything to do with a corresponding exterior landscape and an individual's continual encounters with it. Carolyn Steedman has written that the nineteenth-century concept of interiority used the figure of the child as exemplary of that far-off, but deeply buried realm which we only intermittently encounter as rational adults.[4] Steedman's study, *Strange Dislocations*, pays careful attention to the later nineteenth-century incarnations of the child-figure Mignon from Goethe's novel. As dancer, acrobat, and captive to a troupe of tightrope walkers, Mignon is largely defined by her movements in space, which can be either uncoordinated or highly precise, if not mechanical. Her *Bildung* begins when she requests an atlas: education for Mignon is not about learning to fix the self in words – she hardly speaks and cannot read – but in space. Her movements, however, reveal two antithetical versions of selfhood: while the fanatical, skilled precision of Mignon's famous egg dance demonstrates extraordinary volition, her uncoordinated, puppet-like gestures also reveal the malleability of subjects manipulated by larger forces. In other words, she appears to exist at both ends of the agency/structure continuum by exerting supreme control over her body, even as she is simultaneously molded by larger forces. If Mignon's movements make her both master and pawn of circumstances, one wonders what exactly serves as motor for this complicated, contradictory interaction between self and external influence.

Goethe's novel reveals that what grounds Mignon is paradoxically that which drives her, namely her unfulfilled desires for both Wilhelm and Italy, her homeland. Such contradictory spatial metaphors underscore more generally the irreconcilable extremes of desire, or the manner in which individuals single-mindedly pursue highly individual desires which simultaneously steer them along a given path. Desire provides a powerful example of the volition and malleability which coexist in all subjects as they interact with the world. Yet the difficulties of desire in Goethe's novel require more examination if one considers Mignon's sad death. Ursula Mahlendorf has linked both Mignon's erratic movements and the wanderings of the harper (later revealed to be her father) to a deviant sexuality, whether Mignon's forbidden love for Wilhelm or the harper's incestuous desire for his sister. In other words, desire as motor leaves one dangling like a puppet, unintegrated into the larger surround. Thus Wilhelm's fascination with Mignon coexists with his early passion for puppets; as emblem of Wilhelm's childhood, Mignon must logically die for him to mature. At the same time the novel's numerous prohibitions against desire and female sexuality in particular, as Mahlendorf observes, suggest something more than mere narrative logic.[5] When Natalie, whose altruistic, asexual activities provide the novel's feminine ideal, asks Mignon to forgo her androgyny for a dress, Mignon chooses an angel's costume. Indeed, her most volitional act follows when Mignon exerts herself until her heart literally stops beating. To map herself into a world of chaste and charitable women is to be simultaneously mapped out of a landscape which leaves no space for desire.

Prohibitions against desire not only carry a moral component, but also expose the dangers of wandering souls lost in space, fundamentally unaware of their own or larger, spatial boundaries. Significantly, the harper defines the madness which afflicts him as a loss of geographical coordinates: "I see nothing before me, nothing behind me ... but an endless night in which I find the most terrible loneliness ... There is no height, no depth, no forward, no backward, there are no words to express this unchanging state."[6] Psychoanalytic theory stresses the formative nature of spatial relations, specifically the recognition of the self in the mirror as a separate entity, as the foundation for subsequent identifications with other external objects and symbolic forms. Subject/object relations here remain, however, divided between a love of the image's illusory doubling and/or completion, and hate for its external, inassimilable existence. Desire in the novel resembles the more idealizing impulse towards the mirror insofar as sufficient distance between subject and object is lost, as characters like Mignon and the harper find themselves dangling in a disconnected realm of desire-bound relations. Wilhelm's own narcissistic urges to merge with his desired objects differ only insofar as they still allow him to remain at center stage. Lacking an awareness of self as both separate entity and product of external relations, all three characters have difficulty perceiving, identifying with, and integrating themselves within the geographical coordinates around them. Mignon's fettered existence in particular reveals precisely this difficulty: tied as she is to a single-minded pursuit of both Wilhelm and her homeland, her feet at times barely touch the ground.

For his part, Wilhelm seems buffeted initially by the erratic movements of an unfettered imagination, which often leaves him wandering as if in a labyrinth or awash in a flood of forms and sensations. Unable to stem the tide when he discovers Shakespeare's *Hamlet*, Wilhelm experiences an "unfamiliar movement," or "a thousand sensations and faculties of which he hadn't the slightest concept or idea stir[ring] within him . . . " (3:9:192). What "moves" him is neither concretely perceived nor connected to anything beyond the labyrinth or flood of internal perception. If Shakespearean poetics hinder Wilhelm's ability to distinguish internal from external influence, his passion for puppets adds another important dimension. Significantly, all of Wilhelm's objects – his puppets, his role as Hamlet, and even his first love, Mariane – become mere extensions of self whose "strings" he adroitly manipulates in the realms of both art and love.

Blurry boundaries between art and love manifest themselves very early in the novel, when Wilhelm's "passion for the stage bound itself to his first love for a female creature" (1:3:11). Another early passage describes an embrace as Wilhelm clasping Mariane's red uniform and vest, each part of a stage costume. (Later he will be fascinated by Mignon's appearance and costumes.) If such artificiality seems emblematic of the theater-world in general, the novel links it more specifically to puppetry: "[Mariane] was now absolutely essential to him, because he was tied to her with all the bands of humanity. His pure soul perceived that she was half, more than half, of himself. He was thankful and devoted without boundaries" (1:9:32). Whether Wilhelm truly perceives Mariane is debatable, however, since he hardly registers how his passionate monologues about childhood experiences with puppets put her to sleep. At the same time, Mariane seems the ideal puppet, because her passion for Wilhelm serves as her only means of support: "She had nothing that could lift her up. When she looked inside herself and searched, her spirit was empty and her heart had no support. The sadder this circumstance became, the more fervently she fastened herself to her lover" (1:9:32).

In the world of theater, puppetry provides a rather rudimentary, mechanical version of an otherwise elevated art form, one in which Wilhelm later demonstrates his own wooden acting. That his hand at one point inadvertently appears during a puppet show, prompting much mirth from his audience, alerts us again to the centrality of self over object, as does a later observation that Wilhelm the actor only ever plays himself on stage. A stranger who knew Wilhelm's grandfather and his much vaunted art collection also points out Wilhelm's narcissistic relation to art: "If the collection had stayed in your house, over time your perceptions of the artworks would have developed so that you wouldn't have only seen yourself and your own inclinations in them" (1:17:71). The spatial implications for this nexus of self, art, and love are manifold: in the narcissistic convergence of subject and object, the bottom drops out in numerous respects. If Wilhelm's creative impulses elevate him into pleasing "castles in the air," they also find their support "on a bed of fog whose figures of course flowed into each other" (1:9:33). Such flimsy spatial reference points challenge Wilhelm's control as puppeteer, suggesting that he, like Mignon, flails in his own nebulous fantasy world. Wilhelm's proximity to his audience as puppeteer also keeps him at a physical and visual remove. Ironically, Wilhelm dreams of a National Theater nourished by German soil, a goal which relies upon fundamentally different spatial coordinates, namely an alternative topography where art springs from integration into the surround. What Wilhelm lacks is the connection [*Zusammenhang*] to something larger: "After I had experienced something, it suddenly seemed to me as if I didn't know anything, and I was right: Because I was missing the connection, and that's what everything depends upon" (1:4:16).

Wilhelm's gradual grounding is a more complicated process than his ultimate insertion into the Tower Society and (mostly chaste) marriage to Natalie suggest. His *Bildung* is not simply a matter of moving from narcissistic self-cultivation to integration in the world via mostly "duty-bound activities" (7:9:521). The process begins as Wilhelm observes himself in the metaphorical mirror offered by the Tower Society: "He saw himself for the first time outside of himself, although not like a second self in a mirror, but rather like a portrait of another self. One doesn't recognize one's self in all its parts, but one is happy that a thinking intellect has captured us, that a great talent wanted to represent us in a way that a picture of us as we were will last even longer than we ourselves can" (8:7:535). Wilhelm's response to this portrait reveals not the love of and loss of self in its double, but rather a sobering acceptance of external perceptions as the basis of identity, the first step towards integration. Paradoxically, such referents should enable Wilhelm to return to and know himself, as the character Jarno explains: "when he learns to lose himself in a larger mass, when he learns to live for others and to lose himself in duty-bound activities, he will learn to know himself for the first time" (7:9:521–2). Unlike a simple loss of self in objects of desire, this passage describes a "detour" [*Umweg*] through symbolic and geographical coordinates so anchored in the physical landscape as to prevent a collapse back into self. "Self-cultivation" according to this model of *Bildung* finds its most resonant metaphor in the increasing presence of gardens towards the end of the novel, which, like the soil needed for a German National Theater, serve as both anchor and sustenance for subject formation.

An extended passage on the effects of traveling through Germany reveals the effects of this "detour" in both human and spatial terms: "One went to work, and . . . Wilhelm found much satisfaction evenings in acting and in being with Serlo and Aurelien, and his ideas, which for so long had turned in circles, spread themselves out on a daily basis" (4:17:281). Expanding circles both invoke community and turn back to a self now perceived as connected and unique. And here Wilhelm's return to the lost art collection of his childhood home provides the most resonant metaphor: "It speaks from a totality, it speaks to me from every part without my comprehending the former and without me being able to make the latter my own. What magic I sense in these surfaces, these lines, these heights and widths, these masses and colors" (8:5:573). If Wilhelm strongly identifies with the collection, he still recognizes its essential separateness in all those carefully registered architectural details. Selfhood is mapped into surround here via external forms which nonetheless conjure selfhood as individual and differentiated, or a kind of free-standing edifice. At the same time it is important to recognize what gets lost here. Identity as firmly anchored in spatial coordinates perceived as both separate and different – the more sobering response to the mirror – may counter the dangling, hovering, and wandering which otherwise characterize Wilhelm's *Bildung*, but they also have the effect of burying desire. In other words, such crisp architectural lines create a sense of selfhood in artful, sanitized terms that in no way spark the yearning to merge with and lose one's self in objects which, unlike those above, conjure the illusion of doubling or completion.

How does the apex of selfhood aspired to in Goethe's novel articulate itself within the flattened topography of the road movie? And just how far does *Wrong Move* stray from Goethe's novel? Critics often enlist spatial metaphors to underscore the shortcomings of cinematic adaptations, or their tendency to level off, condense, and move away from their literary sources. Wenders' narrowed compass in *Wrong Move* manifests itself everywhere, beginning with the three locales – the northern town of Glückstadt, Bonn, and Frankfurt – which concentrate the novel's extended travels. Similarly, Wenders reduces the novel's complicated cast of characters to the five who squeeze into the space of a car, as if the imperatives of a road movie take precedence over the novel's vast canvas.[7] Only four of the characters – Wilhelm, Therese, Mignon and Laertes – share their literary predecessors' names, although Laertes resembles less the actor in the novel than the harper, because both he and the harper harbor a dark secret. The effect of such compression also undermines the surging, forward movement of the *Bildungsroman*, creating instead a static, insular world of cramped car scenes sometimes shot at night. The filmic medium's value, however, lies precisely in its ability to capture a novel's expansiveness and profusion of detail within a canvas of highly condensed, yet resonant visual forms. In other words, radical incisions may be more virtue than mere exigency in the adaptation process, depending on how concentrated visual images nonetheless open out verbal domains. For instance, the Glückstadt/Bonn/Frankfurt trajectory not only vaults us from Goethe's to Wenders' Germany, but also from half-timbered houses seen in opening shots to Frankfurt's impersonal high-rises, an architectural style which levels both cultural difference and all traces of the Second World War's destruction. Similarly, shots of characters in darkened cars cut off from the landscape paradoxically point up a lack of grounding vaguely reminiscent of Goethe's puppets. In other words, Wenders' concentrated images both demonstrate an altered historical frame and allude to the novel's dominant visual metaphors.

Numerous critics agree, however, that Wenders' very loose filmic adaptation consciously negates Goethe's novel.[8] The car as visual trope, of course, forces the viewer to ponder the vast distance that the concept of *Bildung* has traversed in two centuries and its contemporary meaning in Germany circa 1974. Wenders' film reveals how far the tradition has meandered from its eighteenth-century origins, with the grand tradition of the *Bildungsroman* long receded. Similarly, the superficial, disconnected voice-overs and monologues spoken by Wilhelm and others in the film pay lip service to the grand tradition of self-cultivation, even as they stray into an increasingly closed off realm ill disposed to integration. Wenders' loose adaptation has everything to do with the historical circumstances in which the film was made, a terrain which deserves close attention.

Richard McCormick's interpretation of *Wrong Move* in his extended study *Politics of the Self: Feminism and the Postmodern in West German Literature and Film* provides the finest and most convincing reading of the film as situated within its own historical context. He pays particular attention to Peter Handke's screenplay for the film, completed in 1973, and the manner in which Handke gives shape to an ongoing debate on the relationship between art and politics which spans two centuries. Handke himself, McCormick argues, had much influence on Germany's New Subjectivity movement, insofar as he took a stance against the subordination of literature to political activism. Wilhelm's isolated, self-centered posture throughout the film reflects a belief in the value and authenticity of subjective experience rather than the impersonal, dogmatic language of politics. Modern *Bildung*, according to Handke's screenplay, consists of an isolated self-cultivation, minus integration, as the means towards the writing, reflecting life. It requires not only solitude, but a shut eye: Handke's Wilhelm boasts his "erotic gaze," which culls "experience," the authentic perception of things, from the "after-image" which appears to the closed eye. Less important are those detours through the complicated landscapes of history and politics: Handke cuts to the chase by privileging a highly individuated self over its wanderings.

Not surprisingly, in Wenders' film verbal domains are less important than visual effects which challenge Handke's premises, not to mention the aims of New Subjectivity more generally. McCormick draws out significant changes which Wenders made to Handke's screenplay, most pointedly in the film's final tableaux; whereas Handke's Wilhelm observes a snowstorm at the Zugspitze accompanied by the sound of a typewriter, Wenders eliminates both snowstorm and typewriter, merely placing Wilhelm at the Zugspitze with his back to the audience. As McCormick argues, "Wilhelm does not succeed in becoming a writer, and his movement into isolation seems just as wrong as his other moves."[9] Wenders also figures Wilhelm's imperviousness to realms of history and politics as his desire to kill, rather than learn from Laertes, who presided over the murder of Jews at Vilna. Wilhelm's "erotic gaze" – that purely private image available to the closed eye – finds negative resonance in those shots of five individuals pressed up against each other in a darkened automobile. Self-cultivation occurs here in a vacuum, as political and historical considerations are jettisoned, much as Wilhelm tries to dump Laertes in the Main River towards the end of the film.

If dangling serves as Goethe's central metaphor for an isolated self, Wenders' Wilhelm and cohorts seem intent on deflecting the various external landmarks – political, historical, and more generally human – which cross their paths. The grand tradition of *Bildung* also serves as an important visual trope which allows Wilhelm to swerve inward, rather than pursue integration. Not only does Wilhelm use his reading material, Eichendorff's *From the Life of a Ne'er-Do-Well* and Flaubert's *Sentimental Education*, as a prop to deflect Mignon's gaze when she sits across from him on a train, but the Zugspitze featured in the film's final scene turns Wilhelm away from his tenuous human connections and also from

17. Rüdiger Vogler as an isolated Wilhelm Meister in Wim Wenders'
Wrong Move

the filmic audience. An extraordinarily resonant image, the Zugspitze shot signifies more than the grand tradition which served as my original guiding metaphor. Rather it provides the most striking mirror of a frozen, static self, utterly alone in those misty heights at Germany's southernmost border. The terrain of the *Bildungsroman* dead-ends here, since experience during New Subjectivity has become so personal, idiosyncratic, and closed off as to be unavailable to a diegetic or extra-filmic audience.

The mirror as trope may not, however, capture the complex interaction between self and surround in *Wrong Move*, since mirrors serve as relay between the self and the world they open out onto, a trajectory which Wenders' characters seem incapable of following. Alice Kuzniar has argued that twentieth-century interiority for Wim Wenders requires not a child, but a car, or rather a windshield which maps a particular relation between subject and external world. Following Baudrillard, she argues convincingly that the external world for Wenders' wanderers exists not beyond, but at the windshield as simulacra, which renders the actual physical landscape superfluous. As Kuzniar asserts, Baudrillard inverts the psychoanalytic paradigm of the mirror scene, since object takes precedence over viewing subject, existing as it does independently in the mirror.[10] In other words, the windshield/screen does not open out spatially onto or refer to a larger world of symbolic, linguistic or geographical forms; it remains the sole point of interface for Wenders' characters with their worlds.

Wrong Move, I would argue, presents an even more extreme version of subjectivity, with its car scenes suggesting less interface with the world via the simulacra/windshield than pure interiority – insular, claustrophobic, unconnected – moving through a sometimes invisible landscape. Such hyperinteriority reveals itself verbally as well, particularly in the superficial, disconnected voice-overs and monologues which permeate the film. Full of non sequiturs and banal information, they are spoken before audiences whose responses – which vary from bemusement to disgust and boredom – are barely registered, even among bodies tightly pressed up against each other in a car. At best the presence of others provides a theatrical backdrop, evident in Therese's desire for a dramatic farewell in the throng, or in a group of strangers with which she and Wilhelm have nothing in common. All characters in *Wrong Move* perform a dynamic described by the industrialist they encounter, namely becoming an "actor of one's self," even while audience as external reference point falls away. One is reminded here of Wilhelm's puppets as conduits of self: isolated and beyond the audience's visual access, he pulls the strings of his own narcissistic fantasies, much as self-absorption in *Wrong Move* spins off into insular monologues.

Given this private encounter of self with self, desire must work hard to reconcile individuals on diverging tracks. An early scene, for instance, shows Wilhelm and Therese gazing at each other longingly from trains aimed at different destinations, a situation more than a result of mere happenstance or bad timing. Later, when Wilhelm and Therese do unite and travel together, Wilhelm searches her out in the dark one night but ends up instead in bed with Mignon. This mistake reveals not the loss of self in an object, but the loss of the object itself, which hardly matters or is registered. Wilhelm's decision to sleep with Mignon even after he discovers his mistake recalls that "erotic gaze," or the ability to transform something within a closed eye, even if this trick requires shrouding Mignon's presence. Like those TVs wrapped in plastic so often seen in Wenders' films, Mignon is reduced to a flickering, muzzled presence, not a window onto the world beyond self. Desire satisfied in the dark by interchangeable objects recalls those car scenes at night, in which the screen/windshield registers nothing of the world. For all his attention to the vagaries of body and soul, Wilhelm remains profoundly immune to visual or tactile contact with others: never do we see him consummate his relationship with Therese, and she chides him at one point with the observation: "For a writer, you really miss a lot."

If such deflection of the external in all forms seems entirely volitional, I would like to suggest that the way characters move through space in *Wrong Move* is never so resolute. And here a second avenue of interpretation presents itself in which even more visual affinities with the novel become apparent. To read the film only as a negation of the *Bildungsroman* or its diminution within a narrowed compass presumes fixed end points – a grand tradition, fixed and immovable, at one end, and the cul-de-sac of German selfhood circa 1974 at the other. Arguments for visual resonances between text and film, however, proceed from the tenuousness of the whole genre, as well as the concept of *Bildung*. As I have argued, understanding *Bildung* requires analysis of the complicated ways in which individuals interact with their surround, where control at the wheel or as puppeteer coexists with skidding and dangling in the face of larger forces. The visual and verbal meandering which permeate the film are thus not merely a form of departure, but part of a larger choreography of irresolute interactions between individual and the world, as characters stop and start, backtrack, and reposition themselves throughout the film, alternately in control and buffeted by larger forces.

Two scenes – a stroll through a Bonn alley and up a hill overlooking the Rhine – are representative. In the first, Therese arrives in Bonn to meet the man she glimpsed from her departing train. She and Wilhelm wear almost identical trenchcoats, like two actors playing a scene. Together they block a self-timed snapshot set up by some American tourists. (If their positioning anticipates Wilhelm's back to the camera at the Zugspitze, it also demonstrates, as I will argue, Wilhelm's imperviousness to the filmic medium, a stance with subtle but significant import for his *Bildung*.) Mignon, Laertes, and Bernhard join them, as Mignon performs impromptu cartwheels in the pedestrian shopping zone while Laertes plays harmonica. Then all five characters meander through a back alley, and point-of-view shots allow them to assume the distanced, all-seeing eye of the writer/camera. At the same time, the camera also remains behind them to capture their movements through space, thus obliquely commenting on their ability to master their surroundings. Three times the group stops and observes commotion: a baby's cry, a physical altercation between a couple, and a mad man's anguished cries. Despite what seems the blueprint for an episodic narrative encompassing birth, marriage, and ultimate infirmity, Wilhelm the would-be writer and the rest flee the scene, then backtrack and run down another alley. Such willy-nilly movements register a variety of irresolute, if not irreconcilable impulses, either an aloof theatricality which sometimes acknowledges, sometimes eschews its audience, or an attempt at observation and integration which then capriciously flees the scene. Skidding this way and that, Wenders' characters resemble more pinballs than sentient, reflective beings responding to surroundings which themselves seem equally chaotic and disconnected.

In a long trudge up a hill above the Rhine, similar choreography debunks Wilhelm's utopian dreams of writing. As Laertes reflects on the complicated relationship informing art, politics, and personal history, Wilhelm expresses his desire for "authentic social interaction" and "intersubjective communication" via poetics, not the "inauthentic, impersonal, and reified" language of politics.[11] Ironically, Therese and Mignon whistle Beethoven's "Ode to Joy" at one point, a choice that for Wenders in particular links art with German history and politics,[12] and Laertes' revelation here that he killed Jews at Vilna inextricably links one man's personal story with its historical backdrop. In other words, false, naive oppositions underpin Wilhelm's artistic ambitions. He further deflates his own utopian dreams in the utterly silly conversation about writing which follows as he strolls alongside Bernhard and they both invent absurd haikus and short stories. And if writing is meant to propel Wilhelm into some intersubjective realm, his subsequent conversation with Therese belies any kind of intimate interaction, as Therese complains to him of his neglect. If verbal banter here completely undermines Wilhelm's utopian dreams, movement through space also undoes whatever insights or narrative progression a slow, meditative, uphill walk might bring as the whole party once again turns, as in the previous scene analyzed, and races down the hill in yet another flight from experience. Returning to the industrialist's house at the bottom of the hill, they find the ultimate form of disintegration, namely his suicide by hanging. Along the way they barely register the sight of a hunter with rifle whose intermittent shots serve as an ominous, accoustic backdrop for the entire sequence. Throughout one also sees several of the characters struggling with an umbrella buffeted by the wind, and the final scene shows children trying to launch a kite. If the sequence captures Wilhelm and company's imperviousness to a violent political backdrop, whether past or present, it also nonetheless reveals an irresolvable antagonism between self and surround, where push continually meets pull, and individuals are not lifted up and invisibly embraced by the surround in the illusion of an independent, free-floating selfhood. Unlike Goethe's architectural trope of self, *Wrong Move* provides no handy visual metaphors to facilitate integration.

Obliquely, however, *Wrong Move* does suggest an alternative medium for *Bildung*, which in turn offers other methods and metaphors for interactions between self and surround. During the walk analyzed above,

Bernhard recounts a dream, all captured by a camera, in which the in-dustrialist runs across a road shouting "Long live the exploited masses," only to throw himself into the sea. Then Bernard is forced to watch in his dream the entire episode as a witness, as the filmic medium com-pels a confrontation with history, politics, and human experience more generally. The point is made more playfully in a later scene before a photo-booth in a crowded shopping zone, in which two would-be jugglers and acrobats in trenchcoats and dark glasses accost Wilhelm with a super-8 camera, obliging him to film their primitive antics. Film's ability to lead Wilhelm out of his artistic cul-de-sac is hinted at in a shot of him uttering the words *"Im Laufe der Zeit"* – the name of a subsequent Wenders film – in his sleep. Yet this wish fulfillment is far from utopian if one considers film's fraught position in German society during Wenders' early years as filmmaker. Eric Rentschler has catalogued the various references to film throughout *Wrong Move* in an eclipsed view of film's expressive pos-sibilities and of the politics of film subsidies and distribution.[13] Most important, what emerges from the overview he provides is film's inte-gration within Germany's complicated terrain of politics, history, and self-reflection, which it both reflects upon and emerges from in ways a grand literary tradition no longer does.

In terms of both method and metaphor, film offers alternatives to Goethe's duty-bound activities and idealistic tropes of self. Unlike the solitary realms of reading, writing, and reflection, making films is by def-inition an interactive process which requires the efforts of many individ-uals, plus numerous forms of connection and collaboration. Simply put, film necessitates that selfhood direct itself outward towards a camera, director, and audience. Metaphorically, film also sutures its spectators into the filmic space, fostering identification classically through point-of-view shots that oblige the audience to take up a particular vantage point. Given the range of conflicting positions one may be obliged to assume, this process is, however, far from utopian.

Yet Wilhelm remains too visually impaired throughout for the filmic medium to provide a viable alternative to literature. His handicap, of course, reflects the downside of New Subjectivity: when subjectivity su-persedes observation and reflection, one ultimately sees nothing. Not surprisingly then, antagonisms between Wilhelm and the visual world of film are everywhere in the film, beginning with the opening shots. In a panoramic, bird's-eye view, we see the Elbe River, then close in on the main square of Glückstadt. Small raindrops collect on the camera lens before a reverse shot, probably from Wilhelm's window, shows us its position in a passing helicopter. McCormick argues that *Wrong Move* self-consciously calls attention to the filmic medium, in a distancing that also marks the film's circumspect attitude toward Wilhelm and Wenders' apparent dislike of him.[14] I would add that one finds in these opening shots two fundamentally mismatched spheres, as the camera appears to approach Wilhelm, but then instead moves on in another direction. Wilhelm remains enclosed not just in his room, but in a literary world which sets him on an alternative path to the one established by that self-consciously filmic frame. In fact, the acoustic shift from general sound-track music to the rock music playing in Wilhelm's room also marks the transition to a domain which the original camera never sees. If Wilhelm's fist through the window suggests a rebellious desire to flee, the scene which follows establishes the insular dynamic that informs the entire film and the apparent triumph of the dead, verbal sphere over the helicopter's more vital visual realm. After Wilhelm sucks the blood from his wound, he and his mother enter the bathroom, where he bandages his hand and she stands before the mirror removing curlers and indulging in a long monologue about the dull round of activities she looks forward to when he leaves. Subjectivity here amounts to cannibalizing one's self, the mother ignoring her audience and becoming an "actor of herself," and Wilhelm feeding on himself in an even more intensively personal way, as rebellion turns in on itself.

Ultimately, in tracing the trajectory from novel to film, it is important to first recognize each as its own discrete landmark bearing a uniquely striated mix of historical, artistic, and medium-bound features. Brian McFarlane's relatively recent study on filmic adaptation, which helpfully jettisons fussy concerns about faithfulness, nonetheless enlists somewhat dated structuralist machinery to trace the path from novels to films. Even though he underscores the necessary transformation involved as literary forms turn celluloid, his methodology rests on narrative and linguistic paradigms, which have the inadvertent effect of reinforcing traditional hierarchies favoring the verbal over the visual.[15] Perhaps the mapping metaphor I've used throughout this essay also optimistically assumes enough common ground, here specifically in the form of visual affinities, to indeed find a path between novel and film. But by placing subjectivity and subject formation at the center of my analysis, I have attempted not only to provide a new map for reading both novel and film, but also to highlight the highly mobile mapping between subjectivity and its surround. Again, it may not be so much a map that we need as a compass which registers very complex interactions unfolding over time. The resting point implied by the ultimate goal of integration is at best achieved metaphorically in ways that novel and film mark as somewhat utopian and thus not as some fixed endpoint. More important, attention to interactions between self and surround in literature and film will help us understand that grand and antiquated concept of *Bildung* in less mono-lithic and more open-ended, provisional ways: as much subject to change as any physical terrain would be over the course of time.[16]

NOTES

1 Steve Pile and Nigel Thrift write: "The question becomes how terms such as body, self, subjectivity and so on, are to be mapped; crudely, positions have been taken up in relation to a particular dualism, namely structure/agency. This dualism expresses the problem of subject formation in relation to, on the one side, social rules, sanctions and prohibitions and, on the other side, the individual's feelings, thoughts and actions." Steve Pile and Nigel Thrift, eds., *Mapping the Subject. Geographies of Cultural Transformation* (London: Routledge, 1995), p. 2.

2 Pile and Thrift, *Mapping the Subject*, p. 1.

3 Generally speaking, these largely autobiographical texts and films showed men and women turning away from political dogmatism towards politics on the personal level, with the body serving as the concrete, authentic locus of political events.

4 Carolyn Steedman, *Strange Dislocations. Childhood and the Idea of Human Interiority* (Cambridge, MA: Harvard University Press, 1995), p. 20.

5 Mahlendorf writes that the new society requires "almost [a] total eradication of female sexuality." "The Mystery of Mignon: Object Relations, Abandonment, Child Abuse and Narrative Structure," *Goethe Yearbook* 7 (1994), 34.

6 Johann Wolfgang Goethe, *Wilhelm Meisters Lehrjahre*, (Berlin: Aufbau-Verlag, 1989), Book 7, Chapter 4, p. 461. Further references are to this edition and will be given in the text: the numbers in parenthesis in each reference refer to book, chapter and page respectively. All translations are my own.

7 Wim Wenders' career as film director extends over three decades and across German and American landscapes. Although he has directed many documentary films, including the recent and highly successful *Buena Vista Social Club*, Wenders is probably best known for his feature films. During the 1970s, many of his films, including *Wrong Move*, *Alice in the Cities*, and *Kings of the Road*, took the form of road movies. A decade later films such as *Paris, Texas* and *Wings of Desire* brought critical acclaim and reached international audiences. During the 1990s films such as *The End of Violence* and *The Million Dollar Hotel* have featured Hollywood actors on their own home turf.

8 Richard McCormick writes: "Both Handke's screenplay and Wenders' film can be seen as postmodern critiques of the ideology of the modern age, which was just beginning as Goethe wrote." Richard McCormick, *Politics of the Self. Feminism and the Postmodern in West German Literature and Film* (Princeton, NJ: Princeton University Press, 1991), p. 155. Eric Rentschler writes: "Wenders, much more radically than Handke, questions the German tradition of self-cultivation in showing Wilhelm's passage through the FRG to be a series of wrong moves, for the would-be Literat fails to consider anything but his personal well-being and intellectual improvement." Eric Rentschler, *West German Film in the Course of Time* (New York: Redgrave Publishing,

1984), p. 178. Kathe Geist identifies superficial similarities between text and film (the journey in search of self, the failures and self-recriminations, the lack of resolution), but also carefully underscores myriad differences among novel, screenplay, and film. Kathe Geist, *The Cinema of Wim Wenders. From Paris, France to Paris, Texas* (Ann Arbor: UMI Research Press, 1988), pp. 47–8.

9 McCormick, *Politics of the Self*, p. 161.

10 Alice Kuzniar, "Wenders's Windshields," in *The Cinema of Wim Wenders: Image, Narrative, and the Postmodern Condition*, ed. Roger R. Cook and Gerd Gemünden (Detroit: Wayne State University Press, 1997), p. 223.

11 McCormick, *Politics of the Self*, p. 154.

12 Wenders has said: "[Rock music] was the only alternative to Beethoven (and I'm really exaggerating here)... because I was very insecure... about all culture that was offered to me, because I thought it was all fascism, pure fascism." Quoted in Gerd Gemünden, "On the Way to Language: Wenders's Kings of the Road," *Film Criticism* 15:2 (1991), 18–19.

13 In his hometown Wilhelm rides his bike past a cinema showing *The Return of the Mounted Corpses*, a "third-rate Spanish horror film from 1973"; in Bonn he stands before a cinema showing Francis Ford Coppola's *The Conversation*; in Frankfurt Laertes and Mignon watch Straub/Huillet's *The Chronicle of Anna Madalena Bach* on television; and finally Therese, Mignon, and Wilhelm watch *La Victoria* at a drive-in. As Renstchler argues, the four films comment on the status of film in Germany, where "foreign-made genre fare gluts the dying provincial houses; American films occupy the more profitable first-run Kinos in the big cities; a German film made by two foreigners with a melange of subsidy money, television funding, and private backing plays on TV and reflects the tenuous existence of another subsidized artist; a political film made by a formerly exiled German Jew about a distant country's social climate unreels in an *Autorenkino*" (Rentschler, *West German Film*, pp. 177–8).

14 McCormick, *Politics of the Self*, p. 162.

15 Brian McFarlane, *Novel to Film: an Introduction to the Theory of Adaptation* (Oxford: Clarendon Press, 1996).

16 Thank you, Alice Kuzniar and Susan E. Gustafson, for reading earlier versions of this essay.

11 *Rob Roy*: the other eighteenth century?

Janet Sorensen

Michael Caton-Jones's 1995 film *Rob Roy* positions itself as radically "other" to previous British and US cinematic representations of the "long" eighteenth century. In its central formal and thematic elements the film stands in marked contrast to some of its well-known predecessors, films made in the 1970s through the 1990s that depict a British age of stability after the English Civil War and before a full-blown age of revolution.[1] Such films as *Barry Lyndon* (1975), *The Draughtsman's Contract* (1982), *Dangerous Liaisons* (1988), *The Madness of King George* (1994), and *Restoration* (1994) all render the period in the opulent, rich textures of the material commodities increasingly available in the late seventeenth- and eighteenth-century's rising imperial consumer culture.[2] These films tend to feature heavily composed shots: beautifully lit interior shots of carefully arranged, brilliantly colored luxury goods and tightly shot (and often oddly shot) close-ups of periwigged and made-up courtiers, whose staged, affected poses serve to emphasize the duplicity of their conspiring characters. All is artifice in these versions of the eighteenth century, and even exterior shots, when they appear, are of spectacular military formations of red coats, deep green formal gardens, or gilded pleasure crafts buoyed on man-made bodies of water. As these films stage excessive consumption, they also invite their viewers to imagine the past as a series of visual confections that are themselves available for consumption.[3]

These films generally depict the haunts of the wealthy and the intrigues of the powerful. Only rarely do they represent a comprehensive field of social strata. *Restoration*, for instance, opens with an exterior long-shot of laborers in a chaotic, thriving London and then cuts to mid-shots of overworked physicians in an overcrowded hospital. *Barry Lyndon* includes sequences of Barry's stint in the British army and briefly refers to the hardship of that life through mention of the poor quality of food served to the troops. Even these seemingly comprehensive visions are compromised, however, much like those of Smollett and Fielding which, as John Richetti has argued, offer "a synthesizing abridgment of an actuality that otherwise yields no knowledge worth having."[4] In their brevity and humor, these sequences signal to viewers that they should not look to them for much insight into the period or into the human condition in general. Merivel, the hero of *Restoration*, despite a chastening period of poverty and displacement, ascends – or is restored – to the majesty of his own stately Suffolk estate. Barry Lyndon is ushered off screen at precisely the moment at which he sinks into unending poverty, and the conclusion of *Dangerous Liaisons*, with Merteuil's fall from polite society, predicts but does not show a life outside of the decorous, resplendent world of aristocratic wealth. Instead, the preponderance of imagery in these films consists of the majestic manors and fine furnishings of the rich and well born. If these films reveal the worlds of the upper classes to be flawed, they do not pose the worlds of the lower classes as alternative and equally interesting sites of representation.

Rob Roy, on the other hand, with its mid-shots of roving toothless Highlanders, and its leading lady, Mary MacGregor, Rob's wife (Jessica Lange), made up to look unmade-up and relieving herself in a lake, seemingly rejects the powerful for the powerless, the artificial for the natural. The landscape, shot in natural light, is wild, and wasting indigence is the norm. The norm, that is, for Highlanders. When the film does offer the stock images of ornate interiors or mannered characters engaging in intrigues, these images are exclusively associated with the English or with turncoat Lowlanders. Images of the marquis of Montrose with his exoticized black slave and his palatial and meticulously maintained grounds, and the artificially lit interior shots of his luxuriantly appointed home serve to contrast his evil, prototypically "eighteenth-century" world with the spotlessly virtuous "natural" world of the Highlanders. In this essay I consider the cultural work these depictions of an "other" eighteenth century might be doing. It is my contention that part of that work is the reincorporation of the eighteenth century into a larger narrative of British heritage that might include much-simplified multicultural "Celtic" elements. *Rob Roy* does this by representing the extravagant, stylized world of class privilege that had functioned as the center point of many cinematic representations of the eighteenth century as unambivalently morally reprehensible. Unlike other films depicting the period, in *Rob Roy* the world of courtly power is no longer both desirable and morally questionable; that luxuriant world is rewritten as fully evil. Further, and perhaps more significant, another world becomes the focus of attention. Offering a sincere, sentimentalized Highland culture as an alternative, the film maps cultural (defined as) ethnic difference over class difference, always an important move within nationalist discourse. The film consolidates that cultural identity by representing it as under attack

by a devious English culture and thereby displaces obvious class antagonisms by representing them as ethnic and cultural ones. Thus, instead of
depicting English aristocrats oppressing English peasants of the period,
the film portrays domination in ethnic and cultural terms, drawing from
a very 1990s emphasis on ethnic and cultural divisions – which always
threaten to become the basis of nationalist struggles – at the expense of
class analysis.

This foregrounding of nationalist and related ethnic motifs in a decade
ridden with nationalist and ethnic strife explains, in part, the appeal
of a film about eighteenth-century Highlanders to a 1990s audience.
Another and related move that the film makes also helps account for
that popularity, and that is its claim, in a period of multiculturalism and
its concomitant revaluation of ethnic cultures, that whiteness, too, might
be an ethnic culture in need of salvaging. The distinct ethnicity of the
Highlanders is put forth as the film makes much of blood purity and its
violent violations; their oppressed status is understood not as a function
of property relations or transforming relations of production but as a
function of their distinct ethnic and cultural position. In this way the film
embraces a multicultural British heritage and even makes the move of
recognizing whiteness as a kind of ethnicity, but compromises that vision
by claiming the status of oppressed victimization for this whiteness. In this
respect, I will argue, the film participates in a new and disturbing project
to "make identity politics . . . safe for the silent majority."[5] The film situates an ethnically exoticized, politically repressed white group within
a sentimental economy, inviting identification with and pity toward an
oppressed group via cultural and ethnic markers.

The most common cinematic representations of the eighteenth century, in their emphasis on its splendid court and neoclassically designed
country estates, have rarely invited identification with the inhabitants
of those lavish dwellings. Less savvy characters – and viewers – learn the
hard way that surfaces, particularly human appearances, often belie hard-
hearted interiors. The shocking nature of the plottings of Valmont and
Merteuil, for instance, alienates the viewer, and close-ups of their pancake
make-up reinforce that alienation from these foreign and distant creatures. *Restoration*, although situated earlier, presents a similarly libertine
ethos less familiar and certainly less inviting of identification to audiences
than the Hollywood love-story formula. Mid-shots of King Charles's
sexual romps with his mistress depict the canopy bed as a kind of stage,
their lovemaking clearly not the conventional filmic scene of heterosexual
intimacy. Such representations, if they amuse the film viewer, rarely invite
his or her sympathy. These films instead direct the viewer's gaze toward
the opulent spectacle of courtly pomp and the trappings of landed gentry

life: rustling silk, Chinese fans, rich oil paintings, fine engravings, and elaborate topiary.

The sensibility is close to camp, as Susan Sontag describes it, a sensibility "of artifice, of stylization," "emphasizing texture, sensuous surface, and style at the expense of content," for camp is "the love of the exaggerated, of things being what they are not."[6] This is a world whose ruling image, after all, is the masquerade. In an early scene in *Restoration*, King Charles II and then Merivel don elaborate horse masks in an episode devoted to tricking one of Charles's mistresses into believing that the King has discarded another of his mistresses by marrying her off to Merivel. While the depravity of the court comes in for some censure later in the film, these early scenes of frolicsome artifice delight rather than scandalize. *Dangerous Liaisons* opens with images of the studied and painstaking toilet of the film's protagonists. And of his film *The Draughtsman's Contract* Peter Greenaway asserts, "the women's hair-styles are exaggerated in their height, the costumes are extreme. I wanted to make a very artificial film."[7] The camp qualities of these earlier films might be said to be true to the period, for Sontag identifies camp's "soundest starting point" in "the late seventeenth and early eighteenth century, because of that period's extraordinary feeling for artifice, for surface, for symmetry," and she concludes, "the early eighteenth century is the great period of Camp."[8] *Rob Roy* rejects that camp sensibility in its depiction of the period, a move that has considerable political consequences. For camp, in its reluctance, even refusal, to assign a moral value to exaggerated artifice and conscious, hyperbolic performance, poses one alternative to an essentialist vision, an alternative that undermines claims to ethnic purity, cultural unity and homogenization, and singular national identity. In contrast to the chest-thumping affirmations of blood and land found in *Rob Roy*, camp offers a reminder of the performative and multilayered character of those or any social relationships.

Such cinematic representations of a forthrightly superficial world have also posed an interesting alternative to classical narrative film, which so often privileges character identification in the cinematic experience.[9] The practiced detachment and studied cruelty of such characters as Valmont and Merteuil make them only objects of observation, rarely subjects of identification. Few of these screen representations of the eighteenth century, furthermore, attempt to recapture another ideological touchstone of the mid-to-late-eighteenth century, sentimentality. Sentimentality, an ethos valuing affective display, fellow-feeling, sympathy, and shared customs, was in this period very much connected to a "chivalric heterosexuality."[10] Yet emotional sympathy and chivalry are noticeably lacking in many standard depictions of the period. While a youthful

Redmond Barry falls prey to sentiment, a mature Barry Lyndon rejects its impracticality as he fortune-hunts for a wife. The goal, in this anti-sentimental economy, is to overcome feelings; the moment when they become "beyond my control," as Valmont puts it in *Dangerous Liaisons*, is the moment when one needs to sever all emotional ties. Indeed, the heavy use of mid-shots and distorting or alienating close-ups work against an economy of sentimental exchange. Thus, in an odd turn of events, while classical narrative film of the twentieth century has developed techniques of representing and inviting sentimental exchange in the shot/reverse-shot formula, that shot sequence and the sentiment it might foster are rarely used to represent English men and women of the eighteenth century, the period in which moral philosophers described the workings and insisted on the social value of sentimentality.[11]

The reluctance to emphasize sentimental exchange or to deploy the filmic techniques that invoke such sentiment might account in part for why the period has generally not, up until now, lent itself to what, following Andrew Higson, we might call "heritage" ideology.[12] The 1980s and 1990s witnessed the rise of British heritage films, films that, as Higson writes, "nostalgically reconstruct an imperialist and upper class Britain" and "offer... visually splendid manifestations of an essentially pastoral national identity and authentic culture."[13] To achieve the design of the heritage film – to instill a sense of continuity with a national past – some form of emotional identification with the characters is important. While representations of the eighteenth century on film have often reconstructed an imperialist and upper-class Britain, however, these have not been "nostalgic" representations, sentimentally calling up a lost wholeness. Depthless and alien in the lack of sentiment attached to them, the men and women of these films offer neither a model national character nor a point of national historic continuity. This absence of a nostalgic British nationalist frame of reference in film representations of the period is, like their devaluing of sentiment, a strange reversal, in as much as historians such as Benedict Anderson and Linda Colley have credited the eighteenth century with the rise of the cultural nationalism with which we remain quite familiar.[14] Nonetheless, the historical periods available for heritage films' reclamations of the national past have tended to fall outside of the eighteenth century. Higson argues that in heritage films based on nineteenth- and early twentieth-century Britain the narrative meaning and character identification often work against the heritage-friendly view of history as "depthless pastiche" and mere "visual splendor."[15] Yet the standard representations of the eighteenth century on film prove that mere visual splendor alone falls far short of suturing viewers to a represented past, an element necessary for the success of the heritage film.

18. Archibald Cunningham (Tim Roth) in a duel in Michael Caton-Jones's *Rob Roy*

The camp sensibility of the films, with their emphasis on surfaces and hyper-conscious performances of manipulated identities, makes notions of an essential "deep" Britishness impossible.

Rob Roy, alternatively, works to reinscribe the eighteenth century within a narrative of British national heritage and as it does so confronts its filmic predecessors' version of the eighteenth century. It includes the sumptuous eighteenth-century world of playful disguise yet consciously sets those images up for viewers' disidentification, recoding images and filmic syntax that viewers have come to associate with the eighteenth century as signs of a corrupt social space. *Rob Roy* reproduces elements of the camp sensibility of earlier filmic representations of the eighteenth century most notably in the exaggeratedly evil character of Archibald Cunningham, who manages to conduct even the most heinous of crimes – from caddish repudiation of his pregnant and penniless lover to premeditated murder – with pursed lips, raised eyebrows, and droll verbal expressions. Other filmic versions of the eighteenth century would reserve judgment on such a stylized character. Moral judgment would not be the point, as he would be played as camp, in which, as Sontag writes, "to emphasize style is to slight content, or to introduce an attitude which is neutral with respect to content... Camp sensibility is disengaged, depoliticized – or at least apolitical."[16] *Rob Roy*'s Cunningham, conversely, is in no way camp. Viewers are not asked to delight in his arch fiendishness. *Rob Roy*'s world might be an eighteenth-century Britain made safe for association with British national heritage.

None of *Rob Roy*'s antecedents fully adopts a camp ethos. Yet if they rather unconvincingly motion towards moral commentary on the dangers of artifice, they spend much more time celebrating the pleasures of style and moral disengagement. *Restoration* juxtaposes a sensuously indulgent court world against the world outside and its worthy poor, but it fudges the issue by placing its hero, wiser for his experience as an impoverished young physician, back into the position of wealthy estate owner and friend to King Charles II. Similarly, a syntagmatic reading of *Dangerous Liaisons* would necessarily stress the conclusion's condemnation of Valmont and Merteuil. Yet most of the film offers their shrewd strategizing and successes for the viewers' delectation. In *Rob Roy*, however, no such doubled message is available. The English and Lowland aristocracy, with the safe exception of the paternal Duke of Argyll, are odious, even or especially as they inhabit the stock imagery of an extravagant, stylized eighteenth century on film. Through this means the film moralizes what had been a rather free-floating set of cultural representations, forcefully insisting on camp's immoral rather than simply amoral quality.

This revaluation of stock film images of the eighteenth century is accompanied by transformation of oppressed Highlanders into ciphers of a Celtic cultural difference struggling to maintain its uniqueness. The film stresses the Highlanders' underdog status as they face heartless repression at the hands of those well-heeled, manicured, and lace-adorned eighteenth-century figures. Partaking in the emotional economy of the sentimental, which, as Robert Markley notes, "implicitly identif[ies] the victims of social inequality – men, women, and children – with 'feminine' powerlessness" ("Sentimentality as Performance," 212), Rob's band are the objects of sympathy. Shot/reverse-shot editing sutures the viewer into a sympathetic relationship to the Highlanders, as in an early scene, in which Rob surveys the huddled and impoverished faces of his clan. A naturally lit exterior shot/reverse-shot sequence shows Rob's rugged face, then pans the group of suffering elderly and very young kinsmen, and then cuts back to a reaction shot of Rob, his saddened eyes registering a deep sympathy. In another scene a young kinsman weeps at the realization that Mary MacGregor has been raped, while he and his fellows were unable to protect her from her English attacker. Rob and his followers, unlike their sophisticated contemporaries, never trade sophisticated verbal barbs in the stylized language of wit. Theirs is an honest language that differs from the verbal manipulation of their social superiors, their moments of jest articulated in earthy folk sayings. Close-ups of the physically beautiful Highland heroes, played by such film icons as Lange and Neeson, foster viewer identification.

What is especially interesting about *Rob Roy*'s respective characterizations of duplicitous, evil elites and creditable, sentimentalized peasants is their inscription within ethnic categories; not structured by class position, these differences are repetitively announced as the differences between Anglo and Celtic ethnicities. The association of Celticness with sentimental alternatives to dominant culture has become a leitmotif in recent films. Catering to what we might call a "metropolitan" center point of view, these films write out the complexities within and historical distinctions between various Celtic sites, conflating Scottish and Irish under a general, sentimentalized oppressed Celticness.[17] From *Titanic* (1997) to *Babe: Pig in the City* (1998), to films closer to the eighteenth century, such as *Restoration*, sentimental images of victimized classes have come to be associated with Celtic culture with noteworthy frequency. One particularly harrowing scene from *Babe: Pig in the City*, for instance, features animal patrollers rounding up a houseful of homeless animals. As the truncheons of the uniformed patrollers come down in slow motion on the heads of defenseless kittens and pups, a mournful Celtic instrumental tune, not unlike one we might hear in *Rob Roy*, plays alongside the shouts of their rapacious captors. In overlaying woeful Celtic strains over images of forced dislocation and the violent suppression of an ephemeral moment of organized resistance, the scene maps Celticness onto the subject position of the socially oppressed, and it does so through motifs of sentimentality. Recall too *Titanic*'s brief foray into the lower decks of the luxury liner – its glimpse at the impoverished passengers jammed together in the ship's hull reveals that these travelers are not only a poor-but-happy crowd, boisterously drinking and singing, but also a brogue-speaking, jig-dancing group, recognizably Celtic. The differences of the oppressed from their dominators are not charted via historically specific events and relationships, such as the Highland Clearances or the history of English occupation of Ireland, but between vaguely coded cultural practices, sublimating historical differences into a generalized "Celtic" victimhood.

Closer to the eighteenth century on screen, the servants and peasants in *Dangerous Liaisons*, bystanders to the alien world of their decadent betters, speak (strangely enough) with Scottish accents. And one of the two key "moral centers" of *Restoration* is an abandoned Irish woman named Katherine. Although half-crazed by her husband's leaving her, she speaks truth in her bizarre gestures and (brogue-inflected) expressions and heroically sacrifices her life for her unborn child – the very zenith of sentimental imagery. The message here, as in similar scenes in *Rob Roy*, is that the stuffy, sophisticated, but essentially fraudulent Anglo society might have the money and power, but the honest "embodied" Celts are superior, especially – and this will be important to my essay – because of their unsophisticated culture and the economy of sentiment that define them. The sincere Highlanders stand in contrast to Anglo characters incapable of knowable and honest identities. Repeated references to Cunningham's history of "buggery" and allusions to an English predilection for "buggery" link Cunningham and his nation to the "homosexual," that figure of dangerously fluid identity itself.[18] They and their world – not the Highlanders – come to represent the "other" in *Rob Roy*.

Rob Roy's representations of the wealthy elite as Anglo (English/ Lowlander) versus the propertyless as Celt (Highlander) ethnicize class difference. These ethnic valuations do not play out in the earlier films such as *Barry Lyndon*, in which the Irish hero can be as duplicitous as his fellows. Though the translation of class into ethnic/cultural difference might be recent, *Rob Roy* draws from an old Saxon/Celtic cultural binary and its distribution of sentimental qualities, which has its origins, as we know it, in the eighteenth century. Terry Eagleton links the image of "the convivial yet melancholic Celt with a song on his lips and a tear in his eye" as well as the discourse of moral sentiment itself to the relation of the periphery to a modernizing economy in the eighteenth century.[19] In this relationship, the rational, bloodless, duplicitous, and powerful Anglo stands in contrast to the sentimental, embodied, honest, and disempowered Celt. In more specific terms, the Anglo/Celt binary emerged in important ways through the drive to "improve" the Highlands in the wake of the Act of Union between England and Scotland in 1707, the Jacobite loss at Culloden, the disintegration of the clan system, and finally the forcible removal of Highlanders from the Highlands during the Clearances. Exhaustively explored by Peter Womack, the binary Anglo/Celtic counterposes mutually exclusive yet reciprocally defining dominant and dominated cultures.[20]

The relationship between these two geopolitical entities, and their role in developing narratives and methods of national cohesion, however, is even more complex, for it is necessary to account for the means by which British heritage discourses, generally dominated by Anglo-Britain, have been able to incorporate this "Celticness." As Katie Trumpener has shown, if England had the power to improve everything from domestic agriculture to empire, it relinquished the power to nurture sympathy and strong collective cultural affiliation, and thus the earliest and most effective cultural productions of nationalism arose not in the center of England but in the Celtic periphery. Most important – and central to my argument about the national heritage ideology of *Rob Roy* – is the fact that the "Celtic Periphery" occupies not simply colonial but also national space in the symbolic imaginary of Britain. Walter Scott articulates this doubled position when he comments on the appealing incongruity of Rob Roy (the early eighteenth-century Scots folk hero who had formed the basis of one of his own novels, a novel that bears no resemblance to the film). Scott describes how Rob Roy "blends the wild virtues, the subtle policy and unrestrained license of an American (native American), [yet was] Flourishing in Scotland during the Augustan age of Queen Anne and George I . . . within forty miles of . . . a great commercial city."[21] As the immediate threat that the Highlands had posed to both colonial and national integration faded after Britain successfully "subdued" them, they could be reclaimed as part of British national heritage. Thus, those powerful cultural modes of social cohesion produced in the Celtic periphery could be appropriated – albeit in a transformed manner – for British narratives of national cohesion. If the film *Rob Roy* suggests that an Anglo eighteenth century might be radically other, it simultaneously maintains the Highlanders' proximity to British culture in order to suggest that a Highlander might be "one of us." It is true that, unlike its counterparts representing the Highlands, from tour books to Scott's novels, the film *Rob Roy* tells its story through the perspective of the Highlanders. Yet they are English-speaking peasants, and it is through abnegating their real linguistic differences and relegating them to representatives of a past and earthy physicality that they offer a much stronger point of relationship than their cosmopolitan oppressors. The film might then be said to reenact the British appropriation of Celtic modes of sentimental nationalism that Trumpener traces in British Romantic literature.

Interestingly, however, the particular type of national subjectivity required by those emerging notions of Britishness in a modernizing, post-Union Britain in the late eighteenth century and early nineteenth century was not one of authenticity or of unmediated identification with the past or the culturally "different." James Buzzard, Ina Ferris, and Ian Duncan have all argued, for instance, that in Scott's novels, the emphasis is on inauthenticity and a consciousness of alienation from remote spaces and times, specifically foregrounding "historical difference from the Gaelic world."[22] As Duncan writes of Scott's novels, "the knowledge of our alienation from 'authentic' cultural identities accompanies our privileged repossession of those lost identities as aesthetic effects" ("Introduction," ix). The film *Rob Roy*, however, cannot afford to acknowledge fully the viewers' alienation from a Gaelic past in its aim at an appropriable multicultural status for Britishness and whiteness. The film differs from Scott's novel not only in the novel's wildly different plot but also in the novel's self-consciousness of translation and fabrication.

In articulating the oppressed status of its (white and British) Highland characters through ethnicity, the film depends on the rhetoric of authenticity that accompanies discourses of ethnicity. The film omits the difficulties and estrangement involved in cultural translation by avoiding those issues in relation to linguistic translation – its Highlanders speak not Scots Gaelic but a thoroughly comprehensible version of English with occasional inflections of Lowland Scots. If theirs is not the abstract, almost placeless language of Standard English, it is an accented English, offering regional specificity within the unifying rubric of a single "British" language. Alternatively, any tensions of representing the foreignness of the Highlanders – the potentially edgy quality of their "alien" character – are dispensed with early on. The film's opening scene, in which Rob travels deep into imposing mountains to retrieve the cattle of Lord Montrose from a band of roving, menacing Highlanders distinguishes Rob and his folk from other bestial, thuggish Highlanders. Rob authoritatively asserts that he "protects" these cattle (in fact, not dissimilar from mafia-style protection), and in stealing from Montrose, they are stealing from him. Here, Rob claims common cause with the Anglo-British Montrose against "criminal" Highlanders. These other Highlanders, such as the drunken, irrational Will Guthrie, who challenges Rob, are dispensed with – two are stabbed to death by Rob, the others disband and disappear.

The Highlands have been – for centuries now – an over-determined mythic site; in 1817 Scott had already resignedly written to James Ballantyne, "You are aware the Highlands are rather a worn-out subject."[23] Yet this film comfortably inhabits the conventional representations of that subject as well as a variety of generic codes – from the Western, with its lone virtuous outlaw hero and its long shots of uninhabited mountainous landscapes, to the 1930s Warner Brothers historical biopic, with its candy-coated hero – and draws from a series of clichéd images of tartan-clad, dirk-wielding Highlanders, all of which should make for great camp. Despite this, it achieves a kind of formal transparency, managing to evade an expected slide into kitsch or even the hint of self-consciousness about its generic borrowings. The film needs to maintain that un-self-consciousness regarding its own conventions because its logic has rejected self-conscious posing and playful doubledness. Cunningham, ruthless and self-serving, is most detestable because of his very relish for self-conscious posing and duplicity. The film marks this "enemy" through his conscious manipulation of identity and its coding of him as sexually suspect. Not the courtiers but the Highlanders function as the point of identification – and object of sympathy – in part through their essential, non-manipulable identity. The film thus offers an oppressed group for appropriation by viewers, an oppressed group, it must be added, which is both ethnically oppressed and white. This is a kind of multiculturalism, but one in which the "Celts" represent a separate and victimized ethnicity with which a white audience might claim affinity. Such claims must necessarily suppress the doubled and parodic quality of camp.

One key scene of Gaelic culture seemingly under attack and a series of sequences of consequent conflicts over blood illustrate the film's mapping of oppression into cultural and ethnic terrains. One of these is the critical scene of Rob's clan celebrating the prospect of borrowing money to buy and sell cattle intercut with Cunningham's murder of one of Rob's group and the theft of that money. Here, class oppression is re-imaged as an attack on Celtic cultural difference. Parallel editing, in a complex series of cross-cuts and dissolves, depicts an egalitarian tribe that suffers not at the hands of another class but at the hand of a culturally distinct interloper. This logic is epitomized in the image in this sequence in which Cunningham, marked as eighteenth-century Anglo by his wig and luxurious clothing (all the more noticeable in the night-time forest setting of this scene) stabs Alan MacDonald, the red-headed, unshaven, kilted Highlander, in whom the clan has entrusted hopes of future prosperity. Images of Cunningham's predatory murder of MacDonald, who is returning to the clan with the borrowed money, are cross-cut with scenes of a traditional Highland fest – a ceilidh complete with dancing and music. The evil English Cunningham hunts down the defenseless Highlander, threatening the destruction of the Highlands, which is figured through images of Scots Gaelic material cultural practices.

The rhythm of this intercutting sequence slows down considerably after the cuts between a lively horseback chase and high-spirited dancing and music. Scenes of a wounded Alan MacDonald valiantly but futilely attempting to elude his English hunter are cross-cut with a dark-haired woman singing a mournful Gaelic song (the only use of Scots Gaelic language in the film). This intercutting reinforces the notion that what Cunningham is really killing is the unique culture of the Highlanders. The camera pans across the Highlander men, women, and children staring into the fire as they listen to the woman's song, and the heat rays of the fire create a dreamlike effect, slightly distorting the Highlanders' faces as they begin to blur together. This is an unmistakably bonded community, graphically represented in the blending together of their individual visages. Not a word is spoken throughout this long, slow sequence; the strength of communal sentiment between these Highlanders exceeds words altogether. Dancing, eating, and trading jokes about sex, this is an embodied group, and through emphasizing this embodiment, along with their cultural particularity, the film establishes that whiteness, like "other"

19. Rob Roy (Liam Neeson) and Mary MacGregor (Jessica Lange) at
the ceilidh in *Rob Roy*

ethnicities, can be marked and embodied, in a sense de-universalized or
de-abstracted.

   This particular form of whiteness is then depicted as being under attack. The slightly distorted firelit image of the Highlanders also makes
them a ghostlike presence; they and their culture exist, the viewer is reminded, only in memory. Such scenes recall James Macpherson's mist-
ified vision of the Highlands in his *Fingal* (1762) or the romantic imagery
of William Collins' *Ode on Popular Superstitions of the Highlands* (1788);
both writers represent the Highlanders and their culture as irrecoverably
past. In the film, the viewer's privileged position in this sequence points to
a similar relation between reading or viewing subject and Highland object.
The viewer experiences the murder and the ceilidh simultaneously. Yet
the Highlanders the viewer watches are unaware of MacDonald's tragic
fate – or theirs – at that point. The viewer might indulge in the sentimentality of the Highland scene, but the true power of the sentiment of
the sequence derives from the viewer being outside of it. The images of
the ceilidh are all the more poignant, all the more sentimentally driven,
by knowledge of the immanent devastation of these Highlanders (unbe-
knownst to them) with a loss of one of their own and the meager hope
for their own improvement. This doubled position of the viewer – both
insider, identifying with the Highlanders and outsider, with distance and

privileged knowledge – replicates the logic of multicultural appropriation, where consumption, often alongside cultural disintegration, underwrites multicultural "appreciation."

The slower segment of this sequence begins with an extreme close-up of the singer's mouth. Despite its anachronistic lipstick, the close-up of the mouth touches on a recurring theme throughout the movie of the Highlanders' essential orality – and a concomitant immediacy and sincerity. This orality is another marker for embodiment in contrast to the abstracting writing and print associated with the English. As the film borrows from many already familiar visions of the Highlands, it perpetuates a longstanding myth linking the Highlanders' orality to a discrete social and economic system. If the Anglo society is one of arbitrary hierarchies in which blood relatives such as Montrose and Cunningham have nothing but disdain for each other, the hierarchies of the Highlanders are naturally recognized by members of the familial clan. Rob's men repeatedly declare that they "are not ruled by Rob but are his friends," and Rob's wife's opinion is sought in clan decisions in this utopic political world. The orality of these Highlanders also reinforces the notion of their being "true to their word" in a way that the literate Anglos are not. It is especially ironic, however, that the Highlanders' insistence on a cultural code of being true to one's word would be of the utmost importance not to a mythic use-value economy but, instead, to the rising credit economy supposedly so seemingly distant from but in fact quite common to eighteenth-century Highland experience.

The Highlanders' integration into an international commerce economy, however, is stubbornly silenced in this film. Scott's novel, as Ian Duncan has argued, reveals the ways in which investment in and prizing of representations of cultural differences are a function of an expanding world-system, a capitalist economy saturating most of the globe, but this ineluctable relationship is unavailable in the film. One of the most important markers of the cultural difference of the Highlanders in *Rob Roy* is their supposed status as inhabitants of an entirely separate pre-commodity-form economy whose insularity could guarantee the ongoing purity of their distinct ethnic and cultural community. Noticeably absent from the visual world of the Highlanders are the self-aggrandizing material goods so much in evidence in other filmic visions of the eighteenth century. The heather beds and rough-hewn iron caldrons of Rob's domestic space stage the fiction of an economy based on pure use-value. The film depicts the Highlanders as inhabiting an economy and culture distinct from a usurping English capital economy, an invaded utopia of barter, where tenants make payments to landlords in kind. In fact, the Highlanders' troubles stem from Rob's entry into private property, specifically into an English/Lowland speculative economy of cattle futures, as he asks for a loan of money from the nefarious aristocrat Montrose – money which is then stolen, initiating the outright battles between the Highlanders and their Anglo foes. Yet the film's denouement finds the Highlanders able to return to this pursuit of property ownership, and the happy ending is pinned on their successful bid to start their own small business in cattle trading.

The notion of "honest" use-value production, as opposed to the deceit and excess of the south, is ethnicized as it extends to the pure Highland sexual economy and its pollution. While the married Rob and Mary engage in natural sex and reproduce, all assortment of allusion is made to the perverse sexuality of the English, from Queen Anne's inability to reproduce (Montrose quips, "I have seen healthier graveyards than that woman's womb"), to Cunningham who is, as he himself puts it, "a bastard who begets a bastard." The link of sexual perversion to commercial money economies is an old one, as evidenced in Ben Jonson's *Volpone*, for instance, and the film seizes on this imagery in its respective depictions of the resolutely masculine and heterosexual Rob in contrast with the fawning foppishness of Cunningham, whose character Janet Maslin, in her *New York Times* review, aptly describes as "small, fussy and fey."[24] As opposed to the blood purity of the Highland Celts, figures such as Cunningham point to the mongrel mix of Englishness that might threaten the pure whiteness of the Celts.

The consequence of their participation in the corrupt English world of speculation and money is grotesquely imaged in the film's graphic depictions of English sexual conquest – as ethnic pollution – in Cunningham's rape of Mary MacGregor. Disruption of blood purity is the necessary consequence of this cultural and economic exchange. Worse still is the seeming endorsement of blood and land nationalism. If the oft-repeated long shots of the mountains foreground land, the close-up images of rape invoke its twin in ethnic–nationalist rhetoric, blood. Interestingly, other films of the eighteenth century, when they depict rape, often do so from the perspective of the rapist – such as Valmont – and subscribe to something like a camp sensibility in the divorce of content from highly stylized seduction. In *Rob Roy*, rape is filled with political content, but it is of a most reactionary kind, a mere figure for violation of ethnic purity, naturalizing ethnic difference as it dismisses other bases of oppression.[25] The greatest horror of the rape, finally, is not the violence against the woman so much as it is the threat of racial corruption, as Cunningham impregnates her.

In a film awash in historical inaccuracies, perhaps the most important and destructive one is its treatment of the Highlands as an ethnically and culturally distinct community making the transition, for better or worse, to an advanced modern British economy. Criticism of the film merely on the basis of its tartan sentimentality might reflect ongoing cultural biases, and surely there is something very easy about an Anglo/center sneer at the pathos generated in these images of persecuted Highlanders. That wrong is not righted, however, in embracing the terms of analysis of that persecution as forwarded in this film. Its sentimentality, its rewriting of a cultural whiteness as the basis of oppression, and above all its dangerous nods in the direction of ethnic separatism do a disservice to the historical complexities of the geopolitics of Britain in the eighteenth century and in our own period. If, for instance, as Peter Murphy has shown, ruling Highland chiefs had sophisticated economic dealings with the English and French, dealings that often sold out the tenant farmers of their clans, a film that ignores this information about class in order to map ethnic over economic identities is no less dangerous because it claims to do so from the perspective of the oppressed.[26] Such a mapping over would be impossible if the film also drew from the many ballads and chapbooks produced in the early eighteenth century depicting the "Highland Rogue" – as Rob Roy was called in the most famous of the broad sheets – as a resistance folk hero in class terms. The film draws selectively from those popular representations, endowing Rob with the generosity for which he was renowned in literature but failing to portray the criminal activities of this Scottish Robin Hood whose freebooting or smuggling would, of course, be intimately tied and perhaps resistant to commercial exchange within the Highlands and between the Highlands and their southern neighbors. In historical depictions Rob Roy stole from wealthy Scots cattle owners, a fact that both foregrounds distinctions of property ownership in the period and situates Rob Roy in a considerably more complex position than that depicted in the film.[27]

If *Rob Roy* is a filmic version of the eighteenth century that looks beyond the sumptuously appointed world of the privileged, its vision of oppression and opposition as ethnically based writes collective identity into a market-based multiculturalism. Now, as in the eighteenth century, the logic of the market has written – sometimes even produced – cultural difference as consumer good. In Caton-Jones's film the erasure enacted by the commodification of cultural difference participates in a consumerist multiculturalism's latest market trend: the writing of white ethnicity as cultural "other," as marginalized victim. In mediating cultural contact through consumption, multiculturalism has bolstered a market in consumer goods of cultural difference. The multi-million-dollar budget of this film, in pitching to that market, sets its hackneyed images afloat in a sea of high production values. Thus, in a film that gets many things wrong, thousands of dollars were spent on getting the artifacts right, the stock and trade of the heritage film.

Rob Roy must seriously play with history in order to use one of eighteenth-century Britain's most disruptive histories as a means of enlisting the eighteenth century in the cultural work of British heritage. Kitsch images of Scots history, what one reviewer called "rampant tartanry,"[28] might suggest a post-modern playfulness, where image replaces reality and boundaries between high and low culture dissolve.[29] Such a reading not only assumes an implicit hierarchization of audiences, but also ignores *Rob Roy*'s efforts to render such playfulness transparent. *Rob Roy* devalues the theatrical and playfully performative aspects of identity, and it must do so in order to represent white identity as fixed, essential, and under threat of attack. When it comes to questions of national and ethnic identities, however, no approach seems more suitable than the acknowledgment of self-conscious artifice and performance apparent in the eighteenth century's camp sensibility and cinematic attempts to reproduce it.

NOTES

1 Here I include filmic representations of Britain before 1700 because these films are generally continuous with representations of a stable, hierarchically ordered, and prosperous (for some) Hanoverian Britain. For a summary of this and other models of periodization of seventeenth- and eighteenth-century Britain see David Cannadine, *Class in Britain* (New Haven: Yale University Press, 1998).

2 In this paper I limit my discussion to films made for theatrical release. I focus on the films that fall into the specific patterns of representations of the eighteenth century I identify, well aware that there are notable exceptions – such as *Moll Flanders* (1996).

3 Peter Greenaway, for instance, says of his *Draughtsman's Contract*, "My film is about excess." Cited in Peter Wollen, "The Last New Wave," in *Fires Were Started: British Cinema and Thatcherism*, ed. Lester Friedman (Minneapolis: University of Minnesota Press, 1993), p. 45.

4 John Richetti, "Representing an Under Class: Servants and Proletarians in Fielding and Smollett," in *The New Eighteenth Century*, ed. Laura Brown and Felicity Nussbaum (New York: Methuen, 1987), p. 91.

5 Mike Hill uses this phrase in his introduction to *Whiteness: A Critical Reader*, ed. Mike Hill (New York University Press, 1997), p. 3. Hill also refers to attempts to "'lactify' ethnic difference" (p. 12).

6 Susan Sontag, "Notes on 'Camp'" in *Against Interpretation* (New York: Dell Publishing, 1966), pp. 275–92. Citations from pp. 277, 278, and 279, respectively.

7 Wollen, "Last New Wave," p. 45.

8 Sontag, "Notes," p. 280.
9 David Bordwell writes, "character-centered – i.e., personal or psychological – causality is the armature of the classical story" (p. 12) and identifies psychological instability, such as "attractive killers, repellent cops" (p. 76) (and, we might add, seductively amoral aristocrats) as working against the conventions of classical Hollywood cinema. Bordwell et al. (eds.), *The Classical Hollywood Cinema* (New York: Columbia University Press, 1986).
10 Claudia Johnson, *Equivocal Beings* (University of Chicago Press, 1995), p. 6. As Johnson notes, "Sentimentality has a long and exceedingly complex history" (p. 12), and Robert Markley (among others) has pointed to the theatrical quality of sentimentality's displayed affect in "Sentimentality as Performance" in *The New Eighteenth Century*, eds. Nussbaum and Brown. My point, then, is not that representations of sentimentality would pose a clear alternative to the concern with surfaces in many standard cinematic representations of the period, but that many of these films neglect any form of depicting sentimentality.
11 James Chandler made the link between sentimental exchange and shot/reverse-shot edits in "The Sentimental Case," a paper delivered at a conference entitled "Exemplary Cases" at the Clark Library, April 28–9, 2000.
12 Andrew Higson, "Re-Presenting the National Past: Nostalgia and Pastiche in the Heritage Film," in *Fires Were Started: British Cinema and Thatcherism*, ed. Lester Friedman (Minneapolis: University of Minnesota Press, 1993). *The Madness of King George*, produced a year earlier than *Rob Roy*, incorporates elements of camp sensibility – particularly in the characterization of the Prince Regent – but it also, fleetingly, depicts a sentimental economy around the King that serves a heritage agenda. While the film points to the artifice of royal display and the discontinuity of the past with the present, in as much as conceptions of monarchy are in transition, it also suggests a grudging respect for the royals. Parliamentary reformers such as Fox are depicted as shadowy and self-serving figures in contrast to the straight-shooting King George.
13 Higson, "Re-Presenting the National Past," p. 110.
14 Benedict Anderson, *Imagined Communities: Reflections on the Origins and Spread of Nationalism* (New York: Verso, 1983) and Linda Colley, *Britons: Forging the Nation 1707–1837* (New Haven, CT: Yale University Press, 1992).
15 Higson, "Re-presenting the National Past," p. 112.
16 Sontag, "Notes," p. 277.
17 This metropolitan point of view, and its reduction of Irish, Scottish, and Welsh to a mere "Celtic" status, has a history we can trace back at least to the late eighteenth century, as documented in Katie Trumpener's book, *Bardic Nationalism: The Romantic Novel and British Empire* (Princeton, NJ: Princeton University Press, 1997).
18 Lee Edelman explores this connection in *Homographesis* (New York: Routledge, 1994).
19 Terry Eagleton, *Crazy John and the Bishop* (Notre Dame, IN: University of Notre Dame Press, 1998), p. 73.
20 Peter Womack, *Improvement and Romance: Constructing the Myth of the Highlands* (London: Macmillan, 1989).

21 Cited in Ian Duncan's "Introduction" to Walter Scott, *Rob Roy*, ed. and intro. Ian Duncan (Oxford University Press, 1998), p. xxii. Much of my thinking for this essay took shape in conversation with Ian Duncan.

22 Duncan, "Introduction," p. ix; James Buzzard, "Translation and Tourism: Rendering Culture in Scott's *Waverley*," *Yale Journal of Criticism*, 8 (1995), 31–59 and Ina Ferris, "Translation from the Borders: Encounter and Recalcitrance in *Waverley* and *Clan-Albin*," *Eighteenth-Century Fiction* 9 (1997), 203–22.

23 Scott quotation cited in Duncan, "Introduction," p. xi.

24 Janet Maslin, "Rob Roy," *New York Times*, April 7, 1995.

25 The same could be said of that other film blockbuster *Braveheart* – which might explain, in part, racist ideologue Pat Buchanan's ringing endorsement of it.

26 Peter Murphy, "Fool's Gold: The Highland Treasures of Macpherson's Ossian," *ELH* 52 (1985). See also Duncan's "Introduction."

27 That the Robin Hood figure has been trivialized in various contexts should not mitigate the early understanding of Robin Hood as "social bandit" – a figure of rebellion against a corrupt social order. In fact, we might see the early commercial success of images and stories of Robin Hood as directly related to this social meaning. See Eric Hobsbawm, *Social Bandits* (Glencoe, IL: Free Press, 1960).

28 "Me Tartan, You Chained to Past," *The Guardian*, January 18, 1995.

29 Here I draw from a discussion of post-modernism and representations of Scots heritage in David McCrone et al., *Scotland the Brand: The Making of Scottish Heritage* (Edinburgh: Edinburgh University Press, 1995).

Filmography

The Adventures of Robinson Crusoe (Ultramar Films; United Artists, 1952)
Director: Luis Buñuel
Producer: Oscar Dancigers, Henry F. Ehrlich
Screenplay: Luis Buñuel, Philip Roll
Cinematographer: Alex Philips
Art Director: Edward Fitzgerald
Music: Anthony Collins
Sound: Javier Mateos
Editor: Carlos Savage
Cast: Dan O'Herlihy (Crusoe), Jaime Fernandez (Friday)
Running time: 89 minutes (US)

The Amorous Adventures of Moll Flanders (Winchester Productions Ltd., 1965)
Director: Terence Young
Producer: Marcel Hellman
Screenplay: Dennis Cannan, Roland Kibbee
Cinematographer: Ted Moore
Production Designer: Syd Cain
Music: John Addison
Editor: Frederick Wilson
Cast: Kim Novak (Moll), Claire Ufland (Young Moll), Richard Johnson (Jemmy),
    Angela Lansbury (Lady Blystone), Leo McKern (Squint), Vittorio De Sica
    (The Count), George Sanders (The Banker)
Running time: 126 minutes

Barry Lyndon (Hawk Films; Peregrine; Polaris, 1975)
Director: Stanley Kubrick
Producer: Stanley Kubrick
Screenplay: Stanley Kubrick
Cinematographer: John Alcott
Production Designer: Ken Adam
Costume Designer: Milena Canonero, Ulla Britt-Söderelund
Music: The Chieftains, Leonard Rosenman
Editor: Tony Lawson

Cast: Ryan O'Neal (Barry Lyndon), Maris Berenson (Lady Lyndon), Patrick Magee (The Chevalier de Balibari), Frank Middlemass (Sir Charles Lyndon), Leon Vitali (Lord Bullingdon)
Running time: 184 minutes

Clarissa (British Broadcasting Corporation; WGBH Boston, 1991)
Director: Robert Bierman
Producer: Kevin Loader
Screenplay: Janet Barron, David Nokes
Cinematographer: John McGlashan
Production Designer: Gerry Scott
Music: Colin Towns
Editor: Bill Wright
Cast: Saskia Wickham (Clarissa), Sean Bean (Lovelace), Jonathan Phillips (James), Lynsey Baxter (Bella), Jeffry Wickham (Mr. Harlowe), Cathryn Harrison (Mrs. Sinclair), Julian Firth (Mr. Solmes)
Running time: 156 minutes

Crusoe (Island Pictures, 1988)
Director: Caleb Deschanel
Producer: Andrew Braunsberg
Screenplay: Walon Green
Cinematographer: Tomislav Pinter
Production Designer: Veljko Despotovic
Music: Michael Kamen
Editor: Humphrey Dixon
Cast: Aidan Quinn (Crusoe), Hepburn Graham (Lucky), Ade Sapara (The Warrior)
Running time: 91 minutes

Dangerous Liaisons (Lorimar Film Entertainment; NFH Productions; Warner Bros., 1988)
Director: Stephen Frears
Producer: Norma Heyman, Hank Moonjean
Screenplay: Christopher Hampton
Cinematographer: Philippe Rousselot
Production Designer: Stuart Craig
Art Direction: Stuart Craig, Gérard Viard
Music: George Fenton
Editor: Mick Audsley
Cast: Glenn Close (Marquise de Merteuil), John Malkovich (Vicomte de Valmont), Michelle Pfeiffer (Madame de Tourvel), Swoosie Kurtz (Madame de Volanges), Keanu Reeves (Chevalier Danceny)
Running time: 119 minutes

Falsche Bewegung (English title: *Wrong Move*) (Solaris-Film; Westdeutscher
    Rundfunk, 1974)
Director: Wim Wenders
Producer: Bernd Eichinger, Peter Genée
Screenplay: Peter Handke
Cinematographer: Robby Müller
Production Designer: Heidi Lüd
Music: Jürgen Knieper
Editor: Peter Przygodda
Cast: Rüdiger Vogler (Wilhelm), Hanna Schygulla (Therese), Ivan Desny
    (The Industrialist), Marianne Hoppe (The Mother), Hans Christian Blech
    (Laertes), Nastassja Kinski (Mignon), Lisa Kreuzer (Janine)
Running time: 103 minutes

The Fortunes and Misfortunes of Moll Flanders (Granada Television [UK]; WGBH
    Boston [US], 1996)
Director: David Attwood
Producer: David Lascelles
Screenplay: Andrew Davies
Cinematographer: Ivan Strasburg
Production Designer: Stephen Fineren
Music: Jim Parker
Editor: Edward Mansell
Cast: Alex Kingston (Moll), Daniel Craig (Jemmy), Diana Rigg (Mrs. Golightly),
    Ronald Fraser (Sir Richard Gregory), Dallas Campbell (Master Denniston)
Running time: 216 minutes (UK); 220 minutes (US)

Gulliver's Travels (Channel Four Films [Film Four International]; Jim Henson
    Productions; RHI Entertainment Inc., 1996)
Director: Charles Sturridge
Producer: Duncan Kenworthy
Screenplay: Simon Moore
Cinematographer: Howard Atherton
Production Designer: Roger Hall
Music: Trevor Jones
Editor: Peter Coulson
Cast: Ted Danson (Lemuel Gulliver), Mary Steenburgen (Mary Gulliver), James
    Fox (Dr. Bates), Ned Beatty (Farmer Grultrud), Edward Fox (General
    Limtoc), Robert Hardy (Dr. Parnell)
Running time: 187 minutes

The History of Tom Jones, A Foundling (British Broadcasting Corporation [UK];
    Arts and Entertainment Network [US], 1997)
Director: Metin Hüseyin
Producer: Michael Wearing (BBC), Delia Fine (A & E)
Screenplay: Simon Burke
Music: Jim Parker
Cinematographer: Cinders Forshaw
Editing: Annie Kocur, Paul Tothill

Leading players: John Sessions (Henry Fielding), Max Beesley (Tom Jones), Samantha Morton (Sophie Western), Benjamin Whitrow (Squire Allworthy), Tessa Peake-Jones (Bridget Allworthy), James D'Arcy (Blifil), Brian Blessed (Squire Western), Christopher Fulford (Mr Square), Richard Ridings (Revd. Thwackum)

Running time: 95 minutes (UK [5 parts]); 120 minutes (US [3 parts])

Jacques le fataliste et son maître (Antenne 2; Société Française de Production; French Ministry of Culture, 1983)
Director: Claude Santelli
Producer: Michèle Vidal
Screenplay: Claude Santelli
Cinematographer: André Dumaître
Art Direction: Jean Thomen
Music: Jean-Marie Sénia
Editor: Catherine Gabrielidis, Juliana Sanchez
Cast: Patrick Chesnais (Jacques), Guy Tréjan (His master), François Périer (Diderot), Henri Virlogeux (Gousse), and Catherine Samie (The hostess of the Grand Cerf Inn)
Running time: 123 minutes

Joseph Andrews (Woodfall Film Productions, 1977)
Director: Tony Richardson
Producer: Neil Hartley
Screenplay: Chris Bryant, Allan Scott; screen story by Tony Richardson
Music: John Addison
Cinematographer: David Watkin
Production Designer: Michael Annals
Editor: Thom Noble
Cast: Peter Firth (Joseph Andrews), Ann-Margret (Lady Booby), Natalie Ogle (Fanny Goodwill), Michael Hordern (Parson Adams), Beryl Reid (Slipslop), Peggy Ashcroft (Lady Tattle), Timothy West (Mr Tow-wouse), John Gielgud (Doctor), Hugh Griffith (Squire Western)
Running time: 99 minutes

Les Liaisons dangereuses 1960 (Les Films Marceau-Cocinor, 1959)
Director: Roger Vadim
Screenplay: Claude Brulé, Roger Vadim, Roger Vailland
Cinematographer: Marcel Grignon
Production Designer: Robert Guisgand
Music: Art Blakey, Thelonious Monk, Jack Murray
Editor: Victoria Mercanton
Cast: Jeanne Moreau (Juliette de Merteuil), Gérard Philipe (Vicomte de Valmont), Annette Vadim (Marianne Tourvel), Jeanne Valérie (Cecile Volanges), Jean-Louis Trintignant (Danceny)
Running time: 106 minutes

Man Friday (ABC Entertainment, Incorporated Television Company, Keep, 1975)
Director: Jack Gold
Producer: David Korda
Screenplay: Adrian Mitchell
Cinematographer: Alex Phillips Jr.
Production Designer: Peter Murton
Art Direction: Agustín Ituarte
Music: Carl Davis
Editor: Anne V. Coates
Cast: Peter O'Toole (Robinson Crusoe), Richard Roundtree (Friday)
Running time: 115 minutes

Moll Flanders (MGM; Spelling Films; Trilogy Entertainment Group, 1995)
Director: Pen Densham
Producer: Tim Harbert, Pen Densham, Richard Barton Lewis, John Watson
Screenplay: Pen Densham
Cinematographer: David Tattersall
Production Designer: Caroline Hanania
Art Direction: John Lucas, Steve Simmonds
Music: Mark Mancina
Editor: James R. Symons, Neil Travis
Cast: Robin Wright (Moll), Morgan Freeman (Hibble), Stockard Channing (Mrs. Allworthy), John Lynch (Jonathan Fielding), Brenda Fricker (Mrs. Mazzawatti)
Running time: 123 minutes

Rob Roy (Talisman Production; United Artists, 1995)
Director: Michael Caton-Jones
Producer: Peter Broughan, Richard Jackson
Screenplay: Alan Sharp
Cinematographer: Karl Walter Lindenlaub
Production Designer: Assheton Gorton
Art Direction: John Ralph, Alan Tomkins
Music: Carter Burwell
Editor: Peter Honess
Cast: Liam Neeson (MacGregor), Jessica Lange (Mary MacGregor), John Hurt (Marquis of Montrose), Tim Roth (Archibald Cunningham), Eric Stoltz (Macdonald), Andrew Keir (Duke of Argyll), Brian Cox (Killearn)
Running time: 139 minutes

Suzanne Simonin, la religieuse de Denis Diderot (English title: *The Nun*) (Films Rome-Paris; Société Nouvelle de Cinématographie, 1966)
Director: Jacques Rivette
Producer: Georges de Beauregard
Screenplay: Jean Gruault, Jacques Rivette

Cinematographer: Alain Levent
Costume Designer: Jeanine Herrly
Music: Jean-Claude Eloy
Editor: Denise de Casabianca
Cast: Anna Karina (Suzanne), Gillette Barbier (Soeur Saint-Jean), Francine
  Bergé (Soeur Sainte-Christin), Yori Bertin (Soeur Saint-Thérèse), Hubert
  Buthion (The Archbishop)
Running time: 155 minutes

Tom Jones (Woodfall Film Productions, 1963)
Director: Tony Richardson
Producer: Tony Richardson
Screenplay: John Osborne
Cinematographer: Walter Lassally
Production Designer: Ralph W. Brinton
Art Direction: Ted Marshall
Music: John Addison
Editor: Anthony Gibbs
Cast: Albert Finney (Tom Jones), Susannah York (Sophie Western), George
  Devine (Squire Allworthy), Rachel Kempson (Bridget Allworthy), Joyce
  Redman (Mrs Waters), Diane Cilento (Molly Seagrim), Freda Jackson (Mrs
  Seagrim), John Moffatt (Square), Peter Bull (Thwackum), David Warner
  (Blifil), Hugh Griffith (Squire Western), Edith Evans (Miss Western), Joan
  Greenwood (Lady Bellaston), Micheál Macliammóir (Narrator [voice])
Running time: 121 minutes

Bibliography

Andrew, J. Dudley. *Some Concepts in Film Theory*. Oxford: Oxford University Press, 1984.

Armstrong, Nancy. *Desire and Domestic Fiction: A Political History of the Novel*. New York and Oxford: Oxford University Press, 1987.

Balázs, Béla. *Theory of the Film: Character and Growth of a New Art*. New York: Arno Press; New York Times, 1972.

Barthes, Roland. *The Pleasure of the Text*. Trans. Richard Miller. New York: Hill and Wang, 1975.

Image–Music–Text. Ed. and trans. Stephen Heath. New York: Hill and Wang, 1977.

Bazin, André. *What is Cinema?* 2 vols. Trans. Hugh Gray. Berkeley and Los Angeles: University of California Press, 1967–71.

Beja, Morris. *Film and Literature: An Introduction*. New York and London: Longman, 1979.

Bhabha, Homi K. *The Location of Culture*. London and New York: Routledge, 1994.

Bluestone, George. *Novels into Film*. 1957; reprinted Berkeley and Los Angeles: University of California Press, 1971.

Bordwell, David, and Kristin Thompson. *Film History: An Introduction*. New York: McGraw Hill, 1994.

Film Art: An Introduction. 6th edn. New York: McGraw Hill, 2001.

Bordwell, David, Janet Staiger, and Kristin Thompson. *Classical Hollywood Cinema: Film Style and Mode of Production to 1960*. New York: Columbia University Press, 1985.

Branigan, Edward. *Point of View in the Cinema: A Theory of Narration and Subjectivity in Classical Film*. Amsterdam: Mouton, 1984.

Braudy, Leo, and Marshall Cohen, eds. *Film Theory and Criticism: Introductory Readings*. 5th edn. New York and Oxford: Oxford University Press, 1999.

Burch, Nöel. *Theory of Film Practice*. Trans. Helen R. Lane. Paris: Gallimard, 1969.

Castle, Terry. *Masquerade and Civilization: The Carnivalesque in Eighteenth-Century English Culture and Fiction*. Stanford, CA: Stanford University Press, 1986.

Chatman, Seymour. *Story and Discourse: Narrative Structure in Fiction and Film*. Ithaca, NY: Cornell University Press, 1978.

Coming to Terms: The Rhetoric of Narrative in Fiction and Film. Ithaca, NY: Cornell University Press, 1990.

Conger, Syndy M., and Janice R. Welsch, eds. *Narrative Strategies: Original Essays in Film and Prose Fiction.* Macomb, IL: Western Illinois University, 1980.

Dixon, Wheeler Winston, ed. *Re-Viewing British Cinema, 1900–1992: Essays and Interviews.* New York: State University Press, 1994.

Doody, Margaret Anne. *The True Story of the Novel.* New Brunswick, NJ: Rutgers University Press, 1995.

Friedman, Lester, ed. *Fires Were Started: British Cinema and Thatcherism.* Minneapolis: University of Minnesota Press, 1993.

Giddings, Robert, Keith Selby, and Chris Wensley. *Screening the Novel: The Theory and Practice of Literary Dramatization.* London: Macmillan and New York: St. Martin's Press, 1990.

Harrington, John. *Film And/As Literature.* Englewood Cliffs, NJ: Prentice-Hall, 1977.

Holquist, Michael. "Corrupt Originals: The Paradox of Censorship," *PMLA* 109 (1994), 14–25.

Horton, Andrew, and Joan Magretta, eds. *Modern European Filmmakers and the Art of Adaptation.* New York: Frederick Ungar, 1981.

Hunter, J. Paul. *Before Novels: The Cultural Contexts of Eighteenth-Century English Fiction.* New York and London: W. W. Norton, 1990.

Jackson, Kevin. *The Language of Cinema.* Manchester: Carcanet, 1998.

Jansen, Sue Curry. *Censorship: The Knot That Binds Power and Knowledge.* Oxford: Oxford University Press, 1988.

Klein, Michael, and Gillian Parker. *The English Novel and the Movies.* New York: Frederick Ungar, 1981.

McCormick, Richard. *Politics of the Self: Feminism and the Postmodern in West German Literature and Film.* Princeton: Princeton University Press, 1991.

McFarlane, Brian. *Novel to Film: An Introduction to the Theory of Adaptation.* Oxford: Clarendon Press, 1996.

McKeon, Michael. *The Origins of the English Novel, 1600–1740.* Baltimore: Johns Hopkins University Press, 1987.

McLuhan, Marshall. *Understanding Media.* London: Routledge and Kegan Paul, 1969.

Maeder, Edward, ed. *Hollywood and History: Costume Design in Film.* London: Thames and Hudson; Los Angeles: Los Angeles County Museum of Art, 1987.

Mast, Gerald, and Bruce Kawin. *A Short History of the Movies.* 7th edn. Boston: Allyn and Bacon, 2000.

Mayer, Robert. *History and the Early English Novel: Matters of Fact from Bacon to Defoe.* Cambridge: Cambridge University Press, 1997.

Morrissette, Bruce. *Novel and Film: Essays in Two Genres.* Chicago: University of Chicago Press, 1985.

Orr, Christopher. "The Discourse on Adaptation." *Wide Angle*, 6 (1984), 72–6.

Orr, John, and Colin Nicholson. *Cinema and Fiction: New Modes of Adapting, 1950–1990.* Edinburgh: University of Edinburgh Press, 1992.

Ray, William. *Story and History: Narrative Authority and Social Identity in the Eighteenth-Century French and English Novel*. Cambridge, MA and Oxford: Basil Blackwell, 1990.

Rentschler, Eric. *West German Film in the Course of Time: Reflections on the Twenty Years since Oberhausen*. Bedford Hills, NY: Redgrave, 1984.

Sadoul, Georges. *Histoire du cinéma mondial des origines à nos jours*. Paris: Flammarion, 1949.

Sales, Roger. *Jane Austen and Representations of Regency England*. London and New York: Routledge, 1994.

Simons, John D., ed. *Literature and Film in the Historical Dimension*. Gainesville: University Press of Florida, 1994.

Sinyard, Neil. *Filming Literature: The Art of Screen Adaptation*. New York: St. Martin's, 1986.

Sontag, Susan. *Against Interpretation*. New York: Dell, 1966.

Sorlin, Pierre. *The Film in History: Restaging the Past*. Totowa, NJ: Barnes and Noble Books, 1980.

Stafford, Barbara. *Good Looking: Essays on the Virtues of Images*. Cambridge, MA: MIT Press, 1996.

Stewart, Susan. *On Longing: Narratives of the Miniature, the Gigantic, the Souvenir, the Collection*. 1984; reprinted Durham, NC: Duke University Press, 1998.

Tashiro, C. S. *Pretty Pictures: Production Design and the History Film*. Austin: University of Texas Press, 1998.

Thomson, David. *A Biographical Dictionary of Film*. 3rd edn. New York: Alfred A. Knopf, 1995.

Troost, Linda and Sayre Greenfield, eds. *Jane Austen in Hollywood*. Lexington: University Press of Kentucky, 1998.

Wagner, Geoffrey. *The Novel and the Cinema*. Rutherford, NJ: Farleigh Dickinson University Press, 1975.

Warner, William B. *Licensing Entertainment: The Elevation of Novel Reading in Britain, 1684–1750*. Berkeley and Los Angeles: University of California Press, 1998.

Watt, Ian. *The Rise of the Novel: Studies in Defoe, Richardson and Fielding*. Berkeley and Los Angeles: University of California Press, 1957.

Index

Titles of most works of art are listed under the artist's (in the case of a film, the director's) name, unless the artist's name is not listed in the index, in which case the work is listed alphabetically by title. Page numbers in bold print indicate an illustration.